Boston
Neighborhoods

Second Edition

A Food Lover's
Walking, Eating, and
Shopping Guide to Ethnic Enclaves
in and around Boston

Lynda Morgenroth

Drawings by Carleen Moira Powell

The Globe Pequot Press

GUILFORD, CONNECTICUT

The prices and rates listed in this guidebook were confirmed at press time. We recommend, however, that you call establishments before traveling to obtain current information.

Text design: Lana Mullen and Deborah Nicolais
Maps by M. A. Dubé © The Globe Pequot Press
Illustrations: Carleen Moira Powell
Illustrations have been rendered from photographs taken by Lynda Morgenroth.

ISBN 0-7627-2699-7

Manufactured in the United States of America
Second Edition/First Printing

TX
907.3
.M42
M67
2003

For
my grandparents,
Loeser and Rosa Morgenroth
Jacob and Rose Weisberg

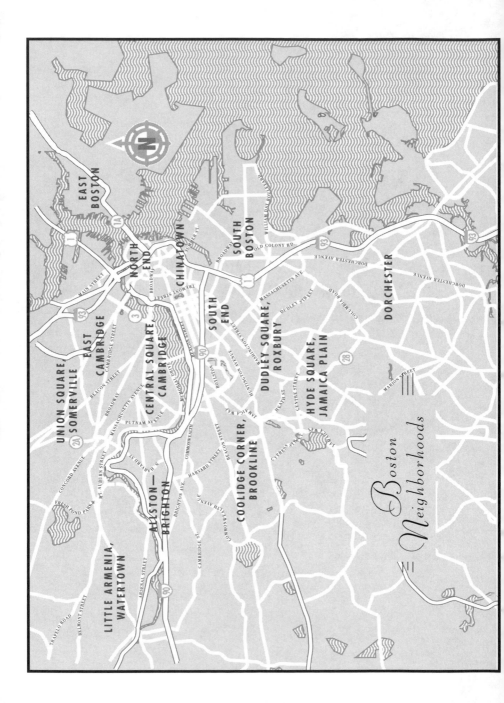

Contents

Help Us Keep This Guide Up to Date

Every effort has been made by the author and editors to make this guide as accurate and useful as possible. However, many things can change after a guide is published—establishments close, phone numbers change, facilities come under new management, and so on.

We would love to hear from you concerning your experiences with this guide and how you feel it could be made better and be kept up to date. While we may not be able to respond to all comments and suggestions, we'll take them to heart and we'll also make certain to share them with the author. Please send your comments and suggestions to the following address:

The Globe Pequot Press
Reader Response/Editorial Department
P.O. Box 480
Guilford, CT 06437

Or you may e-mail us at:
editorial@GlobePequot.com

Thanks for your input, and happy travels!

Acknowledgments

A big thank you to the working people of Boston—the men and women who knead the bread, stir the soup, and keep the shelves of markets stocked with goods. I consider it a miracle that people arrive from other countries with little or no money, speaking no English, and knowing nothing of our codes, and within a few years put together a business. Their only capital is enterprise.

During a time when we have become more suspicious of immigrants, we might consider what we owe them—which is just about everything, except the land itself and the ways of the indigenous people. Immigrants are us.

Thank you and hugs to my own indigenous people—my mother, Blanche, and sister, Diane, who are totally obsessed with cooking and food (though Diane cooks and Blanche just eats).

Colleagues at Globe Pequot—including Managing Editor Liz Taylor and Assistant Managing Editor Josh Rosenberg—have been patient, professional, and kind. A special thank you to close friends who have stood by me through cycles of fertile and fallow fields. And where would I be without fellow food-hounds, who gobbled up the first edition of *Boston Neighborhoods*? Thank you for your support, and please keep walking and eating!

Finally, a heaven-sent hug to my grandpa Jake, who taught me that honesty, integrity, and smarts are important, but that above all, it's a blessing to be a good eater.

Preface

Next to eating and reading, I've always loved walking best. Even as a young child, I was attracted to this silent, graceful, invigorating activity. My parents were overly cautious, and I was overly curious. The explorations allowed by walking proved to be the compromise.

By age eight, I was taking the long road home from school. By ten, I'd learned to keep my own counsel; to never request privileges that were likely to be denied, a useful lesson for a reporter, which I later became. As a teenager during the 1960s, I wasn't doing sex, drugs, or even rock 'n' roll (my parents associated record players with sedition), but was instead walking my feet off, in sensible shoes with good support. But like my peers on drugs, I wanted to see how far I could go.

Boy, did I go—ambling into Catholic churches to gaze upon statues and inhale incense, pawing through matted leaves in New York City parks to find mushrooms and humus, and sidling into record stores to listen to the gravelly voices of black musicians. In late summer, a fine time for walking, I accepted fresh figs from silent Italian grandfathers. They protected their Mediterranean trees through northern winters by swathing them in burlap or sometimes, most remarkable to my eyes, the discarded print dresses of their daughters and wives.

At eighteen I arrived in Boston. Finally free of parental surveillance, I started walking big time, including into Cambridge, Brookline, and Somerville. I didn't learn to drive a car until I was almost thirty. Like, why would I? Trying to get the feel of a neighborhood from a car is like dancing in a chair.

Boston proved to be a paradise for walking, not to mention for reading and eating. I could walk from Coolidge Corner to Kenmore Square (bagels to baklava) in a half hour, from Central Square to East Cambridge (kibbe to kale soup) in ten minutes, and in the space of one afternoon visit Chinatown and the North End, gathering Asian and Italian groceries and observing the similarities between Chinese and Italian bakeries, even though bean cakes and cannoli are different. Food neighborhoods were the most alluring because they were cultural centers, and also because I was always hungry.

Last year, in urgent need of privacy, quiet, and space, I uprooted my urban self and transplanted her—root ball packed solid—just north of Boston. In the early months I feared eternal condemnation to chain supermarkets and living out my days strapped and sedentary in my car. But lo, before too long I discovered a steamy Indian restaurant (I was driving, of course, but scented-out the vindaloo), an Italian produce and grocery store (where most of the customers were Asian), and a family-run Vietnamese restaurant—all in a neighboring town. Soon after, I found I could walk from my new home to the last stop on the MBTA's Orange Line, Oak Grove in Malden, which stops in Haymarket near the North End, Chinatown, the South End, Jamaica Plain (Jackson Square near the start of Centre Street), and Roxbury (Roxbury Crossing near Dudley Square). By changing to the Green Line at Haymarket, I can easily get to Lechmere, at the edge of East Cambridge.

I am not leading a suburban life, but a trans-urban one. I have a porch and a yard, with lilacs and forsythia. But I am riding the rails regularly and—hail to ancestors past!—schlepping bags of food once more.

Salute, salúd, saude, l'chaim!

—Lynda Morgenroth

Introduction

Over the years, as I trekked through Boston and environs—buying Syrian cheese in the South End, colossal green olives in the North End, and smoky eggplant spread and breakfast cookies (what an invention!) in Watertown—I thought it odd that most of the attention went toward the traditional corridors of Boston, supposedly the home of the bean and the cod. I never once ate Boston baked beans, and the cod I generally saw was bacalhau, the dried salted variety stocked in wooden barrels.

Boston's celebrated trinity—the Back Bay, Beacon Hill, and the Freedom Trail—were not my hot spots. My kind of living history was more concerned with the Portuguese community in East Cambridge (crusty Portuguese corn bread, aromatic bowls of kale soup, old-fashioned fish markets with white tile walls); the Jewish bakeries in Coolidge Corner (chocolate babke, prune Danish, round raisin challah); and the Caribbean groceries in Union Square (bricks of aromatic bitter chocolate to pulverize with sugar and whisk into steamed milk).

I want to pass these places on to other urban explorers. My concern, or perhaps I should call it the guidebook writer's dilemma, is whether these "off-the-beaten-path" enclaves should be presented as consumer venues—places to visit for shopping or dining—or as fully constituted neighborhoods to explore, embrace, and understand. Not to stand on a soapbox (although I enjoy everything associated with groceries), but my attitude is generally more civic than consumerist: Go, buy, enjoy, order what you will, and run up a tab, but pay attention to where you are and with whom you're speaking. I'm a little cranky on this subject. I have a panethnic-neighborhood feeling, or maybe I should say I support a panethnic-neighborhood platform. I think we should welcome everyone to our own neighborhoods, expect the same wherever we go, and feel at ease.

In *Boston Neighborhoods*, I've had to be selective, never easy for a good eater. But as a discerning editor once said to me, "Lynda, how much can you eat?" (I can't remember if we were trying to focus an article or ordering lunch.) Had time and space allowed, I would have wandered into additional neighborhoods: Hyde Park, Roslindale, Everett, Chelsea, Revere, each of which has its own élan. But I am not a political or a regulatory agency, not a Chamber of Commerce or a Better Business Bureau. I'm just me, enthusing, occasionally exclaiming, escorting you through.

How to begin? Depending on your temperament and stamina, you might start your explorations in Chinatown, or reserve this gem as your touring finale, an exemplar of the small foreign countries that exist in American cities. If you're the "dive-right-in" type, Chinatown is perfect, you are whisked into an alternate universe. But if you're more the "working-up-to-speed" type, better to ease in with a neighborhood such as Coolidge Corner (Jewish, Russian, Asian) or Central Square (Indian, African-American, Latino). These are more expansive settings, geographically more spread out, and inhabited by a mix of "typical Americans" and more recent émigrés.

All the walks are pretty safe, which is to say, have a great time, but don't imagine you're on a South Sea island. In my thirty years of walking hither and yon, using public transportation, and ranging into neighborhoods considered "questionable" by some, I've had just two bad experiences, each in daylight in fancy venues. Still, I am always vigilant.

Don't explore urban neighborhoods alone at night. Stay where there are plenty of people, and know what you're up against. Dense neighborhoods, such as Chinatown, might seem scary if you're not used to a press of humanity, not to mention the muffled screams of chickens, but any area with so much retail and restaurant traffic has a built-in safety factor. When exploring long avenues—Harvard Avenue in Allston, Dot. Ave. in Dorchester, Mass. Ave. in Central Square—be alert to the changing densities of people and buildings. When activity thins and you feel edgy, pay attention to the feeling. Walk quickly and with confidence. If someone seems a little creepy, look at him or her and say hello. If they are "thinking the bad thoughts," as a Jamaican friend of mine puts it, you will have either blown their cover or perhaps startled them into civility. Most likely, the stranger is another local traveler, a human being taking a walk.

Each of this guidebook's thirteen chapters is devoted to a small section or sections of a neighborhood where there is a concentration of retail activity. As the neighborhoods are so different, the "pin-points" vary in scale. Sometimes the featured section is small. In Boston's Roxbury neighborhood, I concentrate on Dudley Square; in the city of Somerville, I focus on Union Square; same deal with Coolidge Corner in Brookline, and a mere few blocks in Watertown. Why? Because (in the last case) that's where the lavash and lamejune are. In the first case that's where the limbo pies, hair braiding, and Christmas cards with brown-skinned angels are. By contrast, I schlep readers along 5 miles of Dot. Ave.—in a car for once, so be happy!—from South Boston through Dorchester to the Milton line. And in East Boston I tool around three not-quite-contiguous squares. In each case I selected these excursions because they seemed the most doable and the most likely to provide a quality experience.

Each chapter has a short introduction that will give you a sense of the place, followed by instructions on how to get there. A brief history of the neighborhood—some sections of which go back 350 years—follows and then the walking tour. Sidebars pop up periodically. These asides are generally about ethnic cuisine, but also deal with green spaces and other local attractions.

At the end of each chapter is a list of suggested restaurants; these are not comprehensive, but I've tried to provide a range of prices, flavors, and atmospheres. I've used a "dollar symbol" key to indicate the price range of entree items: $=under $10; $$=under $20; $$$=under $30; $$$$=under $40. Most restaurants in ethnic neighborhoods are modestly priced. You'll rarely encounter the high-end tabs, except in the South End and some North End posheries. Even there, don't let the entree prices discourage you; most of the pricier restaurants offer appetizers, firsts, or tapas—often the most imaginative items on the menu—from which you can fashion an eclectic dinner. Plus, in ethnic restaurants, small plates present the hallmarks of the cuisine, the leading food indicators.

While exploring these neighborhoods, I strongly suggest the use of public transportation. It's fast, convenient, and economical. I discourage the use of cars. Boston's streets are narrow, crowded, and byzantine. It's difficult to find parking, and the looming presence of Big Dig maneuvers has created many traffic problems. (The Big Dig is an ongoing mega-construction project to depress Boston's Central Artery and create new bridges and tunnels. The multi-billion-dollar project is happening in the very heart of the city, with excavation sites from the North End to South Station and Chinatown. Pedestrian and motor traffic continues *over* massive tunnel construction and *surrounding* several surface sites.) Now more than ever, use Boston's mass transit system, the T. Short term MBTA passes are available; call (617) 722–3200, or (800) 392–6100, or TDD (617) 722–5146.

One more thing: Wherever possible, I've provided addresses and phone numbers of even the tiniest bodega. But in a few cases, where owners use home phones or do without, or where addresses are nonexistent (as in the case of fruit stands), I've noted the establishments anyway. If you go there, you are likely to find them, or something else of edible interest.

$\mathscr{C}$hinatown

THROUGH THE DRAGON GATE

*C*hinatown is multifaceted and intense, even a little overwhelming to some first-time visitors, because so much life is packed into such a small space. Over 4,000 people live in a neighborhood not much bigger than a few square blocks. Contrary to its name, it is multiculturally Asian, home and workplace to people from China, Vietnam, Laos, Cambodia, Thailand, Korea, and Japan. The predominant population is from mainland China, Taiwan, and Hong Kong.

The markets, murals, restaurants, banks, bakeries, groceries, pharmacies, clothing stores, gift shops, and video and book stores are all Asian. Even the telephone booths are faux red pagodas. Bakeries sell buns with sesame seeds, newspapers are in Chinese, and music in restaurants and stores is Asian. Dunkin' Donuts' sign is in Chinese characters.

On Beach Street I sometimes feel I've tumbled into a provocative, surreal world—a long bright hallway with a zillion doors. Walk in one door and an elderly man is mixing a pile of dried roots and herbs for a customer who is chronically tired. Walk in another door and a fierce-looking fellow cuts off the head of a wriggling chicken with the resounding slash-thud of a cleaver. Another door admits me to a bakery with neat glass shelves of plump pastries—crimped golden squares stuffed with red beans, black beans, or custards.

The dreamlike quality of Chinatown is intensified by its incongruous surroundings—so close they're juxtaposed. At the eastern end of Beach Street, near the handsome Chinese Dragon Gate, your toes may be sheared off if you stray too close to the road, part of the Southeast Expressway. To the southwest, on Washington and Kneeland Streets and on Harrison Avenue, New England Medical

Center, a major Tufts teaching hospital, sprawls, with its legions of men and women in white coats and scrubs, patients in wheelchairs, and their families. On Tremont and LaGrange Streets, Boston's Theater District and remnants of the old "combat zone" infiltrate. A block from the Washington Street side, Boston Common beckons. It's more bucolic than LaGrange Street, but no less odd. Colonial pastureland meets contemporary Asian bustle.

The complexity and incongruity of these environs are pure joy for hard-core urbanites—always a bit perverse in our appreciations—but no thrill for the space-poor, harried inhabitants of Chinatown, who must endure not only physical crowding, but also the sounds of highway traffic, automobile horns, ambulance sirens, airplanes, and the underground pounding and vibrations emanating from the Big Dig, the huge highway and tunnel construction project, and the renewal of lower Washington Street.

Nevertheless, within the silky cocoon of this community, thousands of residents and visitors work, shop, and eat every day. Most restaurants and bakeries are open seven days a week, and no matter what the season, weather, or time of day, someone is buying blocks of bean curd at See Sun, slurping tangled noodles at Sam Hop, or haggling over miniature TVs (or those the size of a wall) at an electronics store.

Still, even on festival days—in the swirl of people, street vendors, and lion dancers—you can always find oases: an informal restaurant where a Chinese family eats silently but with gusto, an almost empty park where a woman in jeans and Chinese slippers practices t'ai chi, or even a shadowy aisle in a grocery store where you can gaze on the decorative cartons of boxed teas, savoring the Chinese symbols for ginger, ginkgo, and ginseng.

How to Get There

By public transportation, take the MBTA Orange
Line to Chinatown or the Green Line to Boylston Street.
Folks who don't mind a short walk could also take the Red
Line to Park Street and walk along the Tremont Street side of the
Common, taking a left on Boylston Street. You can also weave your
way from South Station, which is on Atlantic Avenue, bearing left
through construction rubble to Essex or Beach Street. There are so
many police officers helping pedestrians and motorists find their way
through the Big Dig, you'll have no problem getting directions.

By car, you are courting exasperation, but here goes: Take
Route 93 to the Chinatown exit. Look for on-the-street
parking or a parking lot. Eventually, this exit may
be eliminated as part of the highway
improvement.

• • • *History* • • •

As Boston goes, the history of settlement in Chinatown is brief.
Most of today's Chinatown didn't physically exist until two major
landfill projects were undertaken during the nineteenth century. This
southerly part of the peninsula of Boston was known as South Cove,
an appellation that still comes up when real estate parcels are being
discussed by the Boston Redevelopment Authority. Beach Street,
which today sounds quaint, was once descriptive; it marked actual
shoreline.

Individual Chinese émigrés trickled into Boston earlier in the nineteenth century, but large-scale immigration didn't begin until the 1870s. Two hundred Chinese were shipped in as strikebreakers at a Lawrence, Massachusetts, shoe factory. When the strike was over, the mill owners acted like true capitalists; they abandoned the Chinese workers. Many of these men made their way to Boston, pitching tents in the South Cove, a derelict area of harbor and rail depots. Their scruffy encampment became known as Ping-On Alley. You can find its approximate site today: Ping-On Street runs off Essex Street.

Chinese immigration to the United States was severely restricted by the Chinese Exclusion Act of 1882. Fifty years later there were still only about 1,200 residents in Chinatown. After World War II, when restrictive laws were repealed, immigration increased, though many of those who were successful in Chinatown left for Boston-area suburbs.

Starting in the 1960s and continuing to the present day, Southeast Asian settlers—Vietnamese, Cambodian, and Thai— arrived and settled in Chinatown. The community has been greatly enriched by their presence, as has the city. Their wonderful cooking has inspired many Boston chefs to create fusion menus.

Today, community activists have "taken back Chinatown" for its residents—agitating against the expansion of New England Medical Center, demanding a purge of the prostitutes that spilled over from the "combat zone," and gaining leverage in downtown real estate projects.

When the Big Dig is complete—all present holes-in-the-earth replaced by roads, bridges, tunnels, and a verdant linear park— Chinatown will change. The Route 93 South exit into Chinatown will likely be eliminated. A plaza may be developed for community events such as the August Moon Festival and Chinese New Year. It is possible that residents will have more room to roam, but the neighborhood will not become less cohesive. The community is like a net that changes size and shape depending on external forces. But the knots of the net are tight and will not become undone.

... *A Walking Tour* ...

At its most compact Chinatown is bounded by Washington, Essex, Hudson, and the area around Oak and Pine Streets. Beach Street is the spine of the community and a good anchor street to remember. One end of Beach holds the gleaming white **Dragon Gate,** an architectural gateway. But if you approach from the Boston Common side, as many visitors do, you won't see the gate until a bit later.

Chinatown is so packed with restaurants and stores that rather than guiding you in the conventional "walk here, turn there, stop now" fashion, I'll lay out the main streets and a few of their highlights. Feel free to deviate and backtrack. Better still, feel compelled. Cast your eyes above first floors—to balconies, second-floor restaurants, and studios. In Chinatown you're always missing something.

To get oriented and see an interesting adaptation of an old building, stop at the **China Trade Building,** 2 Boylston Street, near the corner of Washington and Essex Streets. On the lower level, the City of Boston's **Chinatown Main Street Program,** Suite G1, (617) 350–6303, has an office where you can pick up maps and brochures and arrange for reserved-place tours. Loiter in the ground-floor lobby. Look down. Artist Lilli Ann Killen Rosenberg—whose murals I've followed through Boston neighborhoods like so many glowing pebbles in the moonlight—has arranged sizable pebbles here. Twelve mosaic markers, individual signs of the Chinese Lunar Zodiac, are embedded in the floor. A mosaic plaque, erected by Rosenberg and her husband Marvin, is on the lobby wall. The plaque

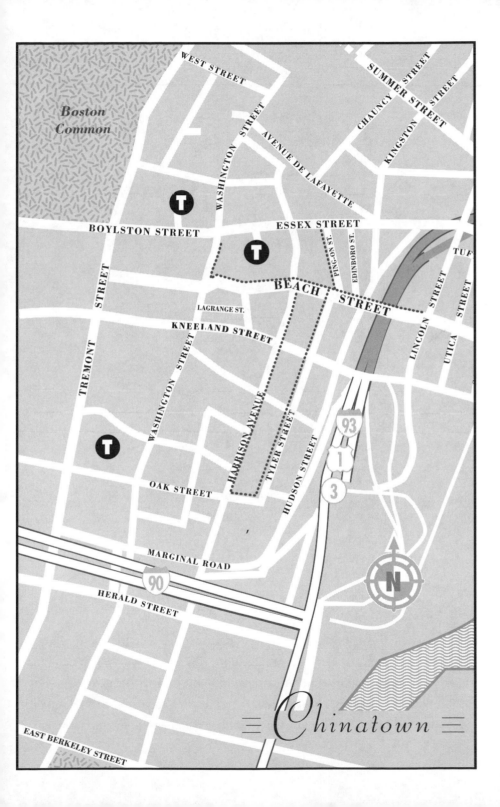

An elderly Chinese merchant carries a repotted plant into his store.

unifies all the signs and explains their properties. In the ancient Chinese system, each year is represented by an animal that bestows aspects of personality and temperament on those it governs.

Several Asian businesses and services are located in the China Trade Building, which houses a substantial music-video store, travel agency, and acupuncturist and dentist offices. The building itself is handsome; it was constructed in 1887 by Carl Fehmer, a major architect of Boston office buildings and grand homes. The Liberty Tree once stood nearby. Planted in 1646, the vase-shaped elm lived for over a century, assuming majestic girth and near mythical status. The Sons of Liberty met beneath its sheltering branches. In this tent of leaves, secluded, they hatched the plot for the Boston Tea Party, which took place in nearby Boston Harbor. In 1775 the Tories and Redcoats destroyed the tree, though not its symbolism. Today a bronze plaque is imbedded in the sidewalk in front of the China Trade Building on the corner of Essex and Washington Streets. If Chinatown Main Street can raise the necessary funds, a single large elm, a living commemoration at the patriots' site, will be planted at **Liberty Tree Plaza** at the intersection of Washington, Boylston, and Essex Streets.

Beach Street

Take a right on Washington Street, and you'll reach the intersection with Beach, Chinatown's main street. Almost on the corner, **Thai Binh Market,** 15 Beach Street, (617) 426–2771, is a Southeast Asian supermarket with tens of thousands of products. The entrance is a little tricky to find—it's on the unmarked side street parallel to Washington (and, yes, you enter the supermarket through a small jewelry store with flashy jade). The market contains teas, spices, sauces, and marinades; tanks of fresh fish (separate water-quarters for lobsters and crabs); and aisles of Asian produce, including hard-to-find kohlrabi, a globular member of the broccoli family, delicate in taste and impressive looking, like a celadon-green sputnik. Don't miss the root vegetables stashed near the floor. The segmented white veg that looks like a string of clay knockwurst is lotus root. When sliced like a carrot, its lacy segmentations appear.

Housewares galore occupy a corner of Thai Binh. Tins of exotic fruit are amazingly well priced—a one-pound, four-ounce can of loquats from Shanghai costs under $2.00, with similar prices for jackfruit and rambutan. Look for paper products, incense, sundry exotic pickles (eggplant, radish, mango), an amazing array of noodles, and what I call the "Wall of Meat." It's an imposing, clear glass display case of grilled beef, pork, poultry, other parts of things, and rangy octopods, which turn bright coral when cooked.

Some counterintuitive advice: If you have trouble adapting to the sight of animal innards, birdies on skewers, and large ducks hanging by their long necks, the Wall of Meat at Thai Binh is where you should start. Either freak out and stop eating critters, freak out and admire another culture's cuisine, or get with the program and buy succulent grilled meat.

I find standing at this wall tantalizing. It smells delicious, and the items are fascinating: quail on skewers, beef livers the color of cordovan shoes, coiled pig intestines, and racks of red-glazed pork ribs that look like the interior of a piano. Dawdle here. A customer will soon come along and a transaction arranged. You'll see high-caliber meat cutting. A butcher takes a rack of spareribs, arranges them vertically, and using a cleaver on a block, makes a series of rapid, precise, karate-like chops that sever the junctures between the bones. In a whir of motion, he lines up the ribs horizontally—almost twirling the bones—and zaps them again. He then gently places the 1-inch-square cut-up meat bits in a Styrofoam box. In thirty seconds, a hanging rack of pork turns into what look like canapés.

Similar activities take place in the fresh fish area, especially when a home chef who knows her business requests a cut-up head. The sound of the chopping is unnerving, but as my friend George Moy notes, "We eat the soup. So?"

Onward to commerce. An oasis of refinement, **Cathay Corner,** 56 Beach Street, (617) 426–7449, offers old-style Chinese treasures, the kinds of carved jade figures, august ceremonial bowls, and hand-painted deities that you imagine in the homes of old Bostonians. In this small-scale, decorative arts gallery, the dapper, silver-haired proprietor is informative on the subject of his objets d'art. Many of the ceramic figures are wonderful to behold, but you must learn to visualize them in a calm, draped, austere setting. Even in this elegant store, there's so much stuff, it's hard to concentrate on individual pieces. Cathay Corner sells jewelry, too, and ginger jars that some clients convert into lamps. Sometimes the store is inexplicably locked. Come back later, after a pastry-pick-me-up.

Other than being made with flour and shortening, Chinese pastries differ quite a bit from American-style goodies. **Hing Shing Pastry,** 67 Beach Street, (617) 451–1162, offers a pleasing palette of plump, round delicacies. The bakery is small, without tables, and the door to the kitchen is open—allowing fascinating glimpses of a floury world. Try an almond or walnut cookie. They're so short as to crumble at your touch and are lovely with slightly bitter tea. If you visit Hing Shing in August and September, you'll find my sentimental favorite, and I am hardly alone, mooncakes, wonderfully decorated individual cakes about the size of a tart. Mooncake pastry is a mix of flour, lemon, sugar, and oil, which is nudged into a mold and filled with one of many luscious leguminous mixtures: black bean paste, lotus seeds, or nut mixtures. Mooncakes are not for every taste, but as I am a starch devotee, they please me very much. I also enjoy the sesame-seed-swathed doughnuts filled with black beans. I've convinced myself that they're laden with protein; a kind of Asian energy bar.

Hing Shing also sells pork buns and beef buns. Some construction workers from the nearby Big Dig have shifted their allegiances from the Big Mac to the beef bun. Some eat both—a Big Mac or cheeseburger followed by a tidy beef bun.

Touristy gift shops are scattered throughout Chinatown and carry similar merchandise. One of the most pleasant—primarily because its proprietors are so low key—is **Oriental Fortune Gift Land,** 95 Chauncy Street, (617) 350–6132, located on a street north of Beach and Essex. Travel along Chauncy, which crosses Summer, to get a sense of how Boston's old retail district and Chinatown connect. At Oriental Fortune you'll find inexpensive embroidered slippers, tea sets (including miniatures), stationery, small toys, and the ubiquitous Bee & Flower toilet soaps (rose is best). If you live in a drafty house, or your landlord is cheap with heat, one of the nicest small pleasures is an inexpensive but fetching porcelain mug with close-fitting cover, also sold at Oriental Fortune. Some have dragons and make an appealing gift when paired with a tin of Chinese tea.

HARRISON AVENUE

Harrison Avenue is a very long street, running parallel to Tremont (along Boston Common) and Washington (the retail district of Downtown Crossing a few blocks north), and perpendicular to Beach Street. Harrison is an "everything street"—restaurants, bakeries, stores, and apartments, along with New England Medical Center. I like wandering down Harrison after shopping at Filene's Basement—following Washington Street south, taking a left at Essex, Beach, or Kneeland Streets.

Several Chinese bakeries are also cafes and offer restorative drinks and pastries. **Eldo Cake House,** 36 Harrison Avenue, (617) 350–7977, makes nourishing hot and cold drinks, including chilled Ovaltine, quite good, and a reminder of Hong Kong's British incarnation.

In some fundamental way, all good bakeries are alike, an ineluctable combination of staff, customers, atmosphere, and edibles. For these reasons, Eldo Cake House reminds me of Mike's Pastry in the North End—another popular hangout—except that at Eldo the people and the cakes are Asian, eclairs and napoleons notwithstanding. Try the almond and walnut cookies, stuffed buns and cookies, and well-priced almond bars. Packaged in clear plastic boxes, they taste like thin, short pie-crust cookies bedecked with sliced almonds. The coconut pudding is worth taking home on the subway and serving in glass or porcelain bowls.

The scene at Eldo is commendable: An Asian cop with his beeper on is taking a coffee break. Two middle-aged Chinese ladies are sharing three desserts at 10:00 A.M. Three office workers, young Caucasian women in their twenties, come in for coconut pudding and coffee. Several elderly Chinese men are reading Chinese-language newspapers—and eating nothing. An Asian medical worker rushes in for the wrapped "rice meals," which he carries out. These triangular packages, brown paper tied with string, contain rice, vegetables, and bits of pork. Once you see these nifty wraps—origami sculpture filled with food—your sandwich in a baggie looks pitiful.

Check out **See Sun Oriental Foods,** 25 Harrison Avenue, (617) 426–0954, across the street. It's so calm and neat you'll forget about the mayhem at Filene's Basement (Boston's legendary emporium for the frugal) and find other sorts of bargains, including the scores of herbal, medicinal, and black teas (especially Quing-brand Keemun tea, the king of teas, at once smoky and flowery); packaged peanut-sesame candy, made in Taiwan; and the charmingly wrapped Bee & Flower toilet soaps (ginseng, jasmine, rose, sandalwood—the latter ideal for scenting linens and blankets). See Sun may be the cleanest, neatest, most serene market in Chinatown. It's of moderate size, not a supermarket, but extremely well organized, well stocked, and pleasing to the eye. Aisle by aisle, there is consistent, logical product organization and plenty of room to walk. The frozen food section stocks frozen lotus buns and other pastries. The array of smoked and dried fish looks tempting, as does the creamy-white fresh tofu. If you're interested in exotic fruit, compare fresh, dried, and tinned versions of the same thing: longans, for example, like a grape with a shell; lychees; rambutans; and durians, the latter only in tins. If not civilized by processing, durian smells like a mixture of aged cheese and reeking garlic. The rind of this football-size fruit has porcupine-like quills that can lacerate fruit partisans to the quick. Why bother with a football-size smelly fruit that's treacherous to peel? Durian is a potent aphrodisiac, and unlike Viagra, tastes delicious mixed in ice cream, according to devotees.

Though I'm largely ignorant of Asian cooking techniques, the produce at See Sun is so outstanding—young, tender versions of everything (small kohlrabi, not basketballs; slender bitter melons, not boats)—that I periodically buy mysterious vegetables and wing it, Betty Crocker in the Orient. The greens are irresistible. Whatever looks like cabbage or broccoli I buy, wash, cut up, and sauté with garlic. Choy-sum, a bok choy (Chinese cabbage) relative, has a sharp but mellow taste; sometimes it bears small yellow flowers in the center. I have no idea whether one is supposed to eat them, but I always do and continue to live. Their intense yellow hue sometimes moves me to boil eggs, which I eat with the choy-sum and a bit of hot sauce (Asian or Caribbean), a satisfying if eccentric meal. I finish with ginseng tea. As the song says, I feel good.

Glitzy Asian-style furniture can be found at **Eurasia Furniture,** 31 Harrison Avenue, (617) 350–0128, everything from conventional rosewood dining tables and carved chairs to the Hong

Kong hotel look of gleaming white modern beds with oriental design motifs, lamps with fanlike shades, and movie set oriental color combos—red and black, coral and turquoise, and lots of black and white lacquer.

I never met a commercial cookware store I didn't like, and when the wares displayed serve specialty cooks, even more excellent oddities can be found. Who wouldn't love a wok as big as a car hood, or a 4-foot-tall soup pot with a shovel-like spoon? **Chin Enterprises,** 33 Harrison Avenue, (617) 423–1725, stocks common gadgets and cookware, along with everything necessary for Asian-style cooking—woks of conventional size, ladles, whisks, bamboo steaming baskets, electric rice cookers, and steel cleavers. You can also find wooden highchairs and well-priced Eagleware cast-aluminum cookware. If you look like a browsing housewife, you will be completely ignored by the proprietors, Asian men who are immersed in their steaming takeout at all times of day. I like this screen of invisibility, which allows close inspection of culinary equipment without being bothered.

In Chinese culture jade is prized. The glowing, semiprecious stone is generally soft green, but exists in many other hues. **K & T Jewelry Company,** 42A Harrison Avenue, (617) 482–3383, carries a large assortment of jade jewelry, along with lavish eighteen-carat-gold sparklers.

TYLER STREET

If you're searching for a restaurant, Tyler and Beach are the streets to navigate. On Tyler, in particular, look up. What appears at street level as a jumble of restaurants is often revealed to be a series of splendid period buildings when viewed as a whole. Several of the restaurants have lavishly decorated upper stories. **Peking Cuisine** restaurant's building, 10 Tyler Street, looks like an Asian villa, with a

Little Treasures

Dim sum is the ultimate poo-poo platter. Seductive and mysterious bits of food, mainly in artful, edible wrappings—such as those on the outside of eggrolls—arrive in a steady, fragrant stream at your table. Generally, they are bussed by servers who swing through the restaurant with carts of offerings. In some places, servers pause at your table; in other more raucous settings, customers hail the food carriers, sometimes loudly. You can eat whatever you want. You will only be charged for your selection.

Translated variously as "little treasures" or "touches the heart," dim sum is a combination appetizer/cocktail snack/hors d'oeuvre. The ancient Cantonese custom of gathering for bite-size delicacies, originally at a teahouse, now as likely as not at a huge kitschy restaurant, has spread all over the world. Businesspeople do dim sum as a part of deal making. Lovers do dim sum as part of courtship and play. Families do dim sum because they're hungry, get a kick out of eating together, and don't want to cook such labor-intensive delicacies. You can also talk your head off over dim sum and not be heard, an advantage for some families.

Okay, here come the carts. You choose. You chomp. What are you eating? Well, hundreds of possibilities, from the recognizable crispy spring rolls and succulent dumplings—vegetable or shrimp or pork—to mystery packets that may contain a crunchy chicken foot. Balls of sticky rice with veggie bits are wrapped in lotus leaves. Prawns are served with heads intact and look like golden sea horses. The steamed buns filled with red bean paste are intense, filling, and satisfying; the slightly doughy exterior and sweet interior offer great

*textural contrast and deliver a carbo high, followed (for some of us)
by falling eyelid syndrome. Regardless of how stimulating the setting, whenever I eat steamed buns, I feel like slipping under the table
and falling into a deep sleep.*

*In some restaurants, dim sum selections are identified; in others,
not. If you're timid, or vegetarian, it's best to start with larger
restaurants accustomed to the naive tastes of non-Asians. And if
perchance in spite of precautions, you bite into a rice paper-swathed
claw or hoof, what's the diff? Consider what you might be eating
when you bite into an ordinary hot dog.*

*As for cost, it's hard to say what you're spending, as prices of items
are in Chinese. But it would be hard for a group of four adults—
even eating with abandon—to spend more than $50.*

*All food explorers owe themselves a visit to **Chau Chow City**, 83
Essex Street, (617) 338-8158, a massive three-story restaurant seating 800 (and often filled to capacity, so don't expect quiet), described
by Alison Arnett, The Boston Globe's restaurant critic, as the premier
dim sum house in New England. At Chau Chow City, which is near
South Station, dim sum is served every day, 8:00 A.M.–3:00 P.M. In
several other restaurants, it's served only on weekends. As dim sum is
considered a breakfast or lunchtime custom, the procession of little
treasures generally stops in midafternoon. **China Pearl**, 9 Tyler
Street, (617) 426-4338, serves late night dim sum. Other spots
include **Emperor's Garden**, 690 Washington Street, (617)
482-8898, and **Imperial Seafood**, 70 Beach Street, (617)
426-8439 (see "Suggested Restaurants").*

balcony of flowering vines, potted plants, and garden sculpture. Cleverly, each restaurant's sign is so compelling—colorful and in a competing type face—and so many vie for your attention, that you may overlook nonrestaurant establishments, many of which are worthwhile. **Kok Wa Herbs & Books,** 8A Tyler Street, (617) 695–3228, is a diamond in the rough, a very Chinese mixture of herbal medicine, girly magazines, and gambling. In the front of the store, which has a virtual collage of torn, scuffed lottery tickets on the floor, elderly ladies in kerchiefs rub away at their tickets. In the center, boys and men glean the magazines, which feature anatomically unlikely presentations of slender Asian women with voluminous breasts. In the rear, studious-looking herbalists are preparing prescriptions —mounds of wondrous looking roots, powders, leaves, and flowers— which they weigh and wrap. The lottery-purchasing, magazine-reading, and herbal-remedy-seeking portions of the store's clientele seem not to mix.

A nearby neighbor, **China Arts & Crafts Gallery,** 7 Tyler Street, (617) 423–1725, is a friendly little Chinese folk arts and art store, a fun place for children, though much of the gallery's space has recently been consigned to DVDs.

If you follow Tyler beyond the commercial hub, it leads into the past. The **Chinese Catholic Pastoral Center,** 78 Tyler Street, is a striking brick building with a monument to the Maryknoll order, who served the Chinese community from 1946 to 1992. The **Old Quincy School,** 90 Tyler Street, built in 1847, was the site of a radical experiment in American education. In this building young people were treated more equitably than in public schools of the era. Students had individual desks. Drawing and music were part and parcel of the curriculum. Corporal punishment was discouraged. For over a century the building also housed adult-ed evening classes where tens of thousands of Asian adults learned to speak English. Today the building is used for social services to the community, including education. The freestanding meditative figure in front of the building is Confucius, the ancient Chinese teacher and philosopher. Chinatown's active local public school, **Josiah Quincy School,** 885 Washington Street, is a few blocks away. Its cheerful facade features a huge wraparound mural of children's drawings, visible from all sides. On

A Chinese herbalist measures and mixes a prescription.

Earth Day in 1977, a rooftop garden was created here so that urban children could have some experience with nature.

Continue along Tyler Street. Note the many city-planted **ginkgo trees.** These are prized for their hardiness, grace, and dainty fan-shaped leaves that turn bright yellow in autumn. The leaves have long stems, flutter like flags, and make the street seem more open than it is. Continue to **Tai Tung Park,** a small leafy oasis with a dragon mural. Its back wall almost touches Route 93, another reminder of how the interstate severed Chinatown from the South End. If you continue in this direction, you'll wind up in Boston's South End.

At the end of Tyler, hook a right onto **Oak Street**—in an enclave of "tree-named streets," such as Pine and Ash. Stay on Oak, take a left on Washington or Shawmut, and then a right on East

Berkeley to reach Tremont. Explore! As you walk the streets of Boston's neighborhoods, especially at the margins, you'll be able to mentally reassemble what development has torn asunder.

SUGGESTED 🍽 RESTAURANTS

You won't starve—you'll feast—in Chinatown and see a cross-section of Asian food aficionados. Asian families come in from the suburbs on weekends, arts lovers dine in Chinatown before or after the theater (or dance performances at the Wang), and local chefs and musicians wind up here in the wee hours, as some Chinatown eateries stay open till 4:00 A.M.

What follows is a compact selection among the scores of places large and small, fancy and funky, from Cantonese and Hong Kong style to Vietnamese and Malaysian. All are in the $–$$ category. (Note that many smaller restaurants do not accept credit cards.)

Near the Chinatown gate (highest numbers of Beach Street), **Imperial Seafood Restaurant,** 70 Beach Street, (617) 426–8439, is a huge two-part establishment: upstairs a surreal scene of fleet carts of dim sum whizzing by diners deftly scarfing it down, and downstairs colorful Cantonese dishes. **Chau Chow Seafood,** 41–45 Beach Street, (617) 292–5166, is often mobbed and for good reason—crab with ginger and scallions, bright coral jumbo shrimp in the shell, tender baby clams in black bean sauce. Why such an emphasis on seafood? Many of Chinatown's residents come from Guangdong Province along the South China Sea.

When you're bopping along Beach Street, look up and about, not just at individual restaurant signs. Some eateries such as **Rod Thai**

Cuisine, 44 Beach Street, (617) 357–9188, are on the second floor. Some are in food-court-like groups, affording interesting food and superb people-watching. **Sam Hop** and **Swatow,** are nestled in with Rod Thai. The food court looks a little dingy, but the fare is filling and cheap. There's a natural food store on the ground floor, an antidote if you need one.

Tyler Street is another Asian eating avenue. **Peach Farm,** 4 Tyler Street, (617) 482–3332, does stylish seafood dishes, especially soft-shell crab when in season. The venerable **China Pearl,** 9 Tyler Street, (617) 426–4338, offers fried goodies, Cantonese and Hong Kong classics, and dim sum until the wee hours. Many young chefs in the restaurant biz favor **Peking Cuisine,** 10 Tyler Street, (617) 542–5857, making for a hip scene. **Golden Palace,** 14–20 Tyler Street, (617) 423–4565, is like an eating theater, heavy on the reds, pinks, and stagey dragons. At small but serious **Pearl Villa,** 25–27 Tyler Street, (617) 338–8770, you'll find southern Chinese and Malaysian cooking with lavish spring roll platters, live tank lobster, and exquisitely prepared vegetables. Try a cold soup for dessert.

The restaurants on Hudson may draw you to this historic though truncated back street. One side of it was demolished to make way for the Mass. Pike. It's perpendicular to Beach Street, adjacent to the Dragon Gate, and eerily close to the expressway. **Ho Yuen Ting Seafood Restaurant,** 13A Hudson Street, (617) 426–2316, is almost underground, not in the bohemian sense, but in its elevation view. Enjoy lobster with ginger, shrimp with spicy sauce, and exotica such as stir-fried sole and vegetables served in an edible bowl, not to mention fish stomach soup with sweet corn. **New Shanghai,** 21 Hudson Street, (617) 338–6688, celebrated for its elegant atmosphere and sophisticated cuisine, is the place to go for Peking duck, served with a flourish. Tiny

Wing's Kitchen, 23 Hudson Street, (617) 338–2218, known for the clear tastes of Shanghai cuisine, serves splendid yet inexpensive platters of chicken steamed in wine, mushroom-intensive vegetable dumplings and homemade Shanghai-style meatballs—big, moist ground pork balls on steamed bok choy. This Hearty Man's Meal (listed this way in my mind, not on Wing's menu) suggests a New England boiled dinner: corned beef and cabbage, carrots and potatoes, and a slash of Gulden's mustard. But the cuisine at Wing's is far more sophisticated. The restaurant, at the corner of Hudson and Kneeland, has fewer than a dozen tables and reminds me of eating exceptional food in humble surroundings when I was a student with friends who spent scarce funds on food, not rent.

Harrison Avenue offers **Dong Khanh,** 83 Harrison, (617) 426–9410, a Vietnamese place with almost forty different nourishing noodle soup dishes (favored by medical personnel on the run, especially the chicken-based soups), barbecued meats with vermicelli, and the notorious durian drink, good before a heavy date. Dong Khanh's rice dishes—with beef, pork, chicken, or seafood—are very well priced.

Finally, these are three varied eateries on Edinboro Street: **Moon Villa,** 15–19 Edinboro, (617) 423–2061, is the sprawling choice for hungry night owls. **People's Star,** 21–23 Edinboro, (617) 482–7328, serves mainly buffet-style, and the decor is basic. But the noodles, lobster in ginger and scallions, and clams in black bean sauce are salty, enlivening, and good. **Dynasty,** 33 Edinboro, (617) 350–7777, a kitschy Cantonese place—light, mirrors, columns, decor!—is a haven at 3:00 A.M., serving chicken with cashews, steamed sea bass, and pan-fried shrimp. In the wee small hours of the morning, truck drivers eat with opera stars (different tables, but like appetites).

The
$\mathcal{N}$orth $\mathcal{E}$nd

PANETTONE, PAUL REVERE, AND PORCINI BY THE POUND

The reasons generally cited for loving the North End are food, people, and neighborhood. But there is a deeper draw, as well. A visit to this enveloping enclave makes you feel like you belong to a happy family. The small scale of the place, the affable mélange of families, and their appreciation of beauty, ritual, and celebration felicitously combine. Even the first time I visited—fortuitously finding my way to Dairy Fresh Candies, a family in itself—I felt more at home than at home.

This neighborhood of mazelike streets and craggy outlooks figures prominently in Boston history—the Freedom Trail cuts right through. And as you've no doubt heard, the neighborhood offers a moveable feast of bakeries, restaurants, cafes, and pizzerias. It is also a place to people-watch and be watched by the masters, the elderly Italian ladies hanging out their windows and the gents surveying the streets.

The North End is located on the northwestern sliver of the original Shawmut Peninsula, a thumb into Boston Harbor, and sea breezes waft through the neighborhood, especially near Commercial Street. Now fashionable among urban professionals, the community has its share of gorgeously dressed young men and women sashaying home with shiny briefcases, their expensive shoes pressing into cobblestones and worn bricks. The "kids," as the old-timers call them, eat regularly at local restaurants, where they're encouraged to fatten up, bring in their girlfriends and boyfriends, and get married.

The North End looks like what you expect, but more: a few main thoroughfares (Hanover, Salem, North) with narrow cross streets and little piazzas. Church spires. Antique street lamps. Coral geraniums in pots. Bakeries showcasing every enemy of thinness known: the cannoli shells filled while you wait; the crisp, chewy biscotti packed in a paper bag, lightly closed, ready to munch. Whole categories of food you've never met before. Torrone, for example, a chocolate-nougat-nut confection. Gnocchi, a delicate potato dumpling. A spectrum of eggplants—purple, cream, white—some so tiny the thought of eggplant earrings comes to mind.

Most buildings are brick, not wood, as the narrow and congested streets are a firetrap. In the first-floor shop windows, proprietors display their wares: upright crusty loaves, rabbits hanging on hooks, chains of sausages that sway as shop doors open and close, rectangles of spicy, colorful Sicilian pizza studded with ink-black olives, wheels of cheese big enough to roll a cart.

Leaving no room for doubt that this is a real place, and not a theme park, you have to schlep through pedestrian tunnels, odd walkways, and temporary passages (near Haymarket) to reach the North End. For the next few years, especially if you approach from Atlantic Avenue or Commercial Street, you'll be in the shadow and metallic glint of the earth-eating equipment of the Big Dig. But when the massive construction project has dug its last, the Central Artery—the clogged overpass that severs the North End from the rest of Boston—will be gone. Instead, we'll have a green fairway to pass through before visiting the North End, at least according to the present plan.

If you're a walker, you can also make your way from the Boston Common (Park Street MBTA stop, the main hub serving the Green and Red Lines), following the Freedom Trail. If you're a hiker, or flaneur, and can withstand face-specks from the Big Dig, you might try a long meander from South Station (South Station MBTA stop on the Red Line). I am fond of this odd route; in following Atlantic Avenue, then bearing left through Faneuil Hall Marketplace, Boston Harbor is always on the right. The sea breezes are bracing, and you get a dynamic sense of the shape and flow of Boston.

How to Get There

You should never drive to the North End, especially during the ongoing Big Dig construction. The closest MBTA stop is Haymarket on the Orange and Green Lines, followed by a short (if unscenic) walk to the southern portion of the North End, near the intersection of Salem and Cross Streets.

• • • *History* • • •

Those who go to the North End seeking lasagna or multitiered pastries will not be disappointed. But layers of history, as well as layers of pasta, can also tantalize. Three centuries of immigration—colonials, African Americans, Irish, Eastern European Jews, Italians—and today's stratum of Italian Americans and young career people—are resonant in the streets. The immediate impression is, to be sure, of an Italian-American neighborhood, but as you become accustomed to the visually packed narrow streets, you can see between and beneath the layers. In North Square you are surrounded by a seventeenth-century house, an eighteenth-century street plan, a nineteenth-century Italian church with angels flying off the parapets, and the skyscrapers of Boston.

The North End neighborhood is old, settled in the 1600s, and has structures to prove it. Paul Revere's house, which seems amazingly small when you tour it—especially when you learn he had more than a dozen children, born of two wives—is the oldest house in downtown Boston, built in 1676. Next door is a newish house, built around 1711; it belonged to Nathaniel Hichborn, Revere's cousin. The scale of these houses seems utterly in place with the current neighborhood, especially if you dismiss the skyscrapers in the near distance.

In addition to Revere's home, Old North Church (Christ Church) figured prominently in Boston history and remains a popular touring site. On April 18, 1775, twenty-three-year-old sexton Robert Newman placed two lanterns in the church belfry—almost 200 feet above ground—to alert Revere that the British were making their way to Concord. Revere took off like a shot on his famous ride to Lexington.

During the early colonial period, the Puritans built timber houses reminiscent of the England they had left, and the North End became fashionable. But a century later, following the Revolutionary War, the wealthy Tories fled to Canada, and the community downscaled to become a village of workmen and their families. As the neighborhood is on the harbor, most trades were associated with navigation— sailors, tradespeople, craftsmen, suppliers.

Another phase of North End history began with the arrival of immigrants, starting around the mid-nineteenth century. These desperately poor men, women, and children lived in crowded tenements along the North End's crooked streets. The Irish, fleeing the potato famines of 1845–50, came first, followed by Eastern European Jews, who were fleeing political and religious persecution, as well as poverty. In time, the Jews established a retail and residential center along Salem Street (an anglicized version of Shalom, or peace), traces of which still remain. Today, most of Salem Street's storefronts are a century old. And the mix of tradespeople—bakers, butchers, fishmongers, dry goods merchants—are not all that different from those traders of long ago.

Following the Jews, the Italians arrived, most from southern Italy. By the early twentieth century, they dominated the area. Most of the community's churches, schools, and civic buildings—the Bennet Street School, the North End Union, the VFW—bear the imprint of the Italian community.

As in every neighborhood of Boston, immigrants moved from the inner city to the suburbs as they became more prosperous. Today, on Sunday afternoons, a procession, more cultural than religious, forms in the North End: Urban and suburban families reunite in the old neighborhood. Big sedans and SUVs slow traffic as their drivers stop in the middle of the street to acknowledge the greetings of people on the sidewalk, in the windows, on the balconies, and, of course, in their chairs (see "Chairs, Italian Style").

... *A Walking Tour* ...

Even with a map, you'll get lost walking the North End. Expect it. Welcome it! The sensory vignettes that stay with you come while wandering, an activity that sharpens perceptions. Everyone's "eye" is different. Mine loves the rows of old, crushed, metal mailboxes—a vignette of correspondence over time—visible through a foyer window on Garden Court Street. Keep wandering; you'll find your own version.

The reason you'll almost inevitably get lost is that nobody planned the North End. It's a jumble. But the community is so small that you'll never be lost for long.

Walking from the Haymarket T stop through the pedestrian underpass, Cross Street is "the bottom" of the North End, the southernmost cross street. What I consider "the top" is around Copp's Hill Burying Ground. Just beyond, to the north, Commercial Street, along Boston Harbor, is the northernmost boundary. North Street is the

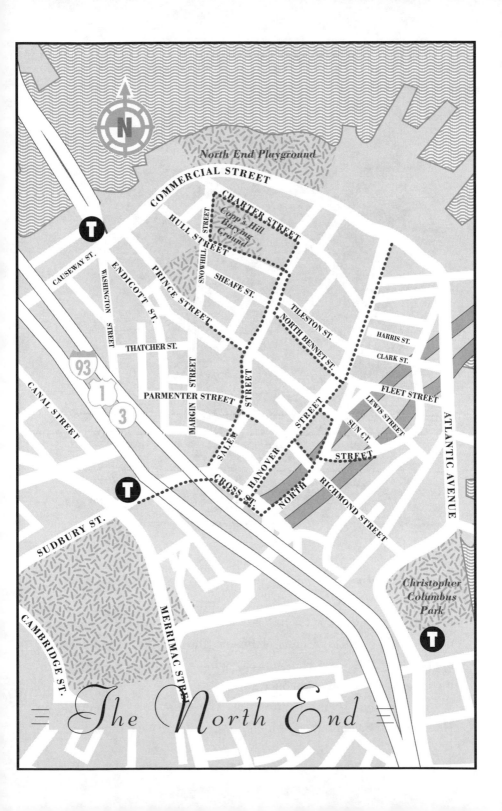

North End apartment gardeners make good use of sunny fire escapes.

eastern edge, adjacent to the Callahan Tunnel. And if you wander down to the residential ends of Prince and Endicott Streets, you're approaching the North Station area, home of the Fleet Center, where the beloved Boston Garden once stood.

During your initial explorations, I suggest you concentrate on Hanover and Salem Streets, which are parallel to each other. Imagine a rectangle, or better still, a triangular pizza slice that you've just bitten into. Hanover and Salem are the long "sides" of the triangle, Cross Street the "point" of the pizza you've taken a bite from, and Commercial Street, to the north, the outer crust. Explore within this zesty slice, and you'll never be hungry.

CROSS STREET

As you arrive from Haymarket, Cross Street conveys an Italian welcome—wine, cheese, ripe fruit, cookies, pastries, bread. Surely you need a lift after passing beneath the turgid Central Artery. Enter **Maria's Pastry Shop,** 46 Cross Street, (617) 523–1196. Other bakeries are bigger, flashier, more advertised, but nobody else has *totos*. Named for an Italian comedian—no one seems to know why—these fudgey balls are the size of Italian plums. Hand-formed, intensely chocolate, and with a light glaze, they can be nibbled, sliced into hemispheres, or stuffed into one's mouth.

Maria's also carries Italian cakes, candies, and an array of butter cookies—the miniature apricot "turnovers" are excellent with iced tea. The crunchy almond biscotti are thin and crisp. The shop refers to these cookies as *queresimole*. "The word is mysterious," shrugs proprietor Maria Merola. But no mystery to the cookies' quality; they're loaded with almonds and baked twice for crispness.

Another specialty is Mustaccioli, fudgy chocolate bars, sometimes with fig filling and always with a dark chocolate glaze.

In warm and not-so-warm weather, **A. La Fauci & Sons,** 46 Cross Street, (617) 523–1158, a bare-bones establishment augmented by handsome fruit displays, thrusts open its doors and moves lavish arrangements of produce onto the sidewalk, including unblemished artichokes that look like something out of a still life. At La Fauci it is customary to point to what you want rather than to serve yourself. If you dare to squeeze the fruit, someone cranky will likely shout, "So how 'bout if I squeeze you? Would you like it?" The most diplomatic response is, "I'm not sure."

Visit **Martignetti's,** 64 Cross Street, (617) 227–4343, for a tempting selection of well-priced Italian and other wines, mainly European. This is an old, crowded, overstocked store—very different from Martignetti's sprawling market in Brighton—but loaded with character. Lots of discoveries here: rough yet silky red wine from Sicily, and luscious Marsalas, including a dry version that makes an enjoyable aperitif when chilled.

HANOVER STREET

Hanover is the heavy-hitter street—lots of sleek restaurants, flashy cafes, bakeries with informal seating. It's the public, ceremonial street, too, the primary location of the North End festivals and processions each summer. Salem, the old market street, has smaller stores, groceries, and butcher shops. Both streets hold historic churches and houses.

This lower end is cafe and hang-out city, with most spots offering coffee, iced drinks, pastries, and light meals. Many North End restaurants don't serve dessert, so diners wander over to cafes for coffee. My theory is that having to move from place to place maximizes the number of people you can see and be seen by. In the North End conversation and social contact are everything.

If you see a crowd in front of a cafe, you're nearing **Caffe Paradiso,** 255 Hanover Street, (617) 742–1768, which televises soccer matches over its bar and is open to the street. Fans scream and applaud. To augment the already absurd amount of vehicular traffic, long sedans slow down in front of Caffe Paradiso to try to catch glimpses of the soccer coverage. Customers with minor athletic interests sip espresso or fruit drinks, devote themselves to rich chocolate gelati, or a lush, spongy tiramisu. On a golden day in November, the doors are thrown open, the marble tables gleam, and small flags of all nations beckon to this cosmopolitan spot.

Next door, and relatively subdued, **Modern Pastry,** 257 Hanover Street, (617) 523–3783, is a small, unadorned bakery with my favorite *biscotti de prati.* During the last decade, as biscotti became "in," they turned into big, thick slices that resemble something a zoo primate would suckle on. Modern Pastry's biscotti are small, dainty, and thinly sliced—and therefore properly crisp. They make ideal accompaniments for cafe au lait, and, of course, *vin santo.* The bakery also creates mythical-looking *sfogliatelle.* The crescent-shaped seashells are a light pastry filled with custard—ambrosial with espresso. Sugar and caffeine can't really be unhealthy. They make us feel so happy.

Modern Pastry's display window is charming: still lifes of marzipan fruit, cookies on doilies, and *torrone,* the exotic chocolate-nougat-almond concoction. It's made by Modern. No one knows how. And they won't tell.

The local **VFW,** North End Post 144, is a heartening outpost. Set back from the street, the modest but proud-looking building is draped with patriotic signs and slogans, and hosts important community functions. A permanent sign on the roof says, in capital letters, WE'D DO ANYTHING FOR THIS COUNTRY.

At **Salumeria Toscana,** 272 Hanover Street, (617) 720–4243, it's hard to evaluate what is most seductive—the fresh pasta, creamy cheeses, and aromatic olives—or the proprietor. He is never overbearing, but he flirts expertly and relentlessly. The sleekly presented foods in this earthy but elegant market create a perfect backdrop. On a recent visit, Signore Flirt and I discussed kissing. He maintained that "middle-aged men are much better kissers than young guys," as

I tried to sample olives. He joined me, announcing that I should kiss him ("It's okay—we both ate garlic.") to test his theory.

You may not like this kind of service, what our mothers used to call "fresh," but the charm of this small store is irresistible. All is artistically displayed, and many of the products—fresh bread, spices, cheeses—are unwrapped. Salumeria Toscana carries a spectacular cheese that I have never seen elsewhere. Not for the faint of heart, Calabria Gold is a firm, somewhat aged, goat cheese with a garnet-colored rind, spiked with hot pepper. When I eat a lot of this cheese, my lips get numb. Probably kissing would be the store's recommendation.

Another upscale Italian grocery is just off Hanover Street. Backtrack a few steps, and facing the direction you've come from, take a left onto Richmond Street. **Salumeria Italiana,** 151 Richmond Street, (617) 523–8743, a gracious gourmet grocer, overflows with imported pastas, cheeses, meats, and sausages; pricey specialty oils and vinegars; and arborio rice worthy of storing on one's desk as a paperweight—so chubby and gleaming are the grains. The cheeses are in good condition here—not dried out. Try the Drunken Goat, a mild Spanish cheese aged in red wine (and yet still a creamy white).

The furnishings of **Caffe Victoria,** 296 Hanover Street, (617) 227–7606, are a little over the top, but who couldn't love operasinging espresso makers? This was Boston's first cafe.

If you've visited the North End, the bakery you probably remember is **Mike's Pastry,** 300 Hanover Street, (617) 742–3050, a big, glitzy, crowded bakery with cafe tables in the window. In contrast to haunts such as Modern Pastry and Parziale's, simple places with just a few specialties, Mike's is a three-ring circus. You can find everything here from a wedding cake and a fresh filled cannoli, to a ricotta pie and tiramisu, to American specialties such as spicy hermits and chocolate chip cookies. Mike's is a big tourist draw and carries an array of seasonal sweets: *panettone* at Christmas time, sculpted marzipan lambs at Easter (with satin ribbons and tinkling bells), and specialties during feast days.

Caffe Graffiti, 307 Hanover Street, (617) 367–3016, is a stylish little place for hanging out over a Campari and soda, an icy cappuccino, or a dark Italian beer. **Caffe dello Sport,** 308 Hanover Street, (617) 523–5063, is nice and sunny, good for people-watching and discussions about Italian soccer teams.

In contrast to the austerity of New England Congregational churches, **St. Leonard's Church Peace Garden,** Hanover at Prince Street, (617) 523–2110, is a cavalcade of flowers, statuary, and festive lights. Maintained by the Franciscans, the sanctuary was designed in 1891 by William Holmes and was the first Italian church constructed in New England.

Past the hubbub of restaurants, bakeries, and cafes, you'll find Paul Revere Mall on the left side of the street and St. Stephen's Church on the right. White-steepled **St. Stephen's,** 401 Hanover Street, (617) 523–1230, exudes purity and virtue. Built in 1804, St. Stephen's is one of just five remaining Boston churches designed by legendary architect Charles Bulfinch. Its transitions follow the religious history of the North End: Originally built as a Congregationalist Meeting House, it became a Unitarian church in 1813, then a Catholic church during the 1860s.

Across the street a long, leafy courtyard—a rectangular park, really—holds an equestrian statue of Paul Revere at one end and an Italian-style fountain at the other. **Paul Revere Mall**—Hanover, Unity, and Tileston Streets—is known locally as "the Prado." In this well-designed Italian-American enclave, North End kids cut-up, parents chat, and seniors play cards and dispense advice, welcome or not. The Prado is a lovely access to the rear portion of **Christ Church,** also called **Old North Church,** 193 Salem Street, (617) 523–6676, best known for its role in the American Revolution. When you arrive at the front of the redbrick building, you're on Salem Street.

No matter what god, gods, or goddesses you worship, you'll likely respond to the presence and character of Old North. The church was built in 1723 for an Anglican congregation, and is today a national treasure. The heraldic white steeple, a Boston landmark, is almost 200 feet high and can be seen from many parts of the city. North-Ender Paul Revere came to this church as a teenager. Along with other parishioners, he regularly rang the eight bells. Their sound was, and is, remarkable. The eight bells, which together weigh over 7000 pounds, are said to be "the sweetest in the nation."

Decades later, as the fiery patriot he'd become, Revere was signaled by the lanterns hung in Old North's belfry to take off for Lexington.

There are tours of Old North. It's cool inside. The walls are painted white. The high pew boxes envelop worshipers. The church clock and organ are almost 300 years old. It is a place of calm, where even the talkative lower their voices.

You can now explore Salem Street, or return to Hanover Street by recrossing the Prado, or cross Salem Street to Hull Street.

If you return to Hanover Street, continue to the end, where the sky seems to open to the harbor. You'll spot the modern **Coast Guard building** on Commercial Street. Enjoy the views of Boston Harbor, glorious "Old Ironsides" (the U.S.S. *Constitution*) in Charlestown, and gulps of sea air.

After visiting Old North, you might cross Salem Street—the Prado leads to Hull Street—to explore **Copp's Hill Burying Ground,**

Olives

When I was a wee lass, olives took two forms: fat black ones in cans and skinny green ones with pimento innards in jars. Imagine my Alice-in-Wonderland delight when I first sashayed down Salem and Hanover Streets, with their shimmering selections of olives: mounded in white ceramic bowls in markets, spiking pizza and pasta in restaurants, kneaded into glossy rolls and breads, and crushed into pale green olive oil. Extra vergine, extra virgin, I soon learned, was the olive oil to buy.

All the olives you'll see belong to one species: Olea europaea. But over 700 cultivars exist, according to Mort Rosenblum, bon vivant author of Olives: The Life and Lore of a Noble Fruit. They grow on stocky trees with fragrant white blossoms and dainty, gray-green leaves all over the Mediterranean, North Africa, and in parts of the Middle East. Like wine grapes, their tastes derive not only from varied growing conditions, but from methods of preparation: dry cured in salt or cured in brine or oil. The same olive may be green when unripe, black when ripened.

In North End groceries and specialty shops, you'll find about a score of varieties, though not all types at all times of year. You'll readily locate the gigantic green Sicilians, lusty black Gaetas, purple-black Kalamatas, and wrinkled, shiny Niçoises, the shining stars of Salade Niçoise.

Some North End stores toss their olives with minced garlic or bits of fresh herbs such as thyme or sage, or set forth family appetizer concoctions, generally best served with chunks of bread and a peasanty rosso.

On a lazy summer evening, take the olives, the bread, and a few cheeses. Uncork the wine. Buon appetito.

Snowhill Street between Hull and Charter Streets. Once a Native American burial ground, it was established as a colonial cemetery in 1659 and holds generations of multicultural North Enders. These range from several members of the Puritan Mathers family (in a brick vault) to Prince Black, an African-American soldier in the American Revolution and an antislavery activist. The high-elevation graveyard is verdant and peaceful and affords splendid views of Boston Harbor and Old Ironsides.

As the burying ground combines aspects of history, poetry, beauty, and even geology, this elegiac outcropping is worthy of a leisurely, thoughtful afternoon. Most visitors take about ten minutes. Though it is hallowed ground, I like to think that the dead are fine with my custom of bringing a bag of biscotti and munching them at **Copp's Hill Terrace,** the adjacent hillside park, after I've walked among the slate headstones, smoothed by time.

SALEM STREET

I love the way Salem Street still feels like a market street. This is not a figment of my imagination, but the presence of more than a dozen specialty purveyors. Meat, fish, produce, coffee, spices, and candies are all sold here. So are cooking accoutrements and good junk. There are nineteenth-century brick buildings with stores on the first floor, residences above.

Heading south on Salem (away from the harbor), handsome, red-brick **North Bennet Street School,** 39 North Bennet at Salem Street, (617) 227–0155—a massive yet tidy Victorian building—still teaches artistic trades such as violin making, metalsmithing, and furniture design and creation. It was founded by Pauline Agassiz Shaw in 1881 as a social service agency for immigrants. Slow down to watch woodworking students through long ground-floor windows open to the street. Admire the gorgeous double oak doors with arched window. Across from the school, **A. Boschetto,** 158 Salem Street, (617) 523–9350, is another classically simple, small North End bakery.

The displays at **Calore Fruit,** 99 Salem Street, (617) 227–7157, which also showcase vegetables, make you want to rush home and cook, or take to your easel. The diverse varieties of mushrooms are inspiring; the portobellos are the size of saucers. Peppers, eggplants, and artichokes almost glow with vitality.

Frank A. Giuffre & Sons Fishmarket, 71 Salem Street, (617) 227–6429, carries a variety of fresh fish and unusual specimens such as fresh sardines and eels—scary looking to some, but the basis of many Italian delicacies.

Saints forbid you would sell bad meat in the North End; you'd be run out of town. Salem Street has several butchers that pass muster with discerning customers: **Paesani Meat Market,** 120 Salem Street, (617) 523–8507; **Abruzzese Meat Market,** 94 Salem Street, (617) 227–6140; and **Di Paolo & Rossi Meat Market,** 56 Salem Street, (617) 227–7878. All look like old-fashioned butcher shops: modest, clean, and with red, marbled meat on display, not cut up and prepared in a back room. In addition to beef, lamb, and pork, North End butcher shops often sell sausage and game, especially rabbit.

When you reach Prince Street, take a right onto a residential block and a small, singular bakery: **Parziale's & Sons,** 80 Prince Street, (617) 523–6368. A better-known competitor, **Bova,** 134 Salem Street, (617) 523–5601, is on the corner. Open twenty-four hours a day, this big bakery carries breads, pastries, pies, cookies, and turnovers. By contrast Parziale's is an old-world spot with just a few products. But their bread is beyond compare—round, crusty, well-baked loaves the size of vintage records; long, oval whole-wheat loaves; and a spectacular cinnamon raisin loaf that is ambrosial when lightly toasted. This place reminds me of village bakeries in the Mediterranean. The family could be having a fight when you enter; they'll pause to sell you the bread, then quickly resume. Their debate—or expression—is far more important than the bread sale, as it is linked to the meaning of life: continuous engagement with intimates.

In a nod to Jewish peddlers past, **Sheldon's Bargain Outlet,** 133 Salem Street, (617) 523–3914, features what my grandmother Rose called *chazzerei,* Yiddish for junk. It isn't junk, but it isn't fancy. Think indoor flea market with the emphasis on clothes, including for kids—also, plastic shoes, hair accessories, household items, and underwear, all displayed on tables and with handwritten price tags. Like many buildings on Salem Street, this one boasts an architectural distinction—it's brick with stone pediments and decorative scroll work.

If you're an architecture buff, you'll delight in the varied small-scale buildings on Hanover and Commercial Streets, including some of the doors. You don't have to dine at **Euno's** (see "Suggested Restaurants"), 119 Salem Street, (617) 573–9406, to appreciate the magnificent carved mahogany door with oval window and cast-brass knob. Created for the restaurant by Boston artist Titus, the bas relief depicts Sicilian-style folk heroes and celebrations of nature, especially food: graceful flat fish, classical scallop shells, grapes, and grain. The carving of the head of Euno, the Sicilian slave for whom the restaurant is named, is museum worthy. But how much better that it's on the street.

To delightfully detain yourself, take a left on Parmenter Street to rest in the **Boston Public Library, North End Branch,** 25 Parmenter Street, (617) 227–8135, no ordinary library. The shelves of books surround a light-filled atrium that has a miniature pond and loads of plants, including palm and fig trees almost two stories high.

Chairs, Italian Style

Where would the North End be without folding chairs? They make statements, mark territory, convey personality, and are only incidentally for comfort.

Elderly men sit on them, sometimes turned backward, their canes hanging on the frames. Pedestrians must squeeze by or walk in the street. Men in chairs rule. From their ad hoc sidewalk cabanas, the men observe people, cars, and weather. They talk about their women, their kids—good kids and no-good kids—potholes, politics, pasta, sauce, and the Red Sox.

Folding chairs also mark on-the-street parking places—especially in winter, when urban snow mountains are dug out by residents thereby conferring ownership (a kind of timeshare). Some fastidious grandmothers, wishing to ensure immaculate and personal seating, slowly carry or drag their chairs into the local parks and piazzas. Sometimes the chairs have been upholstered, "to give a little zing," as one lady told me.

Some neighborhood cats sit on folding chairs, refusing to cede them to humans unless they are swept off with a hand or a light broom stroke. The chair-cats are imperious and crafty. It wouldn't surprise me to discover that they had learned to open the chairs, accomplishing their activities out of sight, as is often the case with cats. I imagine them in late afternoon, applying their dainty but powerful jaws to chair legs and dragging them into the shade.

The children's section is charming, and you can find Italian-language books and diverse volumes on Italian history, cooking, and literature.

Across Parmenter is an ancient and venerable institution, **The North End Union,** founded as a settlement house. Until recently it was a community school for children and adults—with courses in everything from Italian cooking to Italian language—and served a fine lunch to all comers. Regrettably, it's closed, and the building is now used as a theater.

Coffee is the least of it at **Polcari's Coffee,** 105 Salem Street, (617) 227–0786, at the corner of Salem and Parmenter. The handsome, old-fashioned store, heavy on wood and open bins, overflows with spices, grains, dried seeds, and beans—from the seductive vanilla to the chubby ceci—and, of course, coffee and tea. They do not balk when I ask to smell the loose tea before buying it, and pull down the heavy glass canister, place it on the counter, and shake it so the tea leaves will release their perfume. Or not. Polcari's, eighty years old, is the source for elderly home cooks in need of fresh oregano and those new to cooking, learning the wonders of arborio rice, the raw material of risotto.

On this zesty street even the hardware stores have personality. **True Value** has as many different kinds of terra-cotta and faience pots as some suburban nurseries, festively stacked on the street. Inside, in addition to typical hardware store items, the place stocks serious cooking tools and some of the best designer aprons I've ever seen—long, practical, heavy-duty affairs with festive prints, featuring seafood, tropical landscapes, herb gardens, and wine. They also stock huge glass bottles with brass spigots for paisans who make their own vino.

Pablo Neruda wrote the grand poem "Oda al Tomate" ("Ode to the Tomato"), proving that food can inspire great art. If he were alive

Chocolates at Dairy Fresh Candies attract man, woman, and beast.

and I could bring him to **Dairy Fresh Candies,** 57 Salem Street, (617) 742–2639, the multigenerational Matera family enterprise, I believe he would compose another ode. On one side of Dairy Fresh are open bins of glossy dried fruit and wrapped candy and wall displays of romantic boxes of chocolate, including the Perugina line, which all people in love are acquainted with, or should be. (These are to Whitman's Samplers what Sophia Loren is to Doris Day, which is not to slight Doris Day or Whitman's Samplers, both of which I like. But Sophia and Perugina have va-va-voom.) On the other side of the store, it's gourmet land. You cross an alcove where glossy nut brittle is stashed—it's easy to miss, please don't—along with *pane-forte*, a Tuscan delicacy. In glass cases are scores of varieties of fine chocolates, some imported and many locally made in artisans' studios. Nuts galore: The cashews are colossal, not to mention tasty, fresh, and crisp. The nut bark is heavenly. The wall of gourmet products can make foodies late for any and all appointments, including jury duty, speaking for myself. Even when I have no intention of buying, I study these shelves as an art historian would examine a fresco. Here I have found varieties of balsamic vinegar, superb vanilla, fancy olive oils to give as gifts, packaged cookies, and desirable whatnots—gooseberries in syrup, quince jam (very good on toasted bagels with cream cheese), mushroom mustard, capers, cornichons.

NORTH SQUARE

It's best to chance upon North Square, to idly come upon it, as one does neighborhood piazzas throughout the Mediterranean. Of course, its whereabouts is no secret as it's on the Freedom Trail. But there is something precious about stumbling across this zone of quiet and juxtaposed centuries. When we are unprepared, and without preconceptions, we see most clearly.

I offer a compromise: You might try creeping from bustling Faneuil Hall Marketplace onto North Street. In the midst of the noisy, crowded metropolis, you'll find a spot of quiet and green. You are surrounded by cobblestone walks and gas lamps. In the center a formal garden of boxwood hedge and spring bulbs sets off a small statue of St. Francis, an early environmentalist.

Sacred Heart Church, 12 North Square, (617) 523–1225, built in 1833, dominates. Once it was a bethel for seamen. Its Methodist preacher, Father Edward Taylor, a former sailor, drew Walt Whitman, Ralph Waldo Emerson, and Charles Dickens as admirers. In 1871 this seamen's house of worship was sold, enlarged, and became a Catholic church. During the 1870s **Mariners' House,** 11 North Square, a brick Federalist building next door, was converted to lodging for seamen. In that era, before landfill, North Square was at the edge of the harbor, and seamen kept watch from the cupola on the roof.

Across the way, **Paul Revere House,** 19 North Square, (617) 523–1676, a dapper wooden dwelling built in 1676, is furnished much as it was when Revere lived there. In the courtyard is a tribute to Revere's skills as a bellmaker: a magnificent 931-pound bronze bell of his creation. Next door, a brick English Renaissance–style house, the **Pierce-Hichborn House,** belonged to Revere's cousin, Nathaniel Hichborn. It was built between 1711 and 1715 and is quite a contrast to Revere's Tudor-style wooden abode. You can tour the two stalwart houses or just take in the amazing composite view of tidy eighteenth-century houses and mirror-finish Boston skyscrapers.

In between the houses and the church, on a third side of the square, **Mama Maria** (see "Suggested Restaurants"), 3 North Square, (617) 523–0077, a splendid and romantic restaurant, beckons. The turn-of-the-twentieth-century town house is an excellent place to offer or to receive a romantic proposal. Just beyond, please find **Garden Court Street.** Rose Kennedy, mother of President John F. Kennedy and Senator Edward Kennedy, and matriarch to the clan, was born in a humble tenement, Number 4 Garden Court

Street. Her father, whom she idolized, was John F. "Honey Fitz" Fitzgerald, a grocer's son who became mayor of Boston.

If you haven't had time to focus on local history, make a point of coming back to explore further North Square, Copp's Hill Burying Ground, and the Prado, which links the historic churches of Old North and St. Stephen's. Over time, you'll linger in these sacred spaces, cultivating your appreciations as your appetite builds. Cap off your afternoon by shopping for dinner. You'll find everything you need.

SUGGESTED 🍴 RESTAURANTS

If your experience of Italian cuisine leans heavily to spaghetti and meatballs, you are, in a way, lucky. In today's North End, you'll feel like Alice in Wonderland. While you can find traditional southern Italian and Italian-American dishes—lasagna, spaghetti, pizza—regional Italian cooking and "new Italian" (which is to say Italian-inspired, but with wide latitude) are what now draw raves.

Entire books are written on North End cuisine. I will not elaborate on the dozens of restaurants as they're all easily found, and they all post menus. But to get you going, here are eight to consider.

Ristorante Euno ($$–$$$), 119 Salem Street, (617) 573–9406, which bears the carved mahogany doors, is Sicilian in its sexy intimacy. Downstairs there's a fireplace, upstairs background jazz and cushy chairs. The owner is also Sicilian, as is the gold-green olive oil everything's cooked in, though white truffle oil is used in the Rotini e Funghi (pasta with mushrooms).

There are scads of *M* restaurants in the North End, even those that don't begin with Mama. Still, **Mama Maria ($$$–$$$$),** 3 North Square, (617) 523–0077, may top the list in terms of romance, especially if you request Room 99 in the North Square town house—its own little room, where you can whisper sweet nothings or negotiate corporate deals. The classical Italian menu is indulgent, expensive, and rich. Why not start with Budino di Pane e Asparago (asparagus bread pudding with poached egg and toasted walnuts), and proceed to Anitra all'Uva (braised duck cooked in fruit-infused pan juices with Muscat grapes and vegetables)?

Maurizio's ($$–$$$), 364 Hanover Street, (617) 367–1123— romantic, sizzling, with several walls the color of fire—features Mediterranean cooking (the chef-owner is from Sardinia) with lots of flavorful fish and shellfish.

Tiny **Terramia ($$–$$$$)**, 98 Salem Street, (617) 742–4336, presents gorgeous seafood and unusual soups, including a version of lentil from an island near Sicily that combines plump chestnuts with the sweet, nutty lentils. Terramia's lobster fritters involve shelled chunks of lobster dipped in a flour-and-beer batter, deep-fried, and served with a reduced honey and balsamic glaze.

Everyone must eat at **Daily Catch ($–$$)**, 323 Hanover Street, (617) 523–8567, at least once for its genial, sometimes riotous, atmosphere—like eating in the galley of a convivial ship. No menus—fab seafood and pasta dishes are posted on a blackboard. No rest room, no credit cards, lotsa squid.

Sage ($$–$$$), 69 Prince Street, (617) 248–1879, is an exceedingly pretty, homey restaurant near Parziale's bakery. It's a small, narrow room with terra-cotta–colored walls, chic little linen-draped tables with bentwood chairs, and understated contemporary art. Like most of the new breed of Regional Italian/New American restaurants, Sage runs to pricey entrees, but you can make an exquisite meal of appetizers along the lines of tuna carpaccio, Wellfleet oysters, or a luscious fried soft-shell crab sandwich with mango-papaya relish. Pan-seared sea bass and New England shellfish stew are other expressions of the chef's focus on seasonal, local ingredients.

Food snobs may knock **La Piccola Venezia ($–$$),** 263 Hanover Street, (617) 523–3888, but sometimes a gal's gotta put the old feedbag on. Dig into huge platters of Italian home cooking, inexpensively priced—gotcha spaghetti, lasagna, ravioli—and also Italian soul food: tripe, scungilli, baccala (salt cod). The embracing, vaguely Edwardian atmosphere—dark wood paneling, soft lighting, and a handsome bar—seem perfect for this uncomplicated, enjoyable food. No credit cards.

I have also had good dinners at informal but gracious **Cibo ($$),** 326 Hanover Street, (617) 557–9248. Antipasti range from broccoli rabe with smoked mozzarella and garlic crostini to a toothsome shrimp toscano; the critters are sautéed with garlic, tomatoes, and basil, served over white beans. Most entrees are traditional: linguine puttanesca, gnocchi with gorgonzola cream sauce, eggplant parm. There's also a fisherman-style linguine dish—clams, mussels, calamari, shrimp, scallops—that you can order lapped with red, white, or pesto sauce. I savor making these homey choices—it's like being in the kitchen without doing any work.

Dudley Square, Roxbury

An African-American Hub

To the newcomer Dudley Square looks like a series of juxta-posed stage sets: abandoned yet still imposing nineteenth-century buildings, flashy window displays of dollar earrings, small fish mar-kets, huge modern murals on the sides of buildings, and a white-spired New England Congregational–style church on a hill. Currier and Ives meets the 'hood. Dudley has all these sets because it's had all these lives. Today the heart of Boston's African-American commu-nity, and for decades a major transportation hub, Dudley is an old streetcar suburb that fell on hard times during the 1960s and 1970s. These times dragged on, draining the life and livelihood from a neighborhood of once classy department stores, pharmacies with gleaming soda fountains, and swanky after-hours clubs.

Within the last decade, local activists, urban advisors, and the mayor's office have created some inroads in the area's lagging economic development. Every few months, it seems, an initiative is undertaken, community meetings held, and plans announced to rehab a dilapidated building. But there's a long row to hoe. You'll still see vacant lots, scuzzy buildings, and shards of broken glass on some side streets.

But what Dudley Square has going for it—always has—besides its amazing history and stuff to buy that you won't find anywhere else, is its people: individuals of many colors, heights, widths, lan-guages, and ethnicities (most of whom seem to be shopping at Tropical Foods on Saturday, but I'll get to that).

First impressions of Dudley are kaleidoscopic. Fried fish, siz-zling barbecue, red ribs on white plates. Portuguese and Caribbean pastries, the latter heavy on the nutmeg. African art, snazzy caps, bolts of printed cotton fabric, hard-to-find books, videos on African-American history. Nail salon city. Churches humble and grand. Panoramic views of the Back Bay and South Station from a hill where

How to Get There

Public transportation offers many routes.
The tried and true: Take the MBTA Orange Line to
Roxbury Crossing and walk down New Dudley Street past
the high school and the post office; then bear left. Many buses
pass between nearby Ruggles Station and Dudley, including
Numbers 8, 14, 15, 23, 47. The Number 1 "party bus" runs between
Harvard Square and Dudley (see "Fantastic Voyage"), as does the
Number 66.

The brand-new route is literally shiny. Last summer the much heralded
Silver Line was introduced. Long, silver, electric buses now speed from
Downtown Crossing to Dudley's Victorian-era station. The sleek vehicles
travel along Washington Street through Chinatown, the Back Bay, and the
South End to Roxbury, a fifteen-minute slice of the city for 75 cents.

For MBTA information call (617) 722–3200.

By car there are three routes: Take the Mass. Ave. exit off Route 93
onto Melnea Cass Boulevard, and make a left onto Washington Street,
where you'll see Tropical Foods. From the medical area on Huntington
Avenue near the Brigham and Women's Hospital, take Tremont
Street, which becomes New Dudley. From the South End, follow
Washington Street through Melnea Cass Boulevard.

On-the-street parking is available, as well as a big,
free, centrally located lot on Washington
Street across from Payless Shoes and
Boston Foot Locker.

the Puritans settled. An array of architecture spanning two centuries—from gleaming white clapboard First Church Roxbury in John Eliot Square, the oldest standing wood-frame church in Boston, to ruddy brick nineteenth-century building blocks, to futuristic looking Madison Park High School just outside the square.

Dudley is a crossroads and mercantile square in Roxbury, a neighborhood of Boston not far from Northeastern University and Roxbury College. On the map, the "square" is actually more a triangle, bounded by Washington Street—one of the oldest streets in Boston, where many of the stores are located—Dudley Street, and Warren Street. In real life, the area is considered a little bit larger, with Dudley Station the fulcrum, extending up near Melnea Cass Boulevard and west toward John Eliot Square.

"Gone down [or up] to Dudley" in Roxbury parlance means heading for this place.

• • • *History* • • •

Dudley's history is amazing, as in the old-fashioned, dictionary sense, "filling the viewer with surprise and wonder." If you appreciate history—and incongruous juxtaposition—try tooling along in an auto from Boston's South End, heading south on Washington Street. You'll get a visual history course as you pass over Melnea Cass Boulevard. Esteemed members of the seventeenth-century Dudley family, colonial governors, are buried in Eliot Burying Ground, at the corner of Eustis and Washington on your left. The ancient raised cemetery, which contains the earthly remains of John Eliot, "Apostle to the Indians," is just across the street from Kornfield's, the last independent pharmacy in the area, a vestige of the neighborhood's early-twentieth-century Jewish incarnation. For a nineteenth-century visual icon, check out the 1859 Eustis Street Fire Station next to the burial ground. The squarish brick station with granite trimmed windows, designed by architect John Roulestone Hall, is today an official Boston landmark. Dudley Square glints with these historic puzzle parts. Farther down Washington you'll see Looking Good, a modern general store—albeit with loads of personal care products— dubbed "hair-city" by one longtime, well-coiffed customer.

In the colonial era, the place was farmland. As Boston was once a peninsula—before decades of landfill—and Roxbury the only land route to Boston, it became a crossroads. Washington, Warren, and Dudley Streets were laid out in this era, as were Centre and Roxbury. The area became a setting for country estates, including those of wealthy industrialists.

By the mid-nineteenth century, Dudley had become a commercial hub. Ferdinand's Blue Store—a massive five-story, yellow-brick building at the apex of Washington and Warren, now vacant—was *the* place for furniture and housewares. Plans are afoot to rehab the majestic building block for commercial and state office use.

The extension of the streetcar lines during the early twentieth century turned Dudley Square and its Roxbury environs into streetcar suburbs, the eventual home of a large Jewish community, along with English, Irish, and German immigrants and their descendants. During the 1940s and 1950s, the massive migration of African Americans from the southern United States to northern cities— Chicago, Detroit, New York, Boston—turned Roxbury into the hub of Boston's African-American community. By the 1960s most of Roxbury's Jewish families—the children and grandchildren of immigrants—had left for the suburbs.

Today change continues as the city of Boston and community leaders try to develop potentially valuable land parcels. The Boston

Redevelopment Authority is in the process of cleaning up a contaminated 100,000-square-foot property—Modern Electroplating and Enameling, one of Roxbury's most polluted sites—and plans to put in its place a site for office and retail use. A community development corporation is helping local businesspeople buy their own buildings. The state-run Department of Environmental Management curates Roxbury Heritage State Park. The jewel in that crown, another bit of living history, is John Eliot Square, reverberating with civic and spiritual associations, the site of Roxbury's first meetinghouse, built in 1632.

• • • *A Walking Tour* • • •

Roam around Dudley Square for twenty minutes before trying to explore it street by street. There are so many layers, oddly configured street junctions, and highlights in unexpected places that it's best to get the lay of the land before zeroing in.

Dudley Station, designed by Alexander Wadsworth Longfellow, a turn-of-the-twentieth-century architect who did many Back Bay mansions, was built in 1901 as the terminus of the Boston Elevated Railway. It has an artful, grande dame appearance—Victorian, with a stately copper roof turned gray-green, elegant patterned arches, and lavish use of glass brick. When Boston's rickety, rusty old El was taken down, Dudley was turned into a waiting area for buses. Today, the comfortable, well-lighted station is a major MBTA hub.

Explore around the station: Dudley, Warren, and Washington Streets. You'll see that Dudley Square, the retail core, is a triangle formed by two long streets, Washington and Warren, with Dudley Street running behind the bus station. Off in the distance, beyond Tropical Foods, is Melnea Cass Boulevard. Enter this triangular hub-

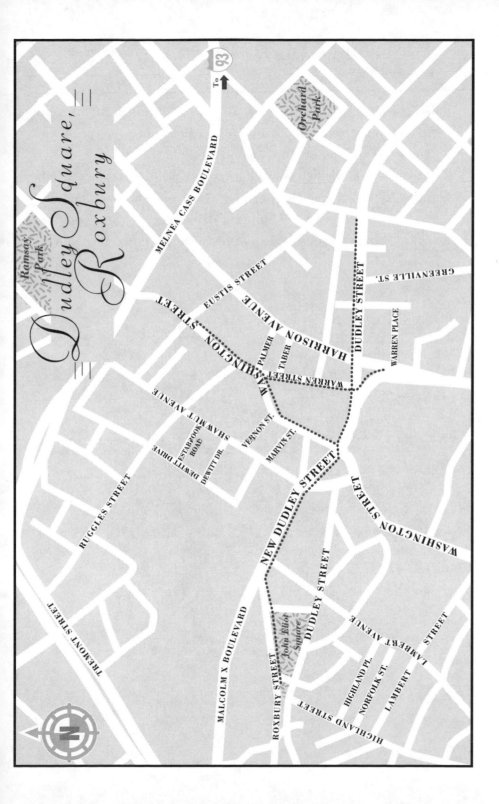

bub—stores, groceries, restaurants—with burial ground on the periphery and a separate area of John Eliot Square a five-minute walk down Dudley toward the Roxbury Crossing T stop.

Once you've oriented yourself, you may need refreshment. **Cafe Dudley,** 2306 Washington Street, serves breakfast, lunch, and dinner seven days a week, including a daily aromatic and bountiful breakfast: Virginia ham and eggs with grits and red eye gravy. I'll get back to this homey cafe in the restaurant section.

Dudley Square take-out restaurants offer spicy meat pies for urban travelers.

If you're a salt-hound who could use a substantial-something that's hot, satisfying, greasy, and good, seek limbo pies (a.k.a. limbo patties). Here and there—restaurants can change month by month in Dudley—you'll see handwritten signs for meat pies, beef patties, or limbo patties. They're one and the same: a savory turnover. Devotees close their eyes when they bite down on limbo patties. Generally, a cook blends bits of beef and cheese and spices, wraps the mélange in dough, and deep-fries the handheld pies until they're golden-yellow. They sell like hotcakes, but smell less polite—more peppery. Invented long before the fashionable "wrap sandwich," limbo patties are perfect to eat in a bus station or seated at a coffee-stained counter near a window, watching humanity through steamy glass.

Behind Dudley station, almost forming a wall with it—near the corner of Warren and Dudley—**A Nubian Notion,** 41–47 Warren Street, (617) 442–2622, is one of the liveliest stores in the square. Though not always at the same location in Dudley, this African-American specialty store has been a neighborhood mainstay for decades. At Nubian you could always find African textiles or hand-made jewelry and accessories to assemble an African-style outfit or add pizzazz to American garb. You still can. You can also choose among hundreds of greeting cards and posters with images from black history and day-to-day life. Nubian Notion's children's books feature characters with brown and black complexions.

Behind the counter, as he has been for three decades, you'll find general manager Jacob C. (Yakub) Abdal-Khallaq, colloquially known as Jake. "We try," he says of the store's enterprise. The store "tries" not only by stocking distinctive merchandise, but also by providing a cozy place. At the entrance a table holds stacks of community announcements. An annex has vintage records, tapes, and video rentals.

Fantastic Voyage

"Give us 75 cents and we'll show you the world," might be the MBTA's motto for the two buses that run between Harvard Square and Dudley Square. These city buses, even without commentary, put tourist buses to shame. With some regularity, there is free-form commentary from the drivers.

"You want a party? Get on, get on—take my bus," exhorts one driver on Saturday night. Dressy couples coming from Symphony Hall, undressy couples coming from Wally's (the South End jazz club), bedraggled young docs heading home from Boston City Hospital, women with saxophones getting on at Berklee, lads with laptops at MIT—they all get on. The full trip (and it is a trip) takes about thirty minutes and makes an amazing slice through the city.

Starting in Cambridge, the aptly named Number 1 proceeds down Mass. Ave. from the wrought iron gates of Harvard Yard, through yeasty Central Square, past MIT and winged Kresge Auditorium, across the Charles River to Boston and Symphony Hall, then onward to the Victorian world of the South End. Pear trees bloom before each ruddy row house, and occasionally a weeping cherry. Next is

On a typical Saturday, Abdal-Khallaq deals with a young woman who rushes in looking for "inspirational tapes for people that are caretakers and need relaxing," a googly-eyed couple looking at silver earrings, and a middle-aged man in need of a cap that "looks fine."

Shoppers can thank the late Malik A. Abdal-Khallaq, Jake's father, who founded the store in the early 1960s. The elder Abdal-Khallaq

Boston City Hospital and Boston University Medical Center on Harrison Avenue. A right onto Albany Street, right on Melnea Cass, left to Washington, and you're at La Dudley.

The Number 66, also a pretty fair bus, begins at Cambridge Common, but it is particularly enjoyable starting at Dudley. After a tamarind-goat-curry, limbo-patty kind of afternoon, it's pleasantly surreal to wait in the British architectural atmosphere of Dudley station, board a bus that careens onto noisy Dudley Street, passes the huge, imposing Basilica of Our Lady of Perpetual Help in Mission Hill, and is suddenly right near Harvard Medical School and the Massachusetts College of Art.

A quick jog left, then spiffy Brookline Village. Good-bye meat pie, hello espresso. Up Harvard Street to the retail citadel of Coolidge Corner—movies, restaurants, books, ice cream, The Gap, a zipper hospital—into Allston/Brighton, including a quirky loop onto Brighton Avenue and Market Street, a trove of Asian, Indian, and Caribbean grocery stores and restaurants. Finally, a brief tour of Allston's North Harvard Street (gas station opposite grocery store that stocks fresh octopus, though unreliably), past Harvard Stadium, and the entrance to academia via JFK Boulevard.

Who needs tourist buses?

began by bringing gift items into his elegant barbershop, known as the Beau Brummell Tonsorial Emporium ("Imagine, we children had to all say this on the telephone," remembers his daughter, Jumaada Abdal-Khallaq-Henry). The Tonsorial Emporium was first located in the space that became Wally's Cafe, a celebrated jazz club on Mass. Ave. in the South End, and then moved to Humboldt Avenue in Roxbury.

Across the street from A Nubian Notion is a flock of small owner-operated stores. Beauty parlors, barber shops, and nail salons abound. Casual clothing and club wear are at **Honey Women's Clothing and Accessories,** 36 Warren Street, (617) 427–5120, part of a series of small, personally run storefronts—steaks, subs, nails, duds—on Warren Street, some of which house multiple merchants and, therefore, offer multiple goods and services.

If you walk to the end of this block away from the terminal and cross Dudley Street, you'll see **CK African Art Market,** 155 Dudley Street, corner of Harrison Avenue, (617) 427–2090. When I visit CK's on weekdays, they're sometimes open, sometimes not. They're always open on Saturday, but it's probably still best to call.

CK's is like an old-fashioned dry goods store cum folk art gallery cum fashion accessories boutique. Racks of imported African clothing are displayed, along with small leather goods, musical instruments, and statues. If you sew or just enjoy swaths of exotic fabric, CK's sells beautifully loomed African textiles. In the midst of wooden sculptures, modestly priced, are handmade earrings. I've bought miniature brass African-mask earrings and dramatic dangles with multiple cowrie seashells. As I tried them on, black women were having their hair braided in the middle of the store. I took a long time choosing in order to see the gorgeous braids and rows emerging.

A whole other thing, **Fatima's African Hair Braiding,** is also located here, 155 Dudley Street, (617) 427–0195, in an annex at the back of the store. Several other Dudley-area shops offer braiding, and some people work out of their homes. You'll need to ask around. Fatima's does all manner of hair design: Senegalese twists, flat twists, cornrows, invisible braids, and African weaving. Guys with long hair are eligible, too.

Gallery G (Boston Metropolitan Artists Guild), 195 Dudley Street (no phone), is a new storefront gallery a few blocks from CK's; continue to the left, away from Dudley Square. Showing the work of over a dozen local artists, this is one jazzy place. Even the floor is artistically painted, and the bathroom is a mini-gallery. Amid the painting, sculpture, photography, crafts, and cards is the atmospheric work of Guadulesa—urban landscapes and jazz-inspired club settings—along with jewelry and leather by Bobby Crayton, and paintings and prints by Shea Ramone Justice. If you continue in this direction, walking into the heart of Roxbury, Dudley Street crosses Blue Hill Avenue and ends at Uphams Corner, an urban hub in Dorchester.

You can't miss **Looking Good,** 2241 Washington Street, (617) 445–3147. I think of it as a general store, but general stores are rarely this jazzy. Let's say it's a hybrid small-town department store/beauty supply outlet/discount house. Customers go in to buy a wig, party goods, a whisk broom, small appliances, a handbag, housewares, or a hot plate.

The prices are good, with some real bargains: flashy earrings for a buck, slinky long silk skirts for under $10, and always some surprising item. Last time I browsed the stationery aisle, I found sturdy red editions of *El Nuevo Testamento* between Elmer's Glue and air-mail envelopes.

On a winter Saturday, Kim McIver, part owner of Looking Good, located hair products for a woman from Framingham, dealt patiently with teenage customers browsing through hundreds of gigantic earrings at the front of the store, and found an appliance bulb for a customer who walked in, stood in the doorway, and boomed, "Help! There's a blackout in my fridge!" Like the owners of A Nubian Notion, McIver and her family have been Dudley Square merchants for decades. "We started with the beauty stuff," she says. "Then we just kept adding on."

Continue along Washington past venerable Kornfield Pharmacy until you reach a hub called **Tropical Foods,** 2101 Washington Street, (617) 442–7439. While it looks a little rundown from the outside, the place is vibrant, clean, and well stocked—a showcase of fruits, grains, and vegetables from all over. For many years, before the advent of "natural grocers" and gourmet stores, Tropical was the only place in Boston where you could get a decent mango and find nonstandard bananas and specialty greens. Even today, once you've browsed, schmoozed, and selected at Tropical, it's hard to go back to chain supermarkets. I challenge anyone short of a botanist to identify all the fruit in this place, a U.N. of squashes and legumes, not to mention people. Don't be put off by the first part of the store where the fare is pretty standard. Continue into the second section—that's where the pods are.

I remember the first time I saw a tamarind pod—a sinuous, fuzzy, beanlike fruit—the way some people remember their first kiss (or perhaps I should say first pleasurable kiss). I knew that tamarind had something to do with seeds and the color orange; whenever it was used as an ingredient, the affected food was orange. But I had never seen its botanical entirety till Tropical. Imagine a cocoa-brown, Möbius strip seedpod—something like the bean-thing on catalpa trees, but made of suede—with plump tender seeds cunningly arranged inside. These pods have many culinary applications, though I still prize them mainly for their beauty. As windowsill sculpture, they reign supreme.

Many small dramas and food missions occur at Tropical. A foodie from Brookline and her children come to browse the produce. They buy a big, strange-looking pod: a breadfruit. An elderly Spanish-speaking customer tries to tell them how to cook it. They smile but do not understand. The little girl tears out pages of paper from her

Greens

At the florist, greens are the sprays of leaves added to set off a floral bouquet. In African-American cooking greens are their own bouquet, though well smothered by the time they taste smooth and good. Leafy green vegetables are "cooked down to a low gravy," to quote the country cook Jessica Harris in Iron Pots and Wooden Spoons, her classic on Cajun, Creole, and Caribbean cookery. In Africa, even today, the greens would be simmered into a nutritious, spicy sauce and served over a starch. In the United States in keeping with our mealtime tradition of a protein, a vegetable, and a starch, greens are served as a separate vegetable on a plate.

Greens can be anything green. African Americans favor mustard, collard, and turnip greens. But there's not a reason in the world you can't use beet tops, chard (even red), or kale. The tried-and-true technique involves cooking bacon and a ham hock with the vegetable—say, four pounds of greens, five wide strips of bacon, a smoked ham hock, and a quart of water—for a good long time.

In this health-conscious era, with high blood pressure being a particular concern in the African-American community, most restaurants now use smoked turkey (wings, generally) instead of smoked pork.

Greens, whether mingling with a pig hock or a bird wing, have a particularly good flavor if stewed in a cast-iron pot. The leaves are iron-rich and absorb even more of the beneficial mineral while in the pot. On a cold winter day, you can leave the pot on the stove for hours, heating up your apartment, humidifying your plants, and making all your neighbors hungry. Once, during such a long, aromatic interlude, an appreciative UPS man rang my doorbell to ask what I was cooking. I told him to come back later, and I'd give him a serving, which I did, packed to go in a recycled kosher herring jar.

school notebook, and the Spanish-speaking woman starts to draw. Eventually, the woman's twelve-ish granddaughter shows up and translates. The breadfruit goes home to Brookline.

One remarkable Tropical aisle is an ode to beans—dozens of different types, including huge bagged sacks, along with grains and flours that encourage culinary experiments: farina, mandioca, and samp (coarse cornmeal). And what carb lover could resist Maiz de Toster, corn for toasting, a product of Peru? So what if it exploded in my kitchen, rocketing from a cast-iron pan, and landing in the ceiling fixture. This is apparently not the way to prepare it.

Back on Washington Street, walking toward the station, you get close to what you might mistake for a vacant lot at the corner of Washington and Eustis. This raised lot is hallowed ground—**Eliot Burying Ground**—holding the remains of seventeenth-century colonial governors, including members of the Dudley family.

Cross Eustis Street. On the same side of Washington Street, the **Hamill Gallery of African Art,** 2164 Washington Street, (617) 442–8204, housed in a huge rehabbed old wallpaper factory, is worth a trip to Dudley Square in and of itself. Entrance to the gallery is in the back, with plenty of parking.

The contents of this spacious gallery knock your socks off. You don't need a degree in art history to see where African-American artists such as Romare Bearden got some of their ideas. On the first floor is a framing studio. The second floor, flooded with light, is display space for expressionistic masks, dramatic sculpture (including carved wooden posts used by nomadic people at tent entrances and to hold down mats), brass and ceramic jewelry, woven textiles, amulets and fetishes, and to some collectors the most beautiful objects of all, the vivid beadwork of the Yoruba people of Nigeria. Crisply articulated turtles, snakes, and birds—all in patterns of tiny bright beads—

festoon sashes and other objects, along with appliqued cowrie shells. At Hamill's I learned that cowrie shells are considered lucky.

Gallery staffers are well informed. Explanation of the work, which changes every two months, is liberally offered. The press to buy is minimal. Many of the pieces are surprisingly affordable. These include striking ceramic beads and small sculptures. Posters are nominally priced.

This well-established gallery winds up being a hub for Roxbury Open Studios, (617) 541–3900, ext. 223, each fall. Artists and craftspeople who work in and around Dudley show work in all media—in studios, galleries, and homes—during a weekend in September or October.

Now continue down to Dudley Street. Follow New Dudley Street toward the white church steeple, which you'll see in any weather, at any time of year. When you get to the post office, cross the street. If you walk past a huge looming building, **Madison Park High School/John D. O'Bryant School of Mathematics and Science,** 55 New Dudley Street, you've gone too far. But take note of the buildings. On occasion local gospel groups perform here.

On the hill, **First Church Roxbury** at John Eliot Square— named for the second minister of First Church, who translated the Bible into Algonquin in 1663—surprises many visitors. "It looks like Newburyport," people say. The classic Federal-style white wood-frame church was completed in 1804.

It is actually the fifth church on the site. First Church Roxbury was organized by the Puritans in 1631. It figures all through American history. During the American Revolution as Paul Revere was making his midnight ride from Charlestown, William Dawes began his ride from First Church. A bell cast in Paul Revere's family foundry still hangs in the belfry.

*Two-hundred-year-old First Church Roxbury occupies a rise of
land in John Eliot Square.*

During the early 1800s First Church became liberal Protestant in character, and eventually Unitarian. "The church's active congregation dwindled during the 1960s," explains Sally Patton of the Unitarian Universalist (UU) Urban Ministry. In 1976 its congregation gave the building—and the rise of land with its extraordinary views of downtown Boston—to the UU's Urban Ministry. Today, after-school programs and antiviolence youth groups meet in **Putnam Chapel,** the smaller 1876 church building. On occasion concert performers, such as Odetta, appear in the church. For information call the UU Urban Ministry, (617) 542–6233.

Across the way, but still in John Eliot Square, the **Dillaway-Thomas House,** 183 Roxbury Street, (617) 445–3399, built as the parsonage to First Church around 1750, has been restored by the Department of Environmental Management (DEM) and is open to the public. Malcolm Wynn, a DEM staffer who helps to maintain the house—painted colonial gold, with a spiffy entryway of white columns and granite stairs—shows off the first floor to all who drop by. He is clearly proud of it.

The 250-year-old house is sparsely furnished, but very like its original self: a parlor and kitchen with three fireplaces ("in their original state," says Wynn), wide oak-plank floors, a delightful window seat, and the view of First Church and statuesque maples and oaks. The house is part of DEM's ongoing efforts to create Roxbury Heritage State Park, and is used to showcase local artists' work during Roxbury Open Studios each fall.

On the other side of First Church Roxbury are memories of a gracious urban age: the stately **Cox Building** (1870) at One John Eliot Square. It's redbrick with granite quoins, set at the end of the block in the manner of New York's Flatiron Building. Its jutting edge is actually six planes. A hundred years ago, during Dudley's boom time, the Cox

Building had street-level stores and hotel rooms on the upper floors. In 1984 it was rehabbed by Historic Boston and today is residential.

Finally, as you wander about the community, don't miss the **murals**. Standouts include "Stay in School" by local artist Dana Chandler on the parking-lot-side wall of A Nubian Notion, and the moody, celebratory paean to blues musicians on the Blue Store Building, part of the old Ferdinand's department store complex. This elegiac work is painted in hues and shades of blue and commemorates Muddy Waters, B. B. King, Memphis Minnie, and others, along with the keepers of the flame, the Warren Street Baptist Church Gospel Choir.

A tribute to blues artists elevates the entrance of the now-empty Blue Store to a streetside work of art.

Soul Food Cuisine

For African Americans soul food means traditional, family-style cooking that—for historic and economic reasons—maximizes the taste and nutrition of inexpensive cuts of meat, readily available fish (fresh-caught catfish, porgies, and perch), seasonal fruit and vegetables (originally homegrown), and locally available starches.

Metaphorically, soul food means savory food—with taste and pizzazz, never bland—cooked with love and heart.

The food is both southern American and African in origin and features liberal use of sugar and fat. Meat is often barbecued over an open grill, fish is breaded and fried, greens such as collards, kale, and chard are cooked with pork. Side dishes might be macaroni and cheese, rice and peas (also called rice and beans), or yams, often with brown sugar and butter whipped in. Pies are superb in this cuisine—with flaky crust and filled with custard, sweet potato, or a banana mélange.

Corn bread, baked in a pan and cut into squares, and fresh biscuits are staples of soul food cooking. The bread, served hot, is moist and crusty and generally made with yellow cornmeal here in New England. The biscuits are buttery and light. Fancier soul food restaurants have taken cues from New Orleans cuisine and feature blackened catfish, gumbo, and jambalaya.

The evocative meaning of soul food has spread. Members of other ethnicities now refer to the cooking of their ancestors as soul food. And so a good spicy meatball might be the soul food of an Italian American; a matzo ball (or, God forbid, derma—garlicky, eerie-looking, stuffed chicken necks) the soul food of an American Jew. Soul food is about taste, memory, pride, and love of culture.

SUGGESTED ▌●▐ RESTAURANTS

Dudley's restaurants are informal, with lots of takeout and eating at counters, reflecting their proximity to Dudley Station. Several spots line the perimeter around the terminal: Arizona BBQ and Ming's Garden on Washington Street, Joe's Famous Steak Sub on Warren Street, Max's Pizza and Ice Cream around the block on Dudley Street. McDonald's is in residence, as is Dunkin' Donuts.

Informal and homey, **The Silver Slipper ($)**, 2387 Washington Street, (617) 442–4853, serves limbo patties, curried goat, and empanadas. The Slipper looks how small-town restaurants used to look all over America—neat, clean, chipper, with bare floors, paneled walls, and tidy checkered tablecloths.

I was fond of the old soul food restaurant once located at the present site of **Cafe Dudley ($–$$)**, 2306 Washington Street, (617) 989–1118, but my lamentations ceased upon conversion to the cafe's garlic mashed potatoes, which are creamy and flavorful, with flecks of red potato skins. The attractive little restaurant next door to McDonald's (the cafe is the one with white tablecloths) serves southern-inspired home cooking with an elegant touch. An informal lunch might feature a meat loaf sandwich, smothered in mushroom gravy with french fries, or grilled chicken with pasta in a red pepper sauce. Dinner, served by candlelight, ranges from comfort food such as chicken livers in a rich, onion gravy and barbecued lamb with fried sweet potatoes, to fancy entrees such as flounder stuffed with crabmeat and a half-pound sirloin steak topped with a blue cheese crust, served with pilaf and vegetable.

In homage to its predecessor, Dudley Soul Food, the sides at today's Cafe Dudley shine. They include red beans, dirty rice, fried sweets and candied sweets, macaroni and cheese, collard greens, black-eyed peas, corn, and cole slaw. On hungry days I order a soulful trio of shiny, flavorful red beans, candied sweets (made from scratch, not with gummy canned potatoes), and deep-green collards—nice with the cafe's hot spiced cider, a New England overlay on southern cooking.

Even if you take the bus to Dudley just once in a while, it's easy to slip into a groove . . . picking up a pastry and a coffee . . . sipping java, munching on a coiled, cinnamony Portuguese roll from Tropical Foods or a wedge of pie from Cafe Dudley. You're eating outside, content and free, crumbs all over your winter coat, as the other bench-sitters chomp on their pastries and chow down on golden-yellow meat pies, held in greasy waxed paper and wadded paper napkins. It's cozy in the rain. Someday some musician will write a tune, "Limbo Pies in the Rain."

South Boston–Dorchester

PUBS AND PHO ON "DOT. AVE."

*S*outh Boston and Dorchester are next-door neighborhoods with intermingled histories. South Boston, once part of Dorchester, is dominated by its Irish-American populace. Today's sons and daughters of Eire range from folks whose ancestors settled in Southie to recent Irish émigrés. Dorchester is more of a melting pot—Irish, to be sure, but also Southeast Asian, Caribbean, Latino, and African-American, with traces of an older Central European community.

The Revolutionary War pasts of these regions are of a piece, so much so that fabled Dorchester Heights, where George Washington faced-off the British, is in South Boston, as is Fort Independence, which overlooks Dorchester Bay. Major streets—Dorchester Avenue, Columbia Road, a stretch of Old Colony Avenue—continue from South Boston to Dorchester with no change in name.

But the two communities look quite different and, at least to this outsider, pulsate different energies. South Boston has a close, orderly, fusty-genteel quality—generations of lace-curtain Irish propriety merged with the property-proud new people, most of whom are young, prosperous, and "not from here," as the old-timers say. To me, an occasional visitor, South Boston seems more comfortable, more homey—its residential streets follow a grid—but also more insular. Dorchester is bigger, messier, with more surprises and jagged energies. A few blocks into a struggling neighborhood, you'll come upon a hub of thriving markets and bakeries or a majestic preserved theater such as The Strand—an eighty-five-year-old movie palace in Upham's Corner now associated with African-American artists and community events.

To get the gist of South Boston, old and new, start with West Broadway, a protean part of the community—with churches, pubs, bars, restaurants, and several fine old buildings—and then head out to Pleasure Bay, the most congenial part of South Boston. Take a

How to Get There
West Broadway, South Boston

By public transportation take the MBTA Red Line to
Broadway station. Bus Number 9 also runs from Copley
Square. By car take Route 93 south into Boston through the
South Station tunnel and exit at Mass. Pike/Albany Street. Bear
left to the Broadway Bridge. In the fall of 2002, traffic was still a
mess because of the Big Dig; periodic unannounced reroutings make
motorists feel like rats in a maze. An adaptation of mine: From South
Station, following Summer Street, take a right on D Street and continue to West Broadway. You'll be a block from American Nut,
which is on the corner of West Broadway and C Street. By the
time you read this, construction on the South Boston waterfront may have begun, making matters worse. Take the
long view: There has been a bridge between Boston
and Great Neck (South Boston) since 1805;
connections will continue.

walk along The Strand, or the Strandway (old names), aka William J.
Day Boulevard (new name). On Sunday afternoons the whole neighborhood seems to parade by: joggers, in-line skaters, dog-walkers, old
couples holding hands, teenagers goofing off, young moms with per-
ambulators sporting their fair-skinned babies: girls in sun bonnets,
little guys in Red Sox caps.

To gain a hold on Dorchester, a more complicated community,
start by exploring a few of its old squares, such as Upham's Corner,
Field's Corner, and Ashmont. Cruise the avenues, especially

Dorchester Avenue, dubbed Dot. Ave. by locals. Cross-cultural travelers will be in their element traveling along this thoroughfare. Dot. Ave. spans an array of ethnic cultures and varied incomes overlaid on a 350-year history.

History

SOUTH BOSTON

A stubby peninsula of Boston proper, now about 4 square miles, as expanded by landfill, South Boston was called Great Neck by the Puritans, who settled Dorchester in 1630. For almost 150 years, farmers quietly went about their ways. Great Neck had fine seaside pastureland, a soft-green landscape for man and cow. Dorchester Street, which leads to Broadway, was the original path to the pasture.

Thinly settled Great Neck was part of Dorchester until 1804, when it was annexed to Boston despite the well-organized protests of Dorchester governors. The crafty Boston developers who'd encouraged the plan immediately set to work. A bridge—at the site of today's West Fourth Street Bridge—was constructed between Boston and its rural adjunct. Great Neck was the first area annexed to Boston during the nineteenth century.

The "neatness" of South Boston—the grid of streets and concentrations of mercantile, municipal, residential, and recreational areas—derives from an orderly history of urban planning. In 1804 Stephen Badlam and Mather Withington, land surveyors, laid out the grid. Starting at today's Broadway Station, the streets were named alphabetically from *A* to *P*, ending at City Point. Cross streets were named First Street, Second Street, and so on.

After about 1825 Southie took off, becoming an industrial center, with iron foundries, machine shops, shipyards, and refineries. By midcentury it had more dwellings than anywhere else in Boston. Immigrants poured in, especially the Irish, fleeing the potato famines of the 1840s. In South Boston they founded churches, schools, and charitable organizations separate from those of Protestant Boston. Before the arrival of the Irish, there were few Catholics in Boston. The Irish were followed by Lithuanian, Polish, and Italian immigrants.

By the late nineteenth century, the northern part of the waterfront had been developed for industry; the southern part was open, meeting workers' increased needs for leisure. Landscape architect Frederick Law Olmsted sought to continue his spread of public parks to this section of Boston. While not wholly successful (his grand plan was to connect Franklin Park with the South Boston waterfront), the creation of Marine Park, the Strandway, and Pleasure Bay ensured permanent water views and water walks for the working people of South Boston.

Today the Irish-American community that established itself during the nineteenth century holds fast. South Boston remains a bastion of Irish social, cultural, religious, political, and athletic organizations—from the score of churches, chapels, and schools; to the pull-out-the-stops St. Patrick's Day Parade; to the L Street Brownies who take their New Year's Day dip just beyond the L Street Bath House. You don't have to be Irish to be a Brownie, but you need to be rugged and laugh a lot.

... A Walking Tour ...

WEST BROADWAY: OLD AND NEW SOUTHIE

The clean, modern **Broadway subway station** incorporates the old mosaic "Broadway" mural in its platform design. It looks dandy with the station's contemporary black-and-white wall art.

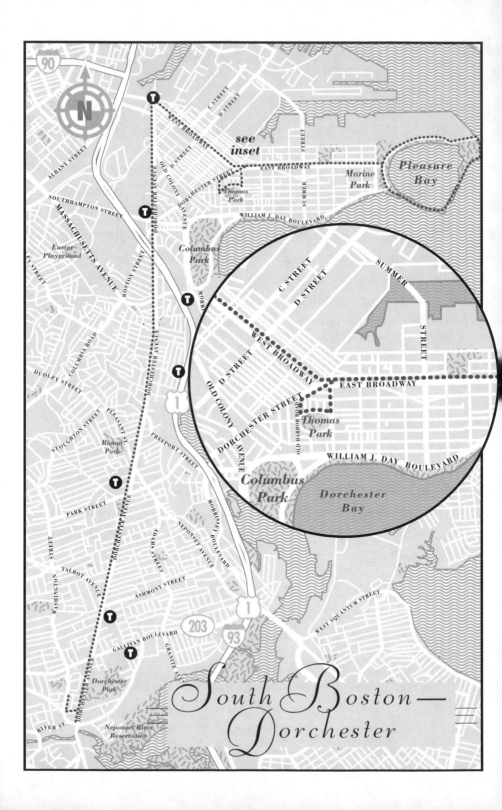

South Boston—Dorchester

Upstairs, you're on the corner of West Broadway and Dorchester Avenue, the Boston skyline to your left. As you begin your walk, the street looks a little shabby, a mix of bars, gas stations, and vacant public housing. Sundry infamous bars, watering holes for Irish gangsters, are just across the way. (Southie natives point these out to visitors in the same fact-a-life way they indicate St. Augustine's, the oldest Catholic church in Massachusetts, and Dorchester Heights, a monument to freedom.) As you make your way, you'll enter more gentrified zones, with several intriguing crossovers, partial integrations, and notable combinations. It's hard not to fall for a neighborhood where you can find biscotti, gourmet coffee, and tofu luncheon specials, Irish soda bread, red strings of licorice, Mary Janes (the shoes *and* the candy), and Teamsters Local 259.

The looming gray granite church, astonishing to see in this modest neighborhood, is the **Church of Saints Peter and Paul,** 45 West Broadway, the first Roman Catholic church in South Boston, built in 1844. The great blocks of stone are Quincy granite. After it closed in 1995, its parishioners moved to nearby St. Vincent's. The building is being turned into condos. Onward to **Mul's Diner,** 75 West Broadway, (617) 268–5748, a local hangout, and **Amrheins,** 80 West Broadway, (617) 268–6189, a grand old family restaurant—redbrick, four-story, with a spiffy, ornate facade (see "Suggested Restaurants").

There's no glitzy facade on **The American Nut and Chocolate Company,** 230 West Broadway, (617) 268–0075, a wholesale nut-roasting and candy supply business. This family enterprise has been around since 1929, when they sold their signature confection—white candy cigarettes with red tips in ciggy boxes—coast to coast, at a cost of 5 cents. On the left side, you got yer nut-roasting and assembly operation; on the right, a dimly lighted, down-to-earth, no-frills retail store, a panacea for aficionados of penny candy, dried fruit, and nuts, which are roasted every day. American Nut's husband and wife owners, Andy and Donna Horvit, make up a high-quality, all-nut blend and also prepare made-to-order gift baskets. The retail store candy is packaged in small plastic bags, most of which sell for under $1.00. Andy says that if the neighborhood ever turns into the gold mine it's supposed to, he'll fix the place up. This little shop could be called "Faves" in its tonier version. It maintains an inventory of candy classics: bags of Mary Janes, nonpareils, spearmint leaves, red hots, multicolored dots-on-paper, licorice strings, gummy bears, jelly-fish, malted milk balls, and chocolate-covered almonds (in choices of milk or dark).

Just after Discount Auto Parts and the Teamsters' HQ, West Broadway starts dressing up. **Oven Door Bakery,** 371 West Broadway, (617) 268–5685, is a merge of Irish hearth (savory Irish soda bread), hometown (old-fashioned black-and-white cookies), and Beantown (cutout butter cookies in the shape of lobsters with white frosting and red sprinkles). I was delighted to find Boston cream pie. If you're new to fuddy-duddy New England cuisine, Boston cream pie is a layer cake with custard filling and smooth chocolate frosting. Oven Door's version looks natty as a tux—it's small in diameter but tall, dressed with a giant long-stemmed maraschino cherry. Many muffins here, too, from apple cinnamon, banana, and bran to pumpkin and triple berry.

When you exit the bakery, pause to view the **Lithuanian Citizens Association,** 368 West Broadway, in a stone building across the street, another clue to nineteenth-century Southie's immigrant mix.

Every time I walk down West Broadway, another old building is wrapped in scaffolding, as though South Boston were being visited by Christo. Check out the majestic High-Victorian, Gothic-style **Monks**

Building, 366 West Broadway, at the corner of E Street, built in 1873 for Monks & Company, a flour and grain dealer. The Mattapan Deposit and Trust Company moved in at the turn of the twentieth century. The four-story redbrick building is now condos. At street level the high-ceilinged former bank lobby is being turned into an art gallery. Gotta say, it looks like a million bucks.

Across the street, the **South Boston Tribune** offices, 395 West Broadway, are near an upbeat, well-stocked CVS—a virtual department store, maybe because of its architectural heritage. West Broadway's CVS, at the corner of F Street, is in a graceful, turn-of-the-twentieth-century building block lavishly trimmed with Indiana limestone, and was once the Falvey Department Store. The CVS of today has an extensive greeting card section. I often see elderly nuns (black stockings and comfortable white shoes) carefully selecting cards. Unlike most customers, they read and reread the words.

Take a turn down F Street. Over time, row houses are being gentrified, one by one. As a result, a group of three or four sister houses will often include one in derelict condition, a couple kept up, and one gussied up, often with an expensive car parked out front.

Across the street note three restaurants, representing faces of Southie: **Cafe Arpeggio ($),** 398 West Broadway, (617) 269–8822, offers coffee, sandwiches, light lunches, and, above all, homemade ice cream. **Jake's Coffee Shop ($),** 402 West Broadway, (617) 269–6049, does pita roll-ups, gyros, and steak-tip subs. On the corner is **Rainbow Dragon,** a typical neighborhood Chinese place with a zillion items on its menu (see "Suggested Restaurants").

Nearby, **St. John the Baptist Albanian Orthodox Church,** 410 West Broadway, (617) 268–3564, is a striking, well-kept, cream-colored stucco building with chocolate-brown doors and trim and well-tended wrought-iron gates.

Olmsted in Southie

You'll hear South Boston's bayside Xanadu referred to as Castle Island, Pleasure Bay, and Marine Park, not to mention Fort Independence. To complicate and poeticize matters further, old timers call it The Strand (as in "I'm going down to the Strand"). These are all the same place. Go there—to the harbor's edge—to an idyllic park and walkway created by Boston's omniscient park master, Frederick Law Olmsted.

Olmsted wanted to extend the "Emerald Necklace" from Franklin Park in Jamaica Plain to his fabricated waterfront park, Pleasure Bay in South Boston. Had his grand design been followed, today's Columbia Road would have become a curve of green. It would have been spectacular, but the present configuration is still pretty terrific. **The Strand,** *the winding path that hugs Dorchester Bay, is now called William J. Day Boulevard. It leads from* **Columbus Park** *and dandy* **Carson Beach** *in the south to City Point Beach.*

Athletes and admirers of stout-hearted men and women should pay attention to the **L Street Bath House,** *nominally a public athletic facility, but in the annals of Southie, home to the* **L Street Brownies,** *a band of hearty swimmers of all ages who take regular dips in the frosty bay, most notably on New Year's Day, when they marshal on Carson Beach in trunks, caps, and goggles and gleefully*

At its junction of East Broadway, take a right on Dorchester Street, passing Marian Manor, a home for seniors, then take a left on Old Harbor Road, with several nicely-kept Victorian-style houses. You'll be climbing a bit of a hill, making the ascent to the inspiring sight of **Dorchester Heights,** the harborside hill from which *pose for photographers. The official name of the L Street Bath House is the* **James Michael Curley Community Center,** *1663 Columbia Road, (617) 635–5104, in honor of the great benefactor, Boston's first Irish-American mayor, who built this monument to health—saltwater showers, handball courts, twin glass solariums— during the height of the Great Depression. Curley had chutzpah.*

Onward along the Strand to **Marine Park,** *with its bandstand and statue of Civil War hero David Farragut. In 1862 Admiral Farragut commanded the flotilla that captured New Orleans. Across the way a circular walkway into Dorchester Bay makes its own idyllic bay-within-a-bay. This is* **Pleasure Bay,** *Olmsted's creation, around which generations of pleasure-seekers have strolled.*

On Pleasure Bay, reachable by the pedestrian walkway or by parking in a lot, **Fort Independence,** *prominent during the Revolutionary War, is the grand stone edifice on the crest of* **Castle Island** *(no longer an island). The pentagon-shaped fort is the fourth on the site, about 200 years old, and was still used during World War II. Local volunteers, many of them retired school teachers, give periodic tours.*

Sullivan's, *on Castle Island, (617) 268–5685, a fifty-year-old eatery and local favorite, sells the foods of the New England beach: ice cream, soft drinks, hot dogs, burgers, fries, clamstrips, and onion rings.*

General Washington defended the emerging U. S. of A. Here a white marble monument designed by Boston architects Peabody and Sterns in 1902 rises 115 feet from the summit. Now a National Park site, where tours are offered, the hill has sheared lawns, where local people lob Frisbees to their dogs and enjoy a fine view of Dorchester Bay.

The adjacent yellow-brick building, trimmed with limestone, is hundred-year-old **South Boston High School,** which became famous during Boston's 1970s bussing crisis, brought about by a misguided, intrusive federal court order, some say, or created by backward, racist social policies, say others. In either or both cases, children and education suffered. The old school is now the site of major educational reforms. In fall 2000, the traditionally run school of more than 1,000 students, 78 percent of whom are minority, was broken into four independent components. Each "learning community" now has its own principal, budget, and autonomy to enable teachers to focus on students with differing needs.

In recent years the property values at **Thomas Park,** the residential area surrounding the Heights, have increased dramatically. My favorite houses include **Number 56,** a sprawling white dowager with red roofs and an ornate widow's walk—you can see it from Dorchester Heights—that overlooks the bay, and **Number 67.** In the latter case it's the front lawn's landscaping that causes me "to go silly," as they say in Southie. Across from the high school, behind a green chain-link fence, a poetic homeowner has created a bucolic scene: A fountain—a cement statue of a water boy—spills water into a small lily pond.

The glossy-leaved trees on this street, aromatic in spring, are lindens, which rarely grow so large, and with such stocky trunks, in Boston. Might be the proximity to the sea. Follow the street around the high school, and come to **Number 1 Thomas Park,** a magnet for lovers of old, eccentric houses. Note the fat chimney set in the middle of the light-gray clapboard house. A matching barn is next door. An ancient catalpa tree—with 2-foot-long pods in autumn—lounges in the front yard. The water you see from the top of the hill is Dorchester Bay.

Walk down the residential G Street, exceptionally pretty and home to several local leaders. Either turn onto East Broadway to explore another sector—complete with the **South Boston Courthouse,** 535 East Broadway, made famous in the movie *Good Will Hunting*—or retrace your steps along Dorchester Street back to West Broadway. If you follow East Broadway, you'll pass through the old municipal part of the city—passing the South Boston branch of the Boston Public Library—and then a residential area of well-preserved Victorian houses, to reach **Independence Park,** between M and N Streets, called M Street Park locally. Within the park the South Boston Vietnam War Memorial was erected in 1981 at the site of an old fountain.

Even on gloomy days the light around you will be changing, you'll smell ocean, and you'll land in the heart of South Boston's Riviera, Pleasure Bay.

• • • *History* • • •

DORCHESTER

Perilously close to one of the craziest patches of Boston traffic—where South Boston, Dorchester, Roxbury, and the South End almost overlap, and Route 93 comes slashing by—a seventeenth-century house stands. Built in 1648, the **James Blake House,** 735 Columbia Road, Boston's oldest standing house, is safe and sound. In an early example of historic preservation (1895), the house was moved to Richardson Park, a few hundred yards from its original location. It is now in the good care of the Dorchester Historical Society, (617) 265–7802, and can be visited two Saturday afternoons each month. Thereby hangs a tale.

How to Get There

⸱ Dorchester Avenue, Dorchester

By public transportation take the MBTA Red Line to
Andrew Square (the junction of Dorchester Avenue and
Dorchester, Southampton, and Preble Streets), the low numbers of
Dot. Ave. The Red Line splits at the next station, JFK/UMass. The four
stations that follow are all in Dorchester: Savin Hill, Fields Corner,
Shawmut, and Ashmont. All are about to benefit from an $88.5 million
reconstruction project. By car take Route 93 south to Andrew Square or
just keep traveling south on Dorchester Avenue from South Boston.

It kills me to recommend driving in the city, but Dot. Ave. is so long,
motoring is the most effective way to do your orienteering. Once
you decide where you want to concentrate, return via public
transportation. The Savin Hill MBTA stop is a good
junction for tooling around the Vietnamese
markets and restaurants.

In 1630 English settlers landed in Dorchester, a few months
before the Boston arrivals, and set up housekeeping on Savin Hill.
Within the next few years, one James Blake, who became a leading
citizen, arrived as a child with his parents. He lived in the house that
today bears his name.

Dorchester, which originally included South Boston and Hyde
Park, was farmland into the nineteenth century, with country estates
for the wealthy, particularly on hilltops overlooking the bay. In 1804
Dorchester Turnpike, today's Dot. Ave., was cut through the town, link-
ing Boston and Lower Mills. Here at the southern end of the town, site

of the sole rapids on the lower Neponset River, grist mills, wool-sizing mills, a gunpowder mill, snuff mill, sawmill, and paper mill all used the harnessed water power, as did the Walter Baker Chocolate Company, which you'll see if you take Dot. Ave. to the end.

The coming of the railroad—the Boston & Providence in 1835 and the Old Colony in 1844—changed Dorchester dramatically, as did the introduction of a horse-drawn streetcar along Dorchester Avenue in 1856. Electric tram service arrived the following year. The old farm community became a streetcar suburb, and, gradually, a dense urban neighborhood. In 1870 it was annexed to Boston.

When Irish immigrant families prospered in South Boston, they would move to larger residences, often relocating in Dorchester. The burgeoning working-class population of the early 1900s led to the development of a distinctly Dorchester house style, efficient and affordable: the three-decker, a beamy wood-frame house with three flats, often with sizable porches, on a single house lot.

After World War II the popularity of the suburbs and the draw of single-family homes sapped Dorchester's lifeblood. Its housing suffered in value and became neglected and rundown. But during the last decades, émigrés from many nations, especially war-torn nations—Vietnam, Cambodia, Haiti, and also Cape Verde—settled in the old three-deckers. Some members of the older immigrant populations remained. Starting during the 1980s, young professionals began staking out the community, buying old houses and their roomy yards, and turning them around.

At Columbia Point, where the Puritans landed, the **John F. Kennedy Library and Museum,** (617) 929–4500, found its place, in a region of immigrants at the edge of the sea. The gleaming modern building contains JFK's presidential papers, many personal belongings, and speeches and tapes of Massachusetts's native son, an

Irish American and a Catholic. The library was designed by Chinese-American architect I. M. Pei. Public housing is also at Columbia Point, as is the University of Massachusetts/Boston.

... *A Walking Tour by Car* ...

DORCHESTER AVENUE, DORCHESTER

When conducting this type of tour, the motor-pedestrian must drive as slowly as traffic allows and expect to make frequent stops. This approach pollutes the atmosphere and is generally not advisable, but how else to get an introduction to Dorchester—its size, dimension, and key neighborhoods such as Field's Corner and Savin Hill?

From its start near the Gillette enterprise in South Boston to its grand finale at the Baker Chocolate Factory in Lower Mills, Dot. Ave. is about 5 miles long. Following this thoroughfare, the motor-pedestrian will receive an introduction to ethnic Dorchester: a mix of owner-run businesses, Irish pubs, Southeast Asian markets and noodle shops, and Caribbean grocers.

Start in South Boston, where you'll drive past **St. Augustine's Church,** near West Eighth Street. The parish includes an 1818 Gothic chapel, attributed to the architect Charles Bulfinch, located in the isolated calm of Boston's first Catholic cemetery. The area is blocked by a locked gate, but the chapel is open on feast days. Drive on, past the **Andrew Square MBTA Station,** mainly glass, with a clock, and past **St. Margaret's** at the corner of Columbia Road. Built in 1894 the Romanesque church was designed to serve Dorchester's rapidly growing Roman Catholic population.

The lower part of Dot. Ave. may look a little grim to the uninitiated, but you'll soon reach the vicinity of **The Banchee ($–$$),** 934 Dorchester Avenue, (617) 436–9747, an Irish pub with shepherd's pie,

Irish-style breakfasts, and Theology Night—talks about religion and philosophy—twice monthly, and with sixteen beers on tap everyday.

Continue onward toward the "thousand block" of Dorchester Avenue. Many things Vietnamese start to appear—pharmacies, dentists, doctors; beauty parlors and nail salons; record stores; auto repair shops; tax preparation services.

Don't be fooled by the sign. Anna's Donut & Bakery, 1035 Dorchester Avenue, is actually **Cong Ty Du Lich,** a Vietnamese coffee shop with Danish, doughnuts, muffins, and bean pastries. Across the street is **St. William's Church,** which offers a weekly Vietnamese mass.

Close to a dozen Vietnamese markets are on Dorchester Avenue. In size they range from corner store to grocery to supermarket. **Phu Cuong Market,** 1051 Dorchester Avenue, (617) 436–5652, is one of the best, a spacious, very clean market—a full-service Asian supermarket with a wide selection of well-priced fresh fish. The fish—clams, salmon, flounder, scup—are not behind or under glass, but set before you, submerged in bins of chipped ice. Customers examine them eye to eye. At Phu Cuong I finally saw fresh durian— after hearing for years how they were never sold this way. On the day I discovered the coveted fruit, they were lodged in the entryway, with crates of bananas and pineapples. Packed in Thailand, each formidable-looking fruit was muzzled by a fibrous net. Try to imagine a huge heavy pinecone, dangerously thorny—the size of a football, the weight of a watermelon—with a stump.

Other markets include **Vien Dong Fareast Supermarket,** 1159 Dorchester Avenue, (617) 265–9131, and **Viet Huomg Market,** 1826 Dorchester Avenue, (617) 265–2553. Both carry similar products, but each has its own personality. Vien Dong is in a small shopping strip with several Vietnamese restaurants, including

A crate of spiny fresh durians lurking in the entrance of Phu Cuong Market.

Sun Rise Rang-Dong Restaurant (see "Suggested Restaurants"), presenting both Vietnamese and Chinese cooking. **Hau Giang ($–$$),** 1155 Dorchester Avenue, (617) 436–6688, in the same strip, is mainly take-out, including some ready-to-go fare. (The mysterious green pyramids swathed in plastic wrap—generally arrayed near the cash register—are steamed rice in banana leaves. The perfumey scent of the leaves permeates the rice as it cooks. Don't eat the leaves, dude.)

Onward past **JD's Irish Pub and Grille, Nash's Pub,** and **T and A Spanish and Asian Market.** In the Field's Corner area (named for nineteenth-century grocer Issac Field, and located near

Vietnamese Comfort Food

Consider the connotations of chicken soup in Jewish cooking and the passion for pasta in Italian cucina, and you'll have a sense of pho's importance for Vietnamese. A protein-intensive broth with noodles, pho is, metaphorically if not literally, both chicken soup and pasta.

In Vietnam vendors prepare and sell the national dish outside. Customers buy a bowl and squat on the street, slurping their noodles and broth. Along Dorchester's Dot. Ave., pho (pronounced "fa") is made and sold in casual, pizzeria-type takeouts, and modest restaurants. During Asian festivals in Chinatown, booths are set up, where many non-Asians try pho for the first time, starting their long, appreciative relationship with Vietnamese comfort food.

Originally a beef soup noodle dish associated with northern Vietnam, the meal-in-a-bowl made its way south as refugees fled the north during the 1950s. The traditional Hue-style recipe features spicy beef broth, rice noodles, and a variety of floating toppings: thin slices of rare beef, well-cooked flank steak or brisket (with alternating stripes of fat and lean meat), or tripe. In southern Vietnam, which is known for its seafood, fish often replaces beef, and the pho is spicier.

Pho is always served with bowls of condiments, such as bean sprouts, fresh basil leaves, coriander, mint, chili peppers, lemon and lime wedges, and an optional, incendiary liquid chili paste. You can scatter or spoon these throughout your bowl or flavor each spoonful as you go, varying the texture and taste of each mouthful. It is acceptable to use chopsticks and a spoon—whatever works. This is not a prissy, fancy dish, but a soulful one, satisfying and nutritious.

the intersection of Adams Street and Dot. Ave.), you'll find noodle restaurants galore, along with **Yum-Yum Chinese Restaurant** and **Mien Tien Gifts,** the last next to **Emerald Isle Pub,** 1501 Dorchester Avenue, (617) 288–0010.

The **Boston Fish Market,** 1484 Dorchester Avenue, (617) 272–2980, that rarity of a neighborhood fish market (which should not be a rarity in Boston), is on the first floor of a bowfront, residential three-decker. The sizable store sells piscine perennials: swordfish, scallops, and shrimp, along with less-well-known, less-expensive fish, such as cusk and scup. Speaking of fish, urban anglers will be pleased to discover **P&J Bait Shop,** 1397 Dorchester Avenue, (617) 288–7917, in Field's Corner.

Once you pass Ashmont Station, the avenue becomes more residential. By the time you're cruising the number 2,000 block, the three-deckers are in prime condition, with window boxes and well-kept yards.

Approaching Lower Mills, you'll segue back into Dorchester's nineteenth-century Irish heritage. **St. Gregory's** (the cross street is St. Gregory) looks like a city, an ecclesiastical village, which includes a sizable school. Nearby **Carney Hospital,** 2100 Dorchester Avenue, was established for the social and medical needs of the poor "regardless of race, color, or religion" by Andrew Carney, a kindly Irishman who made good in his North End clothing store, Carney and Sleeper. The hospital was first sited on Telegraph Hill in South Boston, opening in 1863.

The terminus of Dorchester Avenue is out of a Cecil B. DeMille production. On your left is a redbrick Victorian complex in the opulent Second Empire style, characterized by mansard roofs and elaborate trim; this is the empire that chocolate built. In 1765 a Harvard-educated minister founded **The Walter Baker Chocolate**

Company to grind cocoa beans. Generations of Bakers (and presumably some bakers) ran the business. (Most of us grew up using Baker's Chocolate to make brownies and chocolate cakes.) The successful business led to other mills, such as the Forbes Mill, built in 1911. General Foods acquired Baker's Chocolate in 1927, and in 1965 operations moved out of Massachusetts. The present complex, a sight to behold, was converted to residential, commercial, and light industrial uses. The antiques shops and nouveau pubs in the neighborhood have developed to serve the condo owners in the Baker Chocolate Factory.

In addition to the antiques, boutiques, and homemade ice cream, please note **Common Ground Bakery and Cafe,** 2243 Dorchester Avenue, (617) 298–1020, another feature of Lower Mills. Common Ground has an ambience difficult to describe, a fairy-tale atmosphere, each section of the store part of an arboreal kingdom. The combination

Scones

What could be more Irish than soda bread and scones, especially if served with butter and a full-bodied cup of tea? (No mugs, please, if you wish to emulate an Irish country B&B.) Divine-tasting scones are available at **Greenhill's Irish Bakery,** *793 Adams Street, Dorchester Lower Mills, (617) 825–8187, along with aromatic, chewy hermits and country wheat bread that toasts perfectly. Not all of Greenhill's offerings are Irish; the lavish eclairs are piped with egg custard and a layer of whipped cream. (Go ahead, put cream and sugar in your tea.) The pleasant, family-run enterprise—white walls with dainty emerald-green insignia—also stocks a sampling of Irish food imports and has a few tables for snackin' and gabbin'.*

bakery/natural foods store and cafe bakes good bread—whole wheat, oatmeal, multigrain, spelt, and rye, and homemade-tasting tea breads, such as banana and date nut. The proprietors are members of the Messianic Community Church, whose adherents live communally in Dorchester and elsewhere throughout the country. As church members observe their Sabbath on Friday night and Saturday, Common Ground is closed on the weekends, but is well worth visiting during the week. I must say, at the end of 5 miles of bars and pubs, steamed rice and scones, noodles and lemongrass, and exotic Asian aromas, arrival at Common Ground is a little odd. If I had found cattle grazing here, I would not have been more surprised. Perhaps this is another lesson of the city: Love of bread is a common thing.

Around the block, please find the **Boston Public Library, Lower Mills Branch.**

S U G G E S T E D 🍽 R E S T A U R A N T S

In Southie you'll find old-fashioned pubs with dark wood paneling, informal coffee places, and nouveau pubs (cleaner, sleeker, with dressier accoutrements) such as **Boston Beer Garden ($-$$),** 734 East Broadway, (617) 269–0990, that cater to professional people in their twenties. Yet another declension might be the Southie pubs for younger Irish immigrants, **The Playwright ($-$$),** 658 East Broadway, (617) 269–2537, being one example. These newer meeting, greeting, and drinking establishments can boast good beer, good cheer, and often, striking architecture. Boston Beer Garden is in a gorgeous rehabbed old hall near Independence Park. The Playwright is a dashing-looking yellow building that resembles a public house you'd encounter in an Irish village. Yes, shepherd's pie is on their menu, but also fajitas and pizza.

In Dorchester the best eateries are informal Vietnamese noodle shops and restaurants, and a few venerable pubs such as **Galvin's Harp & Bard ($–$$)**, 1099 Dorchester Avenue, (617) 265–2893, and **The Blarney Stone ($–$$)**, 1505 Dorchester Avenue, (617) 436–8223 (above-average bar food). These eateries are located on Dorchester Avenue and generally are Vietnamese, with a few exceptions such as **Nanina's ($–$$)**, 1578 Dorchester Avenue, (617) 288–2494, a sentimental Italian-American favorite.

In South Boston **Amrheins ($–$$)**, 80 West Broadway, (617) 268–6189, is irresistible because it's so old, so legendary, and so close to Broadway Station. At the oddest times of day, people of all ages are putting on the old feedbag. There's a whole lot of meat in this restaurant: steaks, chops, and wiener schnitzel. Not many *concoctions* (my late father's term for French, Spanish, and Italian entrees or anything other than three discrete units of meat, potato, and boiled vegetable). Drink you must at Amrheins, if only to see the hand-carved, mirrored-back wooden bar, a work of art observed and taken to heart by generations of patrons, and to observe the oldest beer-pump system in Boston.

The **Farragut House Restaurant ($–$$)**, 146 P Street, (617) 268–1212, near Castle Island, is another solid family place with a time-tested menu (no concoctions). The restaurant is on the site of an old inn, the Wave Cottage Cafe, which featured libations (Pickwick Ale drew many a man), fine cigars, and fresh fish dinners.

Home cooking and Irish high style are on the menu at **Shenanigans ($–$$)**, 332 West Broadway, (617) 269–9509, a comfy pub, heavy on the antique knick-knacks, but with soft lighting, booths, and checkered tablecloths. The place is a grabber from the exterior,

Spiffy Irish pubs attract couples and families on West Broadway.

too—a redbrick Federal-style building with a periwinkle-blue facade. Served inside are chicken pot pie, declensions of "surf & turf," simple pasta dishes, and shepherd's pie, a heroic-looking assembly of ground beef and chopped vegetables, topped with mashed potatoes and cheese. The well-named Dublin Lawyer Lobster is luxurious in taste, sophisticated in demeanor, and delivers satisfaction reliant on dissection; technically speaking, chunks of fresh lobster in cream.

Mul's Diner ($), 75 West Broadway, (617) 268–5748, is a must. From the exterior, it's inscrutable. Could be a car wash, its diner sign notwithstanding. Enter, and it's a deep, bustling, clean, and casual restaurant overflowing with couples, families, and local politicians holding court. Big breakfasts and lunches are served (breakfast only, but until mid-afternoon on weekends): omelettes and eggs, pancakes and waffles, burgers and sandwiches, and a few conversation pieces, such as the Hawaiian Omelette (ham and pineapple). Mul's is fast, friendly, and offers good value—with infinite refills of one's coffee cup. (If you'd like a little bite—sandwich, ice cream, or coffee—try one of the neighborhood cafes mentioned in the "Walking Tour: West Broadway and Old and New Southie.")

Rainbow Dragon ($), 412–414 West Broadway, (617) 268–2821, is one of those mainstay neighborhood Chinese places that has hundreds of items on its menu: Cantonese, Mandarin, Szechuan. Lo Mein Peking Noodles is listed with a charming expository note: "This is the original dish that Marco Polo brought back to Italy, which then became spaghetti with meat sauce."

Used to be that two people could eat Asian food for $15 to $20. Now it's $40 and up, even sometimes in Chinatown. In the low-rent storefronts of Dot. Ave., where restaurant owners must honor their patrons' moderate incomes, two people can still eat well for $20. Vietnamese cooking is deft, delicate, and subtly spiced and relies on small amounts of fish, chicken, and meat in a vegetable-and-rice-based cuisine. Pho, or noodle soup, is the staff of life. There are scads of informal Vietnamese restaurants on Dot. Ave., including Pho Hua and Sunrise.

Pho Hua Restaurant ($), 1356 Dorchester Avenue, (617) 287–9746, is a true sit-down restaurant—spacious, with music (Vietnamese pop) and a tank of tropical fish. Noodle soups are served with the requisite mix-ins, including fresh basil leaves and crunchy bean sprouts. In addition to the soups—light, savory broths with meat slivers and noodles—Pho Hua offers rice plates, spring rolls, and a selection of satisfying desserts, including red-bean pudding.

At 10:00 A.M. a chatty, animated Vietnamese family is grouped around a table preparing snow peas at **Sun Rise Rang Dong Restaurant ($),** 1157 Dorchester Avenue, (617) 288–7314. Soon patrons begin filtering into the comfy place—an old storefront with wainscotting, a ceiling fan, and tables decked-out with red checkered cloths—for expertly prepared Vietnamese and Chinese cuisine. The regulars order rice platters, seafood noodle soups, and *goi,* the spritely Vietnamese salads. On the Chinese menu (almost twenty entrees), lo mein (yellow noodles) and chow foon (flat rice noodles) are popular. Sun Rise is homey and sweet.

Shanti: Taste of India ($–$$), 1111 Dorchester Avenue, (617) 929–3900 is a welcome addition to the pub and pho scene, adding the succulent cuisines of India, Pakistan, and Bangladesh to Dot. Ave.'s buffet.

Many a patron discovered Shanti while en route to **Galvin's Harp & Bard ($–$$),** 1099 Dorchester Avenue, (617) 265–2893, a few doors down on the same side of the street. The venerable Irish bar serves quality comfort food: meat and potatoes, nicely fried fish, homemade soups (including French-style onion), and light-as-a-feather Grapenut custard. The bar has its TV tuned to sports, of course, but also keeps an all-odds-all-the-time ticker that prints the numbers on other sporting events. Think of it as an Irish fortune cookie.

The food at **Ba Le ($),** 1052 Dorchester Avenue, (617) 265–7171, makes the pho places seem extravagant. Ba Le is a Vietnamese sub shop—no adaptation to American culture, but a Vietnamese fast-food thang. Eighteen sandwiches are on the menu, and you don't have to speak Vietnamese to order; just point to the item you wish on the pictorial menu over the counter. Vietnamese ham and grilled chicken are among the possibilities. Spring rolls are also available, as are mung bean cakes, tapioca cookies, and prepared desserts.

Coolidge Corner, Brookline

A Little Noshing, a Little Kibbitzing

$\mathcal{S}$ome spouses in their seventies still see each other as they did when they first met. These lingering afterimages of the heart can attach to places, too. Perhaps if I were less fond of Coolidge Corner—if I'd had less fun there—I could describe it more objectively.

Coolidge Corner was the first place I settled in as a young woman in Boston thirty years ago. To me it seemed the height of warmth, charm, and sophistication, just the sort of place to appeal to a girl brought up in New Hampshire and New York, drawn to big trees and quiet streets, but also to well-stocked bookstores, artsy movie theaters, and lavish bakeries. To my eager eyes this crossroad of Beacon and Harvard Streets looked like the best of the nineteenth and twentieth centuries. The so-called subway ran above ground along Beacon Street in an allée of leafy trees. In autumn the maples brushed like red fans against the windows of the moving train.

At the Coolidge Corner T stop stood a Tudoresque structure with a stately working clock. This was the home of S. S. Pierce (pronounced "purse"), grocers to Brahmin Boston. The fancy purveyor sold everything that passed for gourmet in the 1960s: silver tins of tiny peas, French cheese cracker sticks shaped like double helixes (a quantum leap from the Cheez-Its of my childhood), and scores of specialty teas. In spring the store carried fiddlehead ferns; in summer, fresh crabapples. Actual living servants bought the rose-colored fruit and made crabapple jelly for Bostonians with delicate appetites.

As I further explored Coolidge Corner, I discovered majestic, old-fashioned synagogues—the kind with mosquelike domes—and lots of delis, Jewish bakeries, and bookstores. By the 1960s and 1970s, the community had become a residential and shopping hub with a distinctly Jewish flavor, S. S. Pierce notwithstanding. Young families lived in the wood-frame houses on side streets, and well-groomed widows in the tidy brick apartment houses. A few of these apartments were like castles, and many like European residential hotels, complete with small gardens, statuary, and fountains.

Today, Gap and Starbuck's have come to the Corner, along with Barnes & Noble, CVS, and Brooks Pharmacy; fancy dress stores, video "libraries," and swank boutiques. The crowded fruit stores run by cigar-smoking Jewish grandfathers are gone, along with their cranky warnings not to "sgveeze the frucht." The old men glared at me when I would pick up the peaches and smell them. But one of these fruit-dragons taught me how to carve a pineapple.

Fortunately, the splendid town plan and primary edifices are intact (including the S. S. Pierce building, though now housing a monster-drugstore), making Coolidge Corner both cosmopolitan and cozy. Auto traffic proceeds in two directions on Beacon Street and Harvard Street, pedestrians abound, and the streetcar still shuttles along Beacon from Park Street, Boston, to Cleveland Circle, Brookline.

In blocks of well-kept storefronts, many of them early-twentieth-century brick buildings, a zesty variety of stores, shops, and, above all, food purveyors line the wide, pedestrian-friendly streets. Kosher restaurants abound, as do Asian restaurants (including those kosher, vegetarian, and kosher-vegetarian), nouveau delis, bakeries, take-out falafel places, and a slew of cultural offerings: bookstores, art galleries, an independent cinema, and a half-dozen excellent craft galleries—some specializing in the work of well-established local ceramicists, others in Judaica, and one in international folk art. People of all ages throng the streets, along with well-behaved, leashed dogs.

In addition to the well-preserved commercial and residential architecture, including the sweep of nineteenth-century apartment

How to Get There

By public transportation take the MBTA Green Line Cleveland
Circle car (C) to Coolidge Corner. By car follow Beacon
Street, which passes through Kenmore Square, until it
intersects with Harvard Street.

buildings along Beacon Street, and the items to be bought in bakeries and takeouts, I favor Coolidge Corner for its practical streak.
Where else can you find a zipper hospital, shoes for weird feet, and
my favorite underwear store, Lady Grace, that so lustily advertises its
wares: "Bra sizes to 56, Bra cups to J"? Years ago, one of the first
Coolidge Corner wonders I discovered was the team of elderly female
fitters at Lady Grace. They were walking advertisements for their
products—stately, full-figured women, each proceeded by their
prows. Most of these gals are still there, providing counsel, uplift,
and support.

• • • *History* • • •

Architectural historians love to visit neighborhoods such as
Coolidge Corner. Not only are many of the residential and business
structures attractive, but the community looks like it grew there,
evolved, as opposed to being planned and implanted like the centers
of today. Not that there wasn't town planning—how else to explain a
wide main street with trolleys running in both directions, along with

car traffic lanes and wide sidewalks accommodating pedestrians and trees? But the area developed over time, beginning with foot paths and carriage roads.

Harvard Street, which begins in Brookline Village, was cut through farmland in 1662. Called "the road to the colleges," it led to Harvard College in Cambridge, which was founded two decades earlier. As parts of Brookline became weekend estates for Boston bankers, investors, lawyers, and magnates of various stripes, a direct route to Boston became necessary. Beacon Street was developed.

Quite a book could be written—or a razzle-dazzle musical composed—about the late-nineteenth-century developers responsible for Brookline's prominence. In 1886 parks commissioner Henry Whitney hired Frederick Law Olmsted and John C. Olmsted to create a 160-foot-wide boulevard. Just two years later one of the first electric trolleys in the United States began operating on Beacon Street. The town would gain a nickname, "streetcar suburb," from this distinction. In 1889 David McKay bought a large parcel of land in North Brookline. He became a principal developer, building many houses for the businesspeople and managers who traveled daily into Boston. Grand apartment blocks were also built—French flats, Back Bay–style town houses, and spacious rental apartments.

During the eighteenth and nineteenth centuries, most Brookline residents emigrated from Boston including German and Irish immigrants. By the early 1900s a Jewish community had rooted; by the mid-1920s several synagogues were constructed. Jewish migration got a big boost during the 1950s and 1960s. As the sons and daughters of working-class urban Jews improved their situations, many moved from the urban parts of Boston—Roxbury, Mattapan, Dorchester, and the old West End—and settled near relatives in "nice apartments" and wood-frame houses. North Brookline, where

Coolidge Corner is located, became the center of a Jewish community. In recent years Jewish immigrants from the former Soviet Union have added to the mix.

··· *A Walking Tour* ···

HARVARD STREET

A shopper's note: Many bakeries, shops, and restaurants in Coolidge Corner, including all those kosher, are closed on the Jewish Sabbath, which starts Friday at sundown and ends Saturday at sundown. Some shops close Friday afternoon around 2:00 P.M. and don't reopen until Sunday morning. Schedules are also subject to Jewish holidays, which follow the Jewish calendar and so fall at different times each year on the "everyday calendar." In the words of my grandmother Rose, "Who can figure?" Telephone before setting forth.

I never walk in a straight line down Harvard Street. Instead, I zigzag back and forth across the street—perhaps because I prefer the sequence of stores that way, or enjoy getting a little exercise between browsings. I confer this route upon you.

Start your tour near the Coolidge Corner MBTA stop at the **S. S. Pierce Building** at the corner of Harvard and Beacon Streets. Follow Harvard Street toward Allston, where it becomes Harvard Avenue, the street numbers ascending. Later you can wander along Harvard in the other direction, heading toward Brookline Village, where Harvard Street begins.

These days, inside the S. S. Pierce Building, you'll find vials of pills, not cans of peas, but the natty exterior of the old Brahmin grocer is still admirable. Designed in 1898 by Winslow & Wetherell, it replaced a fifty-year-old provisions store on the same site.

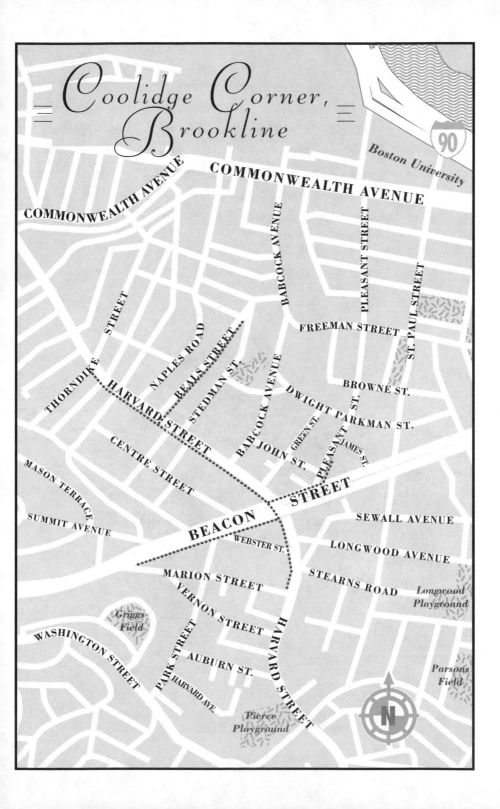

For reasons I have never been able to figure out (bad feet? insistence on comfort? elderly residents?), Jewish neighborhoods generally have good shoe stores, places in which to find quality, durable, unnerdy shoes you can walk in. True to form, the Coolidge Corner neighborhood—with its legion of people of all ages walking, shopping, schlepping—boasts exceptional shoe stores.

The fanciful-looking former S. S. Pierce Building marks Coolidge Corner.

Across the street from the S. S. Pierce Building, **André Shoes,** 275 Harvard Street, (617) 738–1161, carries chic but comfy sandals from Israel, the design-y Arche line from France, and ecco footwear from Denmark. Andre's soft nubuck Mephisto French sandals, which regrettably cost over $130, are the summer shoe of choice for those with odd feet. The colors are soft and painterly.

Simon's Shoes, 282 Harvard Street, (617) 277–8980, is another foot-friendly store, as are **Mel's Capitol Shoe/Too,** 307 Harvard Street, (617) 734–1411, and **Edwin Case,** 1388 Beacon Street, (617) 277–6577, though the latter's wares may appear too orthopedic to fashion plates.

Once upon a time, there was a fine independent bookstore called Brookline Booksmith. Then it became the Paperback Booksmith. Today it's called **Brookline Booksmith and Videosmith,** 279 Harvard Street, (617) 566–6660. It's bigger, slicker, and brighter, with a wing of videos, CDs, and greeting cards, and a spacious downstairs meeting room where authors give regularly scheduled, free book talks. Over the decades this prized independent bookseller, always in the same location, has continued to offer something extra: a wide range of well-chosen contemporary and classic books in all subjects, along with remainders and periodicals, and a courteous and knowledgeable staff. It's an exemplary place to buy cards for Jewish holidays and commemorative occasions—the New Year, Chanukah, Passover, bar and bat mitzvahs (confirmations)—and has an excellent Judaica section.

For devotees of old theaters, the **Coolidge Corner Theatre,** 290 Harvard Street, (617) 734–2500, a bona fide Art Deco movie house, is a treasure. It boasts a classically sized silver screen, as opposed to the postcard-sized views of today's "cineplexes." The gracious old house has rehabbed Art Deco appointments and a snazzy new retro-Deco-style marquee. Most important, the Coolidge is run by a nonprofit foundation and offers a range of artsy and independent new films, revivals, and an array of festivals, including parts of the annual Jewish Film Festival. Other bills range from sci-fi festivals, to award-winning animated shorts, to silent screen classics accompanied by a live orchestra.

Pastryland, 305A Harvard Street, (617) 566–8136, is a small kosher bakery that has a selection of American-style pastries and cookies—your basic muffins and mega-sized chocolate chip cookies— with a few outstanding old-fashioned, Jewish-style pastries, notably cheese Danish. Once upon a time, a plump aromatic Danish—made of slightly sweet yeast dough, filled and folded—was a staple in every Jewish bakery. As the world has been taken over by cheese croissants, strawberry bagels, and chocolate chip cookies with M&M's, cheese Danish have passed from our midst. But at Pastryland, grandma's breakfast sweet lives on. For a modest sum, you can buy one of these babies, fresh and light. Lovers of poppy seed (pronounced "muhn" or "moon" in Yiddish) should also try the poppy-seed Danish.

Shopping arcades exist all over Paris, but in the United States they're rare—especially on sections of urban streets that have been taken over by chain stores. Mercifully and doggedly rescued by local preservationists, the **Coolidge Corner Arcade,** 318 Harvard Street, is a glamorous two-story building of about a score of shops. Some—shoe repair, clothing alterations, insurance—offer down-to-earth services. Others—an Italian cafe, a facial salon, a hair stylist— are more upscale. A few are one-of-a-kind and marvelous, notably, the Zipper Hospital. I have taken many venerable ski parkas, sleeping bags, and even old leather luggage there. I am mad for the small but superb **Encore Exchange Consignment Boutique,** 318 Harvard Street, (617) 566–4544, which specializes in women's clothing and accessories, especially jewelry. If you keep in mind that many of the store's consignees are older ladies (and it would appear from the offerings, ladies with fashion *sechel*—Yiddish for "smarts"), you'll know what to expect: a knock-your-socks-off array of retro pieces. The display of costume jewelry in the small store's window is nothing short of fabulous, like wandering into your Auntie Mame's room-size jewelry box. Devotees might spend thirty minutes in rapt concentration, studying the display: huge faux-gold earrings, chunky coral and jade bracelets, a dazzling velvet cushion of rhinestone pins, earrings, chokers, bracelets, and hair ornaments. Scads of multiple-strand pearl necklaces a la Barbara Bush. An entire tray of animal pins: bees, owls, slinky enameled cats, a cloisonné beetle, an onyx elephant with sage-green eyes.

A few doors from Encore Exchange in the Arcade, look for an entrance to **Fire Opal,** which can also be entered from Harvard Street, 300 Harvard Street, (617) 739–9066. What a serendipitous combination—two scintillating stores so close. While most of what you'll find at the consignment boutique is retro, the focus of Fire Opal is contemporary jewelry and crafts. They show a small selection of artful clothing and decorative arts—fanciful picture frames and mirrors, hand-blown wine glasses, and classical urns for plants. But the jewelry collection is the draw. Almost all of it fits in just three or four cases, but it's carefully selected, in all price ranges and styles: tiny ceramic earrings, totemic hand-forged copper earrings, a ring of intertwined gold and silver bands with an opalescent sapphire. The service is considerate, personal, and low key.

From the outside **Rami's ($),** 324 Harvard Street, (617) 738–3577, looks peaceful, but that's because you can't see inside. You can, however, scent-out something garlicky, seductive, and fried. It's Middle Eastern fast food: falafel, a deep-fried ball of mashed chickpeas, bread crumbs, and spices. The window on this small spicy world is fogged because of the hot stuff within, and because the shop is a long and narrow space, shielding most of the schmoozers, fressers, and kibbitzers (gabbers, eaters, and jokesters) from passersby. But inside—amid the sizzling falafel and fast-moving behind-the-counter assemblers—are small groups of people at tables talking animatedly, or trying to distract each other to play a little trick, or telling long, yarnlike jokes. At one table a handsome elderly man, eating alone, is chuckling as he reads the paper. A slender young woman in a leotard finishes her lunch and that of her date. Behind the counter the proprietor talks loudly in Hebrew on his cordless telephone, occasionally shouting. "Quiet, quiet!" a customer says good naturedly. "Sorry," whispers the proprietor, who cups his hand and continues shouting.

So the public library it's not. But the falafel is famous for blocks, maybe miles. In other places these Levantine chickpea balls taste like collapsed stars. But Rami's falafel are almost delicate, with a crumbly, succulent texture.

Because Brookline is associated with food, education, and history, **The Devotion House,** 347 Harvard Street, a site combining eighteenth-century architecture, twentieth-century education, and impromptu picnics, has a lot of appeal. Across from Rami's, you'll often see neighborhood people seated on benches, munching on pita sandwiches and other "wraps" in front of a children's playground; English classes being taught on the grass; and anchoring the eating and education, a beautifully proportioned yellow colonial house. The house is a well-preserved eighteenth-century structure bought as a site for a new school in 1892. It was taken over by the Brookline Historical Society as a house museum in 1911 and is open for tours on Tuesday and Thursday afternoons.

Behind the house, the **Edward Devotion School,** an actual Brookline public school, is nestled amid the maple trees on the old house property. President John F. Kennedy attended the Devotion School and lived just up the street. From Harvard Street take a right onto Beals Street. **The John F. Kennedy National Historic Site,** 83 Beals Street, (617) 566–7937, is a cheerful, wood-frame house—like many others on the block—where JFK was born. Newlyweds Rose and Joseph P. Kennedy bought their home in 1914 and lived there for seven years. Following JFK's assassination, the Kennedy family bought the old family home. Rose Kennedy herself restored it, recreating her memory of the year the president was born, 1917. The nearby area of JFK Crossing is also beloved for its outdoor murals. Here Brookline's history and highlights can be read pictorially—its transformation from a farming community to a tidy town, the home life of the Kennedy family, and the migration of Jewish immigrants.

Waves of those immigrants have passed through the doors of Congregation **Kehillath Israel,** 384 Harvard Street, (617) 277–9155, which rises up from Harvard Street like a tabernacle of old. The congregation began in 1915 as a group of observant Jews conducting services in private Brookline homes. By the 1920s the need for a synagogue building had become apparent; the present Byzantine-style structure was dedicated in 1925. Its architecture features simple, blocklike shapes, topped by domes and graceful arches. In the ancient world synagogues would have had some of these same features, as well as decorative mosaics. In the sanctuary of Kehillath Israel, twelve gilded mosaic panels depict the twelve tribes of Israel. Outside, to the rear of the building, a small meditation garden, festive with flowering trees in spring, can be glimpsed from the street. In May red tulips bloom and bob before a small plaque on the grounds. THE INA SUE PERLMUTTER GARDEN, it reads.

These days, most full-service takeouts—places where you can buy an entire meal and serve it as your own—are called "gourmet takeouts" to distinguish themselves from fast-food outlets. **Ruth's Kitchen,** 401 Harvard Street, (617) 734–9810, is full service, but not gourmet. It's *haimish*, the Yiddish word for "homey." This is by no means a slur. Take tzimmis, a side dish made of sweetened vegetables—generally sweet potatoes, carrots, and honey. (Linguistic note: In Yiddish, a *tzimmis*, a mélange, can also refer to excitement or confusion: "What's the big tzimmis?" means "What's the big deal?," generally with a soupçon of "calm down" or "chill.") Some fancy shops sell tzimmis that looks and tastes like a pureed veg. Ruth's tzimmis is less refined, more like a busy Jewish grandmother would make, with chunks of potatoes and carrots, a little overcooked, a little too sweet for some—in short, Jewish soul food. All Ruth's dishes are kosher, even the most exotic Asian-style dishes. The latter are also a little overcooked and sweet; not what you'd get in Chinatown, thank God; but for many of us, they convey an American-Jewish je ne sais quoi.

Some people get excited in front of fine jewelry stores, others in front of fine fish stores. I am equally elated in the face of each. **Wulf's Fish Market,** 407 Harvard Street, (617) 277–2506, is the Tiffany's of fishmongers. Perhaps I should say it is the Brigham and Women's Hospital of fishmongers, as the place has a quasimedical quality. The walls are white, the fish are on chipped ice, and the equipment is surgical-quality stainless steel. Fish charts hang on the wall. Old-fashioned fishmongers in white aprons, which look a lot like doctors' coats, carve up stately salmon, halibut, swordfish, and tuna with the aplomb of surgeons. "No fishy smell," my mother, Blanche, pronounced on being escorted for the first time to Wulf's. It's true, there is no fish smell, though there is an oceany aroma and a dampness from the quantities of ice. I love going there on torrid summer days.

Wulf's offers very fresh fish, anatomy lessons, and advice.

Even if I never bought another piece of fish at Wulf's, I would treasure the memory of the man who taught me to clean and cut fish when I was in college and first living in Brookline. The genial fishmonger had a calm demeanor and showed me how to gut the insides, scale the fish, wash it down, make sideways slivered filets, and chop off the head and tail to make stock. He discussed fish eyeballs, an entirely new subject for me, and how fish skin should never be slimy. The man who taught me these lessons is still at Wulf's, and is still patient, soft-spoken, and calm.

The Israel Book Shop, 410 Harvard Street, (617) 566–7113, has some of the same items as Kolbo (a store farther down Harvard), but is more a bookstore than a gallery, though they also carry menorahs, kiddish cups, seder plates, children's toys, and party favors. Israel Book Shop has a traditional, old-world quality, while Kolbo feels artsy and new. A typical menorah from Israel Book Shop would be a magnificent silver candelabra, the type you might see in a synagogue, or a simple brass menorah, like what Jewish children see in a grandmother's house. (By contrast, Kolbo shows menorahs made by contemporary sculptors—those with hand-built figures, one character per candle, and whimsical models that move.) Israel Book Shop is particularly good on scholarly and historical Jewish books, and they carry a rainbow of yarmulkes, the skullcaps worn by many observant Jews.

Bagels come and bagels go, but those of **Kupel's Bake & Bagel,** 421 Harvard Street, (617) 566–9528, are considered by mavens to be among the best. As a result, this corner bakery with a few window sidetables is always hopping. In addition to bagels, look for babke (cinnamon loaf), Danish, egg kichel, strudel, honey cake, rugelach, challah, and a rainbow of hamentashen. Once these tri-cornered, filled pastries were sold only during the Jewish holiday Purim, but now they're available all year round (a mixed blessing, like being able to get gingerbread men not just at Christmas, but anytime). In addition to traditional fillings—prune, poppy seed, and apricot—Kupel's carries hamentashen pumped-up with lemon, raspberry, apple, blueberry, pineapple, and cherry jams.

Skip the pineapple hamentashen, but not the black-and-white mural on the side of Kupel's. This pictorial history of Harvard Street is part social history, part Chagall—in its floating evocations—and mostly David E. Levine, the imaginative artist. Levine manages to combine images of vendors, changing historical moods, and a handwritten recipe for chopped liver, no schmaltz barred, in an elegiac work.

To be Jewish or Italian is to prize good bread. Another bakery, which specializes in crusty, hearth-baked loaves, is **Clear Flour Bread,** 178 Thorndike Street, (617) 739–0060, well worth seeking out. Take a right on Thorndike Street on the right side of Harvard. This small corner bakery has a wonderful atmosphere, a mix of European, free-form and hip, with sourdough and old-world specialty breads artfully displayed. Pies, tarts, muffins, and friendly counter assistance are all part of what you'll find.

The Butcherie, 428 Harvard Street, (617) 731–9888, is not the most attractive or cheerful grocery I've ever been in, but it has a fiercely loyal clientele, as it's a full-service kosher supermarket that also offers catering services. Kosher canned goods and ritual items are here, along with a kosher meat market and deli counter. Look for traditional prepared foods, such as chopped liver and blintzes, and bona fide half-done pickles. Take a look at the store from across the street; the beige deco facade has cream-colored medallions, swags, and classical frippery.

Kolbo Fine Judaica, 435 Harvard Street, (617) 731–8743, an art gallery and bookstore with a Jewish focus, has grown like Topsy. In the beginning, you should excuse the expression, they specialized in high-quality prints and carried a small selection of books and ritual items. Now the spacious, luminous store has become *the* place for elegant glassware, ceramics, Middle Eastern jewelry, posters, paintings, and prints, as well as books. A few years ago they enlarged their already commodious shop to create a separate art and decorative arts gallery, with new space designed as a bookstore. Located on a corner, the store is suffused with natural light. This is the place to look for a sculptural, one-of-a-kind menorah; a handmade ceramic mezuzah, a small ritual item, mounted on a door frame, that sanctifies a house; or a snow-white tallis, the prayer shawl used in the Jewish worship service. It's also a terrific place to while away a half hour listening to Jewish folk music as you choose a book, CD, or card.

MORE HARVARD STREET

Before you explore Beacon Street, check out (at least) the start of Harvard Street on the other side of the trolley tracks, heading toward Brookline Village. On the corner of Beacon and Harvard is a newfangled, interesting wine store, **Best Cellars,** 1327 Beacon Street, (617) 232–4100—very "high concept" as they say in the biz. Its inventory is focused on bottles under $12 and organized by how the wines taste, rather than their country of origin, region, or varietal. Whites, for example, are assigned categories of Fizzy, Fresh, Soft, and Luscious. Each "selection" appears with clear specs and suggestions for serving. It's a great idea, and you never feel like a numbskull, but the plotting-out seems stark to those of us who like to wade through funky bottles and make our own discoveries. Still, Best Cellars drives the point home that a Muscadet, a Sauvignon Blanc, a Vinho Verde, and an Orvietto can be taste relatives.

This part of Harvard Street is a restaurant mecca, with a cluster of Asian restaurants and groceries, along with antiques stores and historic buildings. **United Parish Church,** 210 Harvard Street, (617) 277–6860, comprises its own cocoa-colored kingdom of gables, domes, spires, and arches at the corner of Harvard and Marion Streets. The sprawling church building is truly a united parish, holding three congregations of three denominations, each of which once had their own church buildings. In 1970 the longtime Coolidge Corner neighbors—all Protestant churches that had lost members over the years—gathered together in what had been Harvard Church. Within the building are Harvard Church (United Church of Christ), St. Mark's (United Methodist Church), and the Baptist Church in Brookline.

BEACON STREET

While the nexus of Harvard and Beacon Streets is core Coolidge Corner, the character of the neighborhood continues along Beacon Street, especially outbound, in the direction of Washington Street and Cleveland Circle, street numbers ascending. But if you're feeling vigorous, check out a block or two in the other direction, heading toward Boston, street numbers descending. **Beacon Jewelry,** 1298 Beacon Street, (617) 232–2772, looks like an ordinary jewelry store, but look again. The window overflows with amber jewelry set in sterling silver, a tip-off to the heritage of the store's genial proprietor, Neela, who is Russian. Amber is from the Balkans. Uri, her husband, is a whiz at fixing intricate antique clocks; he learned from his father in Uzbekistan. **Trader Joe's,** 1309 Beacon Street, part of a chain, sells traditional and gourmet grocery items of superior quality for below-average prices, everything from pasta and bread, to candles and cosmetics, to wine and cheese. Their secret: They buy direct and use their own label. Take a quick left off Beacon to the **Coolidge Corner Public Library,** 31 Pleasant Street, (617) 730–2340, a civil space. From the outside it looks unremarkable, but inside are treasures, a combination of people and resources that create a cherished place. Many elderly people living in nearby apartments come in every day to read, generally taking the same chair and looking disappointed if a stranger is in their place. An extensive Judaica section attracts scholars. Behind the collection are vibrant stained-glass windows by Cambridge artist Linda Lichtman. Installed in 1991, *Tree of*

Knowledge/Tree of Life shows red roots, botanical forms, a tempting apple, and a serpent.

If you fancy architecture, Judaica, and history, you may want to saunter down to **Temple Ohabei Shalom,** 1187 Beacon Street, (617) 277–6610. It's the oldest Jewish congregation in Massachusetts, founded in 1842, with roots in East Boston, the South End, and what is today Boston's theater district. The monumental temple has been a Brookline landmark since the 1920s, when the present Byzantine-Romanesque building—with its evocative copper dome, majestic arches, and stained-glass windows—was constructed on the corner of Beacon and Kent Streets. Rabbi Emily Lipof is the synagogue's popular leader and teacher. The temple's name means "Lovers of Peace."

Lovers of trees should take a right on Kent Street to find the surpassingly lovely square of European **copper beech trees,** with grand houses grouped around the ancient beeches. Their trunks are massive, elephant-gray, and smooth, with lengthy flexible branches that curve down to the ground. During light rain you can find protection under these limbs, which form a tent of leaves.

Return to Coolidge Corner. "Outbound" Beacon Street, streetcar lingo for "away from Boston," has several of the best craft stores in the area. **The Pear Tree,** 1355 Beacon Street, (617) 277–9330, a Coolidge Corner mainstay, is a decades-old pioneer in gathering, presenting, and selling crafts from developing nations. The inviting store comes off as a mix of anthropology museum, craft gallery, and bead workshop.

If foreign language books interest you—or classics of travel literature—cross the street to **Mundi,** 1362 Beacon Street, (617) 277–1199. This friendly, bright, proprietor-run store specializes in books *associated* with other cultures. The concept includes English translations of foreign language classics, fiction and nonfiction set in foreign lands, and titles in Arabic, Farsi, French, German, Greek, Hebrew, Portuguese, Russian, and Spanish. There's even a children's section with multicultural books and tapes and a few literary character toys: Babar, Celeste, and Maisy, a girl mouse.

Stone's Throw, 1389 Beacon Street, (617) 731–3773, a few blocks from the heart of Coolidge Corner, is one of Boston's most attractive and inviting craft galleries, featuring a range of ceramics and glass by well-established local and regional artisans. There is almost nothing cutesy or junky at Stone's Throw; the jewelry is elegant and sophisticated, the bowls need nothing in them, and the hand-painted silk scarves can double as wall hangings.

Though it bills itself as a craft gallery, **Wild Goose Chase,** 1431 Beacon Street, (617) 738–8020, is much more a gift store, as it houses an extensive selection of fashion accessories, decorative arts, jewelry, housewares, and tchotchkes. The store is bigger and glitzier than The Pear Tree and nearby Stone's Throw and also more commercial. You can easily find a charming little gift here for under $10—a scented soap or hand cream, candles, or stationery—as well as something lavish. Jewelry runs to the opulent with precious metals and stones, though funkier earrings are part of the mix. Wild Goose also carries small pieces of furniture, lamps, and gift items for Jewish holidays: menorahs (though not as artistic as those at Kolbo), seder plates, and wineglasses.

Beware of cars and trolleys moving in both directions; cross Beacon. One of the most atmospheric bookstores you'll ever encounter is **Petropol Russian Bookstore,** 1428 Beacon Street, (617) 232–8820, which serves the many Russian émigrés who live in the Brookline-Brighton area. It's small, old world, and comfy, basically a medium-size room with books to the ceiling on all sides. These include children's books, periodicals, and literary classics. A

Jewish Cooking

Though the Jewish people carry an ancient culture, they have not had the pleasure of a permanent home. Over the centuries, their cooking has absorbed the flavors of many host cultures. They are a Semitic people, and so the repertoire includes the hallmarks of that cuisine: puffy pita bread, cracked wheat in salads and sides, the retinue of spicy spreads made of mashed chickpeas or eggplant mixed with tahini (sesame paste), and piquant salads of fresh vegetables. All are a part of contemporary Middle Eastern–Israeli food. For thousands of years, you could buy a soul-and-stomach-satisfying falafel, a sandwich of pita and fried chickpea balls, on the street. Today, you can still do so at Rami's on Harvard Street in Brookline.

Over the centuries, as the Jews migrated to Europe and the Mediterranean—not to mention northern China—their vast recipe collection expanded. Sephardic cuisine, the seductive cooking of the Spanish and Portuguese Jews, is a subject in itself. Its romantic unions of sweet and sour, fruit and meat, vegetable and grain has generated a zillion divine meals—and several splendid cookbooks, including Copeland Marks's Sephardic Cooking *and Edda Servi Machlin's* The Classic Cuisine of the Italian Jews.

In nineteenth-century America the two great waves of Jewish immigration were from Germany and Central Europe, including Russia, Poland, Lithuania, and Romania. American Jews descend mainly from these German-Jewish and Russian-Jewish forebears. The German Jews, generally more prosperous and educated than the later-arriving Russians, wanted to assimilate. The Russian and Polish immigrants—hungry, desperately poor, often uneducated—tended to settle together and maintain aspects of their culture, including food.

Knishes, bagels, brisket, tzimmis, kugel, kasha, flanken, matzo-brei, and gefilte fish—where would Jewish jokesters be without gefilte fish?—have Central European roots. Jewish meals of this tradition feature a slow-cooked meat or chicken dish—a pot roast or chicken cooked with sautéed onions and vegetables—served with potatoes or noodles, a simple cooked vegetable, and perhaps a salad. Dessert might be apple cake, rice pudding, or a fruit compote made of dried apricots, pears, peaches, and plums, served with cookies or slices of sponge cake.

Today, even in families where dietary laws are not observed, where no one has "kept kosher" for generations, cultural food preferences often dominate. I grew up in a fairly typical, non-kosher, American-Jewish home. Still, pork was never served, and meat was always well cooked as animal blood is anathema to Jews. (To this day, even though I am supposed to be sophisticated in these matters, when I even read au jus *on a menu, it makes me queasy!) Milk and meat are never served together, hence all the rolling of eyes when non-Jews order a pastrami sandwich and a frosty glass of milk. Dairy products can be served with fish. And so you can enjoy a luchen kugel, a scrumptious noodle pudding made with farmer cheese, at a meal where poached salmon is served. You can eat lox with cream cheese, sour cream with herring, and, only in America, a tuna melt.*

lovely blonde woman sits at a desk. She answers only those questions stated in Russian and speaks only Russian, but she is gracious in gesture and unintelligible murmuring. I pretend to understand what she's saying for the pleasure of browsing in this literary place and listening to the quiet (totally inexplicable to me) conversations among customers. If only they served blini and tea.

If you don't speak Russian, you'll be entering a surreal atmosphere at **Bazaar International Gourmet,** 1432 Beacon Street, (617) 739–8450, citadel of my favorite pastry in the world: the not-too-sweet rolled poppy-seed pastry. In this spacious market—a combination deli, bakery, grocery, and community hot spot—the staff speaks only Russian—and loud. The first few times I entered Bazaar, I thought people were fighting. But how could they always be fighting, when the place seemed well stocked and well managed? Then I realized they weren't fighting, but speaking. Get used to it. Maybe take an aspirin before you go. The food and the scene are worth it. A virtual aquarium of smoked and salted fish. Salamis, sausages, deli meats. Breads, ranging from the excellent Russian rye baked on the premises to Lithuanian and Russian styles imported from Brooklyn, some studded with coriander. A section of prepared foods has salads and entrees with lots of punch. Most are vegetable-based: eggplant salads, squash caviar, and slaws made of cucumbers or cabbage or beets. The meat dishes are flamboyantly displayed: a sliced beef tongue in orange sauce reposes grandly in a red oval ceramic plate.

If grand old apartment buildings interest you, wander on. The **Stoneholm,** 1514 Beacon, is one of the most elegant: a castlelike beaux arts masterpiece built in 1907, designed by Arthur H. Bowditch, rising on the craggy crest of Corey Hill.

S U G G E S T E D 🍽 R E S T A U R A N T S

A book could be written about all the area's restaurants. Here are a few in varied price ranges.

Zaftig is Yiddish for stocky, chunky, and if you're a woman, curvy. It's what you'll be if you make a habit of **Zaftigs ($–$$),** 335 Harvard Street, (617) 975–0075, an old-fashioned deli with much better food, and an airy, spacious, fun room with colorful original art, most of it with local themes. Presumably the spot has deli karma, as way-back-when it housed Jack and Marion's, a boisterous deli where everyone in the neighborhood crossed paths, and where college students would go for après-cinema sandwiches, deli platters, and eggs. Believe me, there was no veggie burger on the menu then, and an order for Salade Niçoise (with artichoke hearts, yet) would have been greeted with "Who's she?" Both of these entrees are on Zaftigs's menu, but the fare is still dominated by knishes, kugel, and kasha; fish plates served with bagel, cream cheese, and lettuce/tomato/onion; and old-fashioned entrees such as chicken in a pot, brisket of beef, and baked meat loaf. Yes, you can still get Dr. Brown's Cel-Ray soda, egg creams, and prune juice. Most wonderfully, you can have breakfast all day, including fried matzoh. It's sprinkled with cinnamon and sugar, however, which would cause my grandmother Rose to proclaim, *"Feh!"* (Yiddish for *yech!*).

Chef Chow's House ($–$$), 230 Harvard Street, (617) 739–2469, is part of the cluster of restaurants on the other side of the trolley tracks on Harvard Street. Good, serviceable, neighborhood Chinese food and a comfy, attractive setting.

Across the street there's a small, charming Greek restaurant, **Niko's**

($–$$), 187A Harvard Street, (617) 277–2999, very informal but with true Greek qualities: sun-splashed yet shady, airy and bright, with attractive art on the white walls and lively Greek music playing. The menu holds typical Greek fare—moussaka, lamb dishes, grape leaves—as well as some unusual items. *Bifteki* is a cheese-filled meatball, served with salad and pilaf. *Fasolatha* is a nice thick bean-and-tomato soup. *Moussaka,* the layered Greek eggplant casserole—with a velvety bechamel sauce that knits ingredients together—is available in meat and vegetarian versions. Folks bring children and grandchildren here, so there are also burgers, grilled cheese, and french fries. Breakfast is served until 11:30 A.M. during the week, weekends until 12:30 P.M. The house omelette overflows its platter and contains savory Greek sausage, pungent feta cheese, sautéed mushrooms, green peppers, and onions. It's served with home fries and toast, and is enough protein for a week.

Pho Lemongrass ($–$$), 239 Harvard Street, (617) 731–8600, is one clever restaurant, having figured out its discerning and demanding clientele very well, and offering a range of traditional Vietnamese fare, freshly prepared and attractively served, with a flexible and diner-friendly menu. Devotees of pho (fa, with a short "a"), the popular Vietnamese noodle soup, can order small, medium, or large bowls of the aromatic broth, with fish or meat, served with the enlivening accoutrements—basil, mint, chili pepper, and fresh lime—that eager eaters add. Chef's specialties include Black Bean Salmon and a tenderized pork casserole with caramelized peppercorn sauce. Freelancers can create their own stir-frys (served with perfectly steamed jasmine rice). I always order cashew nuts so I can say their decisive-sounding Vietnamese name aloud: Hot Dieu.

Takeshima ($–$$), 308 Harvard Street, (617) 566–0200, near the Arcade, is a long-lived Japanese restaurant with soothing soups, sushi and shashimi, and traditional entrees. Try the festive and artistic dinner box special, noodle dishes, and tasty nabe entrees: udon noodles, vegetables, and seafood cooked in a cast-iron pot.

Buddha's Restaurant ($), 404 Harvard Street, (617) 739–8830, is a little weird, but also fun, fascinating, inexpensive, and nutritious. Nominally it's a vegetarian Chinese-Vietnamese restaurant (albeit with plastic red-and-white checkered tablecloths), but the vegetable protein you're eating—tofu in various forms—is disguised to taste, and sometimes to appear, as meat. Vegetarians can consume quite tasty food at nominal prices, but there's the unsettling experience of ordering "shrimp," "beef," and "chicken wings" from the menu, though "boneless gluten pork" doesn't sound much better, I admit. Buddha is great fun, serves brown rice, and has a list of thirty cold beverages worth charging admission to read: guana banana milk shake made with condensed milk, mung beans and red beans with coconut juice, and fresh coconut milk with green beans and ice. On a hot day, they're a meal.

I'm not crazy about **Rubin's ($),** 500 Harvard Street, (617) 566–8761, a Brookline perennial, but everyone else is. Furthermore, it's been in business forever—and is kosher. So obviously there's something wrong with me. The restaurant serves typical Jewish deli food, including sandwiches. So go. Good luck. Enjoy.

Kaya ($–$$$), 1366 Beacon Street, (617) 738–2244, offers fresh, reliable Korean and Japanese food, including very reasonable luncheon specials, artfully served in traditional lacquered boxes (like a supremely elegant TV dinner tray). A typical lunch order of salmon teriyaki is a colorful, satisfying feast—including a nicely cut piece of just-grilled salmon, sautéed noodles, rice flecked with egg and minced vegetables, avocado roll, shrimp dumplings, and assorted pickles and citrus. In addition to traditional entrees, Kaya has two dozen appetizers—temptations from vegetable croquettes to carrot salad to sautéed ginkgo nuts—which can be combined to make a medley of small plates. The service here is soothing and polite, like being cared for by doting daughters.

For several years during the 1980s, I met a friend every single Saturday for breakfast at the **B & D Deli ($),** 1653B Beacon Street, (617) 232–3727. We always sat at the counter and ordered scrambled eggs. They arrived quickly, on heated plates, and the bagels were toasted perfectly—crisp on the outside, chewy inside. The B & D is still good on these details and serves a mean whitefish platter, but I wish they hadn't gone high-hat and remodeled. I like the new place, but I loved the old joint. The eggs were ambrosial—loosely scrambled and creamy—and the counter cook high-strung and gifted. Now the deli is bigger and swankier, and the cooks less mercurial, but also less witty. The B & D is mobbed on the weekends—a great social scene—with big portions of reliable, filling deli food.

 Allston– Brighton

Seoul, Moscow, and Ipanema

*I*t happens fast. You're moseying along Harvard Street in Brookline, heading west on the old "road to the colleges." By the time you reach Commonwealth Avenue, it's as though there's been a clash of cymbals announcing a set change. Good-bye Rubin's Deli, Pastryland, and Zipper Hospital, hello Berezca Market (pork loin sausages), Camino Real (oxtail stew), and E. Shan Tang (pulverized deer antlers). This is Allston, part of the sprawling community of Allston–Brighton—faster paced, more densely populated, more multicultural than Coolidge Corner; and home to members of the Chinese, Korean, Japanese, Southeast Asian, Russian, Brazilian, Haitian, and Colombian communities; and loads of young people.

If you've ever been a student at Boston University or Boston College—or just young and of moderate means in Boston—for sure you've lived in this neighborhood or known someone who did. It has some of the best music clubs in the city and is convenient to the Boston College MBTA. Historically, the rents have been lower (and the apartments dingier) than those of the Back Bay, gentrified South End, and Beacon Hill. College students and young worker bees have flocked here, as have elder Bostonians on fixed incomes and a mélange of new Bostonians.

Asian groceries, markets, and restaurants dominate the scene, along with Brazilian businesses and Russian enterprises. Sauntering down the crowded streets are arrays of people: updated Russian babushkas with high-style platinum blonde or red hair, a smattering of traditional babushkas in cloth coats and sparkly little earrings, Korean college students with nose rings and studs, neatly attired Asian women, Indian ladies in saris, attractive Brazilian couples in leather jackets, and scruffy little boys-of-all-nations on bikes, their mothers screaming at them in various languages to stay out of the street.

The hub along Harvard Avenue, dubbed Allston Village by civic boosters and decorated with pennants, is the spiciest shopping area. Additional restaurants, groceries, and shops spill over to the main cross streets of Commonwealth Avenue, Brighton Avenue, and Cambridge Street. Residential neighborhoods range from brick apartment buildings along and near the MBTA tracks, to modest wood-frame houses on the Boston side of the Charles River near WGBH-TV, to commodious nineteenth-century houses in the outer reaches of Brighton, such as Lake Street.

Where precisely Allston becomes Brighton is a matter of opinion. But the nexus of ethnic communities is undoubtedly Harvard Avenue, where salty feta cheese omelettes, fermented Korean *kimchi,* and ruddy apricots macerated in plum brandy all vie for attention, along with almost-antique furniture shops, low-cost nail salons, and artists' open studios in rehabbed factories where rugs were once made. Here and there, vestiges of the eighteenth- and nineteenth-century meat trade linger.

How to Get There

By public transportation take the MBTA Green Line Boston College (B) car to Harvard Avenue or the Number 66 bus, which runs between Harvard Square and Dudley Station. The Number 66 travels just about the whole route of the old "road to the colleges": Harvard Avenue (Allston) and Harvard Street (Coolidge Corner and Brookline Village). By car drive outbound on Commonwealth or Brighton Avenue to the intersection of Harvard Avenue or follow Harvard Street west.

• • • $\mathcal{H}istory$ • • •

As you experience Boston, it adds dimension to consider how communities were once connected. When the Massachusetts Bay Colony was settled in 1630, what is today Allston–Brighton was part of Watertown. Later, it was given to Cambridge and dubbed Little Cambridge. Farmers used the land for grazing. During the Revolutionary War, beef from Little Cambridge cattle yards fed the Continental Army.

In 1807 Little Cambridge became the town of Brighton, by this time known for its huge cattle market, slaughtering and butchering operations, and commercial gardens. In 1834 the Boston & Worcester Railroad began to run through, making downtown Boston accessible, turning the outpost into something of a streetcar suburb.

Another railroad station opened in the 1860s and a third in 1867 at Cambridge Crossing, the intersection of Cambridge Street and Harvard Avenue. (The former Allston Depot restaurant, today called the Sports Depot and looking not too sporty, is the remnant of the old stone station.) At the urging of depot-proud citizens, this cross-roads—now with its own railroad station, after all—was renamed for local artist Washington Allston. As farming declined, additional connections to Boston developed. In 1873 Allston–Brighton was annexed to Boston.

One of the most intriguing aspects of Allston–Brighton history was the role of the Catholic Church as real estate developer. During the nineteenth century, Roman Catholic immigrants from Ireland and Italy settled in Brighton, where jobs and low-cost housing were available. By the late nineteenth and early twentieth century, old Yankee families were selling their Brighton estates. The Roman Catholic archdiocese purchased large lots from them, turning the parcels into church properties. St. John's Seminary on Lake Street—with its handsome French chateaux architecture, made of nubby pudding-stone quarried from the site—was opened in 1881. Numerous other religious buildings were constructed—convents, monasteries, churches—many of which still stand. These ecclesiastical buildings and landscaped grounds punctuate residential Brighton, a reminder of an earlier pastoral community.

In many ways the growth of Allston–Brighton mirrors that of its neighbor, Brookline. As transportation to Boston became available, a farming community was transformed into a streetcar suburb. But Allston–Brighton developed in a grittier fashion; its sprawling cattle markets and large-scale slaughtering operations continued for two centuries. The slaughterhouses were first located in Brighton Center and later moved to the Brighton Abattoir near the Charles River. During the 1870s these operations were threatened by the innovation of refrigerated cars that brought meat to Boston from the American West. By the 1880s, as Jewish immigration to the area increased, a specialty market developed: kosher butchering, which required fresh meat and local facilities. It may be hard to picture, but there were stockyards in Allston–Brighton until around 1960. (A major thoroughfare still bears the name Market Street.) The Sports Depot restaurant specializes in burgers and steak. Kosher butcher shops linger, and the newer Halal markets prepare meat according to the laws of Islam.

Meat abounds. It can be found as fast food in chain burger joints and music clubs, grilled in Brazilian cafeterias and bistros, and shredded in Korean soups. In an unintentional memento to butchers past, sides of roasted lamb steam up the windows of Greek tavernas, tantalizing customers. On any afternoon folks of varied ethnicities feast on a Greek lunch of savory meat slivers, laid on hot platters or across heated rolls. These meat outposts throughout the neighborhood are Allston's unceremonial Freedom Trail.

... *A Walking Tour* ...

You could spend weeks exploring Allston–Brighton, including enclaves remarkable for their ethnic communities, architectural distinction, and industrial history. For present purposes I'll guide you along Harvard Avenue (the Allston incarnation of Harvard Street), with a few sashays at the intersections of Commonwealth and Brighton Avenues, and along Cambridge Street.

Cross the traffic tangle at the intersection of Harvard and Commonwealth Avenues. Watch out for MBTA trains, cars, motorcycles, and in-line skaters in both directions. Anything can happen. Once, while I was gauging the possibilities of crossing the street, the fiery-hot muffler of a car running a red light fell onto my shoe, branding it. At least my toes were spared.

Keeping a cool head and feet, cross Commonwealth, a wide boulevard at this juncture, and take a right to **Berezca International Food Store,** 1215 Commonwealth Avenue, (617) 787–2837. If only every supermarket could be like this—glamorous but practical, delicious-smelling but clean, with tantalizing, artistic arrangements instead of boring, repetitive shelving. Berezca is a supermarket for Russians and the rest of us. The spacious square store stocks meat, fish, bread, dairy products, produce, baked goods, spices, and condiments. What an array!

Berezca's pastry is lavish—towering layer cakes, tarts with multiple fruit and cordial-flavored custards, Danish pastries the size of books. Nothing is small.

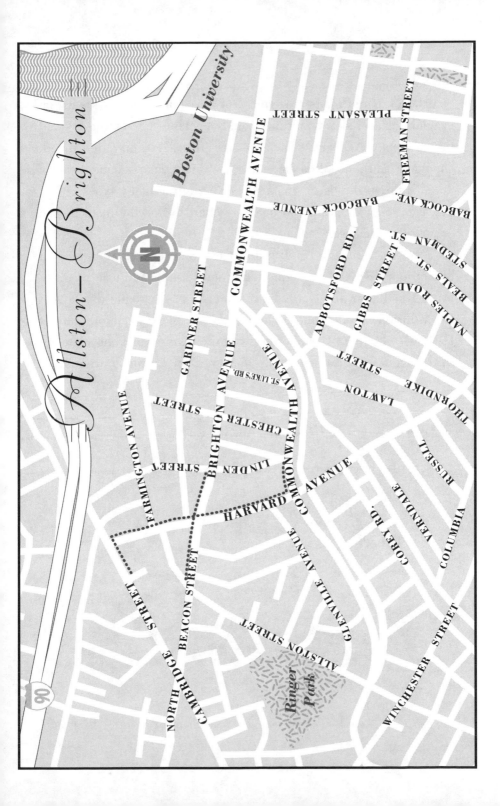

Allston–Brighton

Boston University

PLEASANT STREET

COMMONWEALTH AVENUE

FREEMAN STREET

BABCOCK AVENUE

BABCOCK AVENUE

STEDMAN ST.

BEALS ST.

NAPLES ROAD

ABBOTSFORD RD.

GIBBS STREET

GARDNER STREET

THORNDIKE STREET

LAWTON

ST. LUKE'S RD.

CHESTER STREET

BRIGHTON AVENUE

COMMONWEALTH AVENUE

RUSSELL

FARMINGTON AVENUE

STREET

LINDEN STREET

HARVARD AVENUE

VERNDALE

COLUMBIA

COREY RD.

COMMONWEALTH AVENUE

STREET

NORTHRIDGE STREET

BEACON STREET

CAMBRIDGE STREET

GLENVILLE AVENUE

ALLSTON STREET

Ringer Park

WINCHESTER STREET

90

The prepared foods are typical of Russian groceries, heavy on eggplant salads, slaws, and marinated vegetables. Root veggies and tubers—potatoes, carrots, beets—are showcased; prepared diced, shredded, and minced, alone and in combinations. I counted over a dozen different kinds of smoked fish, including many types of lox. The meat counter is like an anatomy chart. Name the main bovine organs. They're here.

I am not usually a candy eater. I make exceptions if stimulated by opulent displays (or seductive aromas, such as those at Dairy Fresh Candies in the North End). Berezca has baroque displays of boxed European chocolates, making it a fine place to go for Mother's Day and Valentine's Day offerings. But the main joys of chocolate are in the candy shrine—an array of tiered baskets of individually

The deli selections at Berezca International Food Store are positively glamorous!

wrapped bonbons, amazingly well priced. You gather your goodies and weigh them yourself. Unlike dainty Peruginas, each Berezca bonbon is massive. The Plum in Chocolate (actually a prune, wrapped in purple foil) is the size of a baby bird. A cone of chocolate wrapped in midnight-blue foil is 3 inches tall. Most of the candy is impossible to identify until you eat it. Almost everything is heavily draped in dark chocolate, with innards of peels, fondant, fruit, or booze. Like a French pig, I have learned to recognize the (chocolate) truffles: hefty spheres, sheathed in medium-blue foil.

Tucked next to Berezca, **Lavka Chitatelia,** 1217A Commonwealth Avenue, (617) 783–1590, is a Russian bookstore, a fine place to browse and to collect yourself as you make your transition from sausage, chocolate, and slaw back to the street.

Marty's Liquors and Gourmet, 193 Harvard Avenue, (617) 782–3250, a real find for foodies, is located on the corner of Harvard and Commonwealth Avenues. Marty's has an almost-secret parking lot in the rear, and stocks a superb selection of cheeses, crackers, and gourmet items, along with well-priced wines. Check out the dozen radiant shelves devoted to hot sauces—from Death Rain to Chipotle to Last Rites Scotch Bonnet.

Now proceed down Harvard Avenue.

Healing begins as soon as you enter **Shan Tang,** 157 Harvard Avenue, (617) 787–3600, a traditional Chinese pharmacy. It smells invigorating yet soothing, of herbs, earth, wood, mushrooms, and roots. Almost silently, the male and female apothecaries weigh, mix, and blend prescriptions of berries, herbs, powders, tubers, rhizomes, and roots. This tranquil shop is a wonder—a wall of wooden drawers with scores of barks and roots, topped with dozens of large glass jars filled with medicinals, ranging from pulverized rhizomes to desiccated deer antlers. The staff is gentle, friendly, and polite.

Women's health, Chinese-style, can be found at Shan Tang.

Chinese herbal medicine appears to offer remedies for every malady known to man (especially pertaining to sexual dysfunction) and woman (especially pertaining to menstrual disorders and menopause), along with complaints of modern life (anxiety, insomnia, and obesity). The store stocks packaged teas and prepared blends, but the bulk of trade is in special preparations.

It can be a little awkward, not to mention dangerous, to try to explain one's condition to a pharmacist who doesn't speak English, but in Eastern medicine the reading of the pulse is considered vastly diagnostic. In addition, a surprising amount of physiological information can be conveyed by an active demonstration of symptoms—coughing, sneezing, shortness of breath—or in a manifestation, such as dandruff or acne. On-site diagnosis and discussion take place; the pharmacists confer and prepare your potion.

A comprehensive catalog is available. It lists and describes herbal blends according to ailments and contains illustrations and instructions on qi gong, a traditional Chinese exercise form.

It can be an assault on the nervous system to go from Shan Tang to **Flyrabbit,** 155 Harvard Avenue, (617) 782–1313, next door, but then again its stimulating contrast may act as a toner. Here you will find everything from rubber chickens, to pressed butterflies, to natural history posters of beetles, to jars of animal eyes in formaldehyde. Also candles, Mexican folk art, message buttons, squirmy rubber toys that kids of all ages love, and artsy postcards. It's an edgy store—Goth, urban, creepy, self-indulgent, and fun—with artifacts of pop culture, plus mainly commendable natural history resources. The raccoon penis bones we could live without.

Across the street the addictive aroma of Korean pickles at **Mirim Trading Company,** 152 Harvard Avenue, (617) 783–2626, draws you in, and it's pleasurable to begin your browsing with Mirim's selection of cookware and pottery serving pieces. Seeing and touching porcelain and lacquered trays establishes an Asian mood and enables you to visualize how various foods might be served. You might choose a pale-green cucumber soap and a deep-green porcelain condiment dish that would serve very well as a soap dish.

The medium-size Korean grocery carries amazing varieties of noodles—many of them artistically wrapped and suitable for inexpensive gifts—as well as grains, condiments, spices, and, of course, rice. Feast your eyes on the shelves of soy sauces, all attractively packaged, and the near-humorous array of snack foods, many of them rice crackers in various shapes. Mirim is the perfect place to pick up an electric rice cooker for friends who cook Asian style or a handsome Japanese covered casserole. Check out the freezer for exotic flavors of ice cream and boxes of mochi—festive ice-cream novelties—available in mango, red bean, strawberry, and green tea flavors.

Moscow International Foods, 133 Harvard Avenue, (617) 782–6644, carries similar products to Berezca, but is much smaller, less bustling, and more elegant, set up to look like a gourmet grocery with mirrored walls, displays of gilded ceramics and laquered bowls (all for sale), and glass bottles and jars displayed to good advantage. It's quicker to shop here than at Berezca, though the staff is on the haughty side. The store seems to cater to impeccably attired Russian

Moscow International Foods is small, stylish, and slightly haughty—a food boutique.

ladies in their sixties with blonde hairdos and heavy gold jewelry—very Zsa Zsa looking.

For fortification you might stop at **Seoul Bakery,** 56 Harvard Avenue, (617) 787–6500, which is also a cafe. Almond pastries and a kind of raised doughnut filled with bean paste are enjoyable pick-me-ups with tea. American nibbles are also sold.

Brighton Avenue is the heart of Allston Village, with **Herrell's Renaissance Cafe,** 155 Brighton Avenue, (617) 782–9599, on the corner. The neighborhood hangout is festooned with work by local artists, and the bulletin board overflows with neighborhood news, needs, and imaginative, sometimes plaintive, calls for roommates. Expect excellent ice cream—the shop is still associated with Steve Herrell, the true Steve of Steve's Ice Cream. In the morning Herrell's morphs to become **Birdy's Cafe ($).** Old-fashioned breakfast favorites—French toast, waffles, egg sandwiches—are served till noon.

Diskovery, 113 Brighton Avenue, (617) 787–2640, looks worse than my office—dustier, messier, more cat fur—but don't be put off by its derelict appearance. Make your way carefully. You must walk sideways when the bookshelves get too close and when the piles of unshelved books threaten to crush you. Swamplike areas of comic books may make you sneeze. But what a rebuff to the sterility of chain bookstores. Secondhand CDs, LPs, and tapes compete for attention with the thousands of paperbacks and hardcovers on every imaginable subject, especially fiction, philosophy, and cooking. Majik, a long-haired furball of a black cat, yellow eyes ablaze, lounges on the swaying piles of novels. The hopes and dreams of students past are in every corner of this store. I hope my favorite place is still there for your examination: in the rear left corner, an entirely toppled cascade of books, a waterfall of words.

Brazilian Cuisine

Most Americans know more about Brazilian music than they do about Brazilian food. A pity, as the cuisine is as sexy as a samba, as beguiling as the bossa nova. Whether a deep-fried snack, a snazzy sit-down dinner, or a comforting cafeteria lunch with the ubiquitous fluffy white rice and slow-cooked black beans, this is seductive, lively, and unusually diverse cuisine.

Snacks available in many groceries—sometimes in the refrigerated foods area, sometimes near the register—might include risoli, a turnover stuffed with chicken, cheese, or shrimp, or empadinha, a muffin-shaped pie filled with chicken, cheese, or hearts of palm, this last a starchy yet delicate vegetable.

Look at Brazil on the map, and you'll see why the cooking is so varied. It's a huge nation (3,286,540 square miles), with a long coastline on the South Atlantic, a vast interior, prodigious rivers, and a jungle. Its multicultural population includes people of indigenous, Portuguese, and African descent. Barbecues are popular in the southern states, pork and simmered black bean dishes in the middle states, and fiery seafood dishes (laced with the peppery dende oil, extracted from the fruit of the African palm tree) in Bahia on the eastern coast. Even the influence of the Amazon surfaces in such dishes as wild duck soup and tortoise stews.

Brazilian food is heavy on meat and seafood, ranging from the spicy, robust flavors of Portuguese-style sausages to the luxurious-tasting moquecas—seafood stews that use coconut milk, cilantro, and a hit of dende oil. Speaking of hot flavors, malagueta are fiery hot Brazilian peppers, which are often bottled in a rumlike liquor or vinegar. Beef parts less familiar to North Americans are prized. Lingua fresca (tongue in a white wine and parsley sauce) is one such dish.

The Portuguese influence is strong (the first Portuguese explorers landed there in 1500), and so a Mediterranean and Iberian panache *flavors both the cooking and its presentation. You might find simple, robust dishes served formally on a white tablecloth. Or, in a humble cafeteria, foods of delicacy and complexity, such as light, succulent croquettes made of codfish, potatoes, or chicken. (Entrees are generally accompanied by black beans and rice, and a side of fried plantains.)*

In the Boston area a Brazilian restaurant often has clientele from the Azores and Cape Verde, other nations where Portuguese is spoken. African influences—such as the Calabaza squash, yuca, and other indigenous root vegetables—creep in. Greens are favored: couve a mineira *is kale sautéed with bacon fat. As the greens are lightly cooked, maintaining their crispness and bright color, they make a fine accompaniment to* feijoadaò, *a famous Brazilian dish of shiny stewed black beans, fluffy white rice, and an array of meats ranging from grilled steak to smoky sausages.*

Hearts of palm are one of the most distinctive indigenous ingredients. This edible core of the cabbage palm's stem is expensive, as the entire palm is felled to get at this delicate, delectable nugget (what hubris we human eaters express!). Salada de palmito *(hearts of palm salad), which features the ivory-colored shoots, is a classic. The coveted hearts can also be used in, and alongside, soups, stews, and turnovers.*

Though we think of coffee and tea as the two everyday, international beverages of choice, Yerba maté *is widely consumed in parts of South America, including in Brazil. Made of the leaves of* Ilex paraguayensis, *a South American holly tree, the stimulating brew has loads of vitamins and minerals, as well as caffeine, and can be found in American health food stores and Latin groceries. Yerba maté is steeped and strained, just as Indian or Chinese tea are, then served plain* (maté amargo), *with sugar or honey* (maté dulce), *or with lemon slices, or milk, or cream. When iced* (maté tetre), *it's presented with sugar and wedges of lemon or lime. Most refreshing!*

Sunrise Market, 152 Brighton Avenue, (617) 783–1988, is a gem, great for people-watching because of the cross section of Spanish, Asian, Indian, and Haitian products displayed side by side. A typical Sunrise experience: As I wait at the counter with my chicory coffee from New Orleans, my gaze shifts to a display of Korean candy and fried pork ears. I see what looks like shrink-wrapped human tongues next to Indian spices. For the sake of scholarship, I force myself to scrutinize the tongues, which turn out to be thick diagonal slices of preserved banana. Nearby, spring roll wrappers nestle beneath corn tortillas. Fresh crab is available, as are frozen frog legs, quail, and a rainbow of Goya tropical drinks.

I like bananas very much, even very ripe ones, but the fragrance of overripe bananas and plantains at the **Brazilian Corner Grocery,** 192 Brighton Avenue, (617) 787–4407, makes me dizzy. Still, it's a cute place, with some take-out Brazilian snack food in the rear and lots of bananas.

Return to Harvard Avenue and continue down to the end, where Cambridge Street crosses it. Several secondhand furniture stores are fun to explore. The mobility of students in the neighborhood and older people selling family houses make for a lot of furniture on the local market. **Antique Revival,** 1 Harvard Avenue, (617) 787–4040, specializes in moderately priced oak and mahogany furniture. **Lush Life,** 13 Harvard Avenue, (617) 787–7878, is chock-full of forties and fifties stuff. At **The Collector,** 63 Harvard Avenue, (617) 787–5952, a more individualistic store, the knowledgeable owner gathers paintings, china, and musical instruments, especially violins. The store looks like a warehouse—objects stashed rather than arranged—but you can prowl about at will.

S U G G E S T E D 🍽 R E S T A U R A N T S

Most of Allston's restaurants are on Brighton Avenue. They range from a Brazilian buffet in a shopping strip to a hip Vietnamese restaurant celebrated for its flavorful, nourishing noodle soups.

Pho Pasteur ($–$$), 137 Brighton Avenue, (617) 783–2340, started the trend of stylish, affordable, accessible Vietnamese restaurants, built on the goodness of floppy white noodles in beef, chicken, or fish broth, laced with onions and fresh cilantro, and served with crisp bean sprouts, fresh basil, sliced lime, and chili peppers, to be tossed in at the diner's discretion. The menu has been rounded out to include salads, appetizers, and entrees featuring beef, chicken, fish, or tofu with liberal use of Asian vegetables and subtle spicing.

As Italians are part of Allston–Brighton's population, so is **Carlo's Cucina Italiana ($–$$),** 131 Brighton Avenue, (617) 254–9759. The small, cozy restaurant—with a mural of an Italian villa—serves traditional Italian specialties and tends to be crowded. Fried calamari appetizers; linguini with clams, mussels, squid, and shrimp; fusilli in old-fashioned red sauce—everything is moderately priced.

Across the street the handsomely appointed but informal **Sunset Grill ($–$$),** 130 Brighton Avenue, (617) 254–1331, offers casual American favorites and South of the Border eats, but the real draw is the beer: 400 varieties of suds, 112 of them on tap. Check out the two-story mural on the outside.

Rangoli ($), 129 Brighton Avenue, (617) 562–0200, has stolen a lot of the Indian food mavens who used to stick to Central Square. Rangoli serves marvelous *dosas.* These hard-to-find South Indian crepes are made of lentil and rice flours and stuffed with mixtures of potatoes and lamb, potatoes and chicken, or potatoes and onions, served with garnishes of coconut chutney and lentil stew. In addition to well-prepared, more typical Indian dishes, Rangoli offers lentil dumplings, shrimp cooked in coconut-tamarind sauce, and kebobs of chicken pâté, herbs, and nuts.

Viet Majestic ($), 164 Brighton Avenue, (617) 782–6088, is not majestic. It's a dive with fewer than a dozen tables, a frowning waiter, and very good Vietnamese food. There's a flimsy tropical feeling to the setup; the atmosphere is created by the food and spirit of welcome, not the decor. The menu overflows with surprises, including over a dozen green bean dishes, organized in two categories: Fresh Green Beans (sautéed with various mix-ins—could be tofu, could be squid) and Fried Green Beans (same deal, that is, tossed with protein bits). Majestic has a small kitchen and over 150 items on its menu, so God only knows what's going on. It's a little perverse, but I confess to ordering based on the oddness of the entree titles here and never being disappointed. Glowing Tofu was not incandescent as I had dared to hope, but nevertheless luscious and plentiful: marinated tofu, rice noodles, mint, cucumber, carrot, radish, bean sprouts, and peanuts. Many dishes are described with the adjectives *homemade* or *special* and mean different things in different situations. Go for it.

To economize still further, or to dig your canines into meat, visit **Cafe Belo ($),** 1243 Commonwealth Avenue, (617) 202–6277. The Brazilian cafeteria is bare bones—a big white room with a buffet table with all sorts of spit-roasted meats, including fresh roast pork and spicy sausage, and lots of home-cooked vegetables. The sliced fruit is very fresh, and the barbecue smells delicious. Cafeterias are a way of life in Brazil, and at lunchtime a mix of Brazilian émigrés and college students are draped over their hefty platters at Cafe Belo. You pay by the weight of the food on your plate: around $5.00 per pound. It takes a heap-a-food to make a pound, even taking into account the savory gravy. A fancier version of the same restaurant—same cooking and friendly service, but with linen-draped table-cloths—is located at 181 Brighton Avenue.

For those who must have meat—be it to summon Allston–Brighton's past or to satiate animal protein lust—**Cafe Brazil ($–$$)**, 421 Cambridge Street, (617) 789–5980, is the place. Simmered oxtails, fried cassava and linguica, and chicken croquettes are all featured at this festive, romantic restaurant, which is "fancier"—as my mother would say—than most Allston dining spots. On special nights a Brazilian guitarist-vocalist sings beguiling samba melodies, which cause some of us, the lucky ones, to drink too much red wine. Impromptu dancing is permitted. (I only do a few steps, then return to my seat. Others do much more.)

A little out of the way, but still in Allston, **Grasshopper ($–$$)**, One North Beacon Street, (617) 254–8883, is nirvana for vegetarians and other healthy eaters. The menu in this storefront restaurant is entirely vegetarian-Vietnamese, using lots of fresh vegetables, spices, and sauces, with soy-derived "meats." Try the chewy but delicate vegetarian dumplings, well-prepared Chinese broccoli, and fried taro with a medley of artistically slivered vegetables and faux-meat.

I'm fond of little Greek places with counters, old booths, and limited menus. **The Grecian Yearning ($)**, 174 Harvard Avenue, (617) 254–8587, has all the verities: souvlaki, lamb, moussaka, spinach pie, and a nice scrod plate. The well-turned omelettes are reliably good, especially the feta, served with home fries and toast, and here's a place you can have your gyro sandwich, sliced down from the tantalizing grilled meat hunk.

Tokyo City ($–$$), 90–92 Harvard Avenue, (617) 562–8888, offers Japanese, Korean, and Chinese cuisine and is a great choice for friends with diverse tastes or for office buddies. The menu features many atypical dishes, at least for American audiences: Rock Crab with Curry Sauce in a Hot Pot, Potato Croquette with Pork, and a Japanese dish with a catchy name that begs to be repeated nonsensically, Kaki Fry, fried oysters with tonkatsu sauce and vegetables. Tokyo City has a sushi bar (with a few vegetarian items) and a stunning array of appetizers, thirty in all, which you can make a meal of, saving room for red-bean ice cream.

Camino Real ($–$$), 48 Harvard Avenue, (617) 254–5088, is a casual Colombian-American restaurant with the ubiquitous wall-mounted TV, not much on atmosphere, but as my late father said, "You can't eat atmosphere." Focus on your plate. The down-to-earth Colombian specialties include breakfast, not so easy to find in gringo land. Order the simple rice and beans with a hit of Colombian coffee, and you'll be energetic and alert all day. Arepa con Queso is a corn cake with melted Colombian cheese. The truly heavy hitter is Calentao con Carne Asada, rice and beans with grilled steak. Dinner entrees range from down-home platters of liver with onions and grilled tongue to elegant Mariscos, which are seafood dishes. Filete Marginado is grilled cod with shrimp; Cazuela de Mariscos is a casserole of six seafoods. All are hearty, yet pretty. For the ultimate in hearty, consider Paella Real, which combines rice, seafood, sausage, chicken, and pork.

Central Square

A U.N. OF FOOD, FUNK, ART, AND CRAFT

*T*he T stop, the traffic, the whir of construction; the spicy allure of Indian restaurants and falafel frying in pint-size cafes; house-size murals on the sides of buildings; stores for vintage furniture, vintage records, secondhand books; wigs, wands, love potions, nutritive flower essences; hand-carved African musical instruments and delicate Asian bells. Down an alley, aromas of Ethiopian bread baking. Above a bar, a bigger-than-life-size phoenix rising. In a barbershop window, tomato plants growing in red espresso cans.

Central Square is not for the faint of heart. A typical half block includes a police station (with clusters of squad cars, parked at weird angles), a Greek travel agency, an Indian restaurant, a futon store, a hole-in-the-wall falafel takeout, and a major construction project. It's crowded, noisy, funky, fast moving; a retail and residential cross-roads—one T stop after Kendall Square, one before Harvard Square.

Most of the buildings are handsome nineteenth-century store-fronts, mainly stone and brick, with several grand edifices, including Cambridge City Hall. On the side streets off Massachusetts Avenue (universally known as Mass. Ave.) are wooden houses—more of the worker's cottage variety toward the Charles River, more of the larger, pastel-painted, gussied-up Victorians on the Broadway side.

In winter old-fashioned Christmas lights, strung in patterns across Mass. Ave., illuminate Central Square. In summer a series of cultural festivals take over the streets. In autumn the students return from summer breaks; avenues you could walk along on hazy, silent summer mornings are once again crowded with rattle-trap Toyotas, Hondas, Subarus, and the now-fashionable vintage pickup trucks. Restaurants you'd been able to laze in all summer long are teeming with young people—their energy, appetites, attitudes.

In early spring the churches in the area—A.M.E., Baptist, Korean, Eastern Orthodox—celebrate Easter and decorate their altars and entryways with pots of lilies. A small synagogue on Tremont Street throws open its doors for Passover. Matzos appear in the markets next to Caribbean-style corn bread, Portuguese sweetbread, braided Russian Easter loaves, and old-fashioned, hippie-style spelt. In late spring the farmers' market opens in the parking lot behind Harvest Cooperative Supermarket. The crowd looks a lot like the pictures in artist David Fichter's building-size mural in the lot.

Buses into Boston (toward the Back Bay, Symphony Hall, Dudley Square) head inbound on Mass. Ave.; those to Harvard Square outbound. Caution! In addition to buses, watch out for cabs, bikes, inline skaters, and the occasional MIT experimentalist, moving along at a good clean clip in a one-of-a-kind electric-powered vehicle.

How to Get There

By public transportation take the MBTA Red Line to Central Square; buses are also available from various locations—the Number 1 on Mass. Ave. runs to and from Harvard Square. Central Square is midway between Kendall Square and Harvard Square. By car both can be reached by Memorial Drive or Storrow Drive. From Memorial take the River Street exit.

... *History* ...

In spite of recent commercial invasions, clues to Central Square's early history linger in the overlap of a nineteenth-century commercial center amid the almost suburban atmosphere of large-scale Victorian houses, most of which have been converted to multifamily use. These contemporary and historic aspects create a time-travel quality that residents cherish. Leaving their Queen Anne Victorian homes, they saunter past 200-year-old sugar maples and beneath oaks that have upended the sidewalks—brick, concrete, asphalt, whatever—to arrive at coffee bars with imported espresso machines or markets that make Indian food. Or they slip into a poetry reading at a 200-year-old church, now a Korean-Congregational place of worship.

Like all of Cambridge, Central Square was farmland in the eighteenth century. Over time Harvard Square became an academic and administrative center, with industry concentrated in East Cambridge and Cambridgeport, near the Charles River. Central Square, in the middle, developed a suburban residential quality. As early as 1793 omnibuses began a daily run along Mass. Ave., traveling from Boston through Central Square and Harvard Square. By 1826 hourly service was in place. And by the mid-nineteenth century, horse-drawn cars crisscrossed the area, clip-clopping along Mass. Ave., Prospect Street, Cambridge Street, and Broadway.

From the 1850s on, immigrants from North, South, and Central Europe arrived, along with Canadians from Nova Scotia, Chinese, and African Americans moving up from the southern United States. (Some of New England's oldest black families live in Cambridge, including Central Square, mid-Cambridge, and North Cambridge.) As Central Square became more densely populated, apartments and multifamily dwellings were built to house the new migration.

The Square developed an outré quality, a different atmosphere from that of Harvard Square, locus of Old Cambridge. Religious groups considered "unacceptable" in Harvard Square's established churches set up shop in Central Square. In 1817 the Cambridge Baptist Church built its sprawling structure on Magazine Street.

During the 1970s critics decried the sorry state of Central Square's housing and crumbling businesses. During the 1990s critics decried the loss of the funky and the indigenous, as rents skyrocketed, forcing craft stores and small restaurants to close. Still, Central Square is one vital place. One medium-size Starbuck's hasn't turned it into an urban mall, though affordable housing is badly needed. The city workers, students, members of the historic African-American community—who never thought the appearance of impoverishment was cool—and the legions who come in every day to get a good curry, all feel there's still spice in Central Square.

... A Walking Tour ...

If you arrive by T in this hubbub, you'll be at the crossroads of Mass. Ave. and Prospect Street, officially Central Square, though the definition frays a bit to include a stretch of Mass. Ave. and a few other cross streets: Western (where the police station is located), Magazine (several grand churches, including First Baptist and the Greek Orthodox), River (Indian grocery), and intriguing side streets such as Brookline and Pearl, locations of ethnic restaurants and music bars.

Get your bearings and take a short walk away from the square toward Western Avenue: India Pavilion Restaurant and the police station. Cross to Magazine Street to take a peek at some of the many churches in the neighborhood and to scan the various styles of residential buildings.

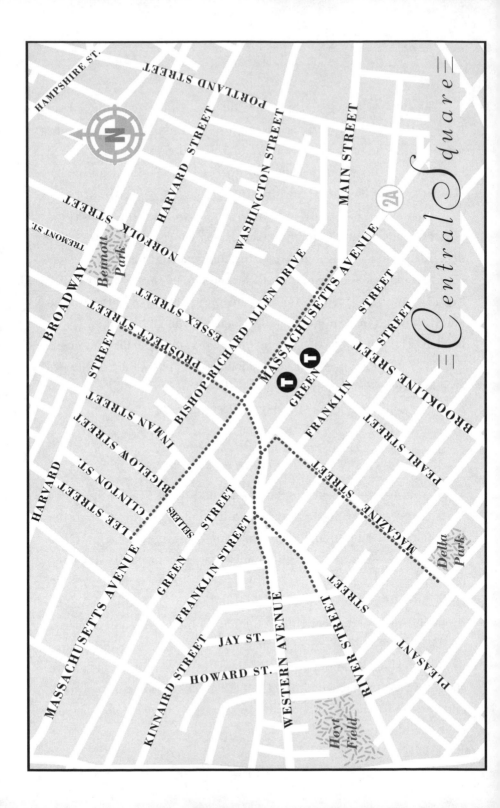

Everywhere you look, you'll see evidence of the square's past and present. Though Greek restaurants and groceries are gone, the historic Greek community is represented by the majestic **Greek Orthodox Church of Sts. Constantine and Helen,** 14 Magazine Street, and the **Greek Music and Gift Shop,** 22 Central Square, (617) 354–6890, which has everything from dates to tapes. If you live in the area, keep an eye on the local paper—or the bulletin of the Greek church—for announcements of seasonal Greek festivals.

If you're interested in religion, churches, or church architecture, Central Square is a trove of denominations: **First Baptist,** 5 Magazine Street; **The Korean Church/Congregational,** 35 Magazine Street; **Grace Methodist,** 56 Magazine Street; **St. Paul A.M.E. Church,** 85 Bishop Allen Drive off Prospect Street; **St. Bartholomew's,** 239 Harvard Street (a splendid old Episcopal church with a mainly black congregation); and **Christ the King Presbyterian Church,** 99 Prospect Street. For good measure, visit the evocative sanctuary of **Temple Beth Shalom,** 8 Tremont Street. The small synagogue—known for its diverse, socially active congregation—is the site of an annual Holocaust Remembrance Day sponsored by the city of Cambridge, its schools, and ministries.

Back on Mass. Ave. heading toward Harvard Square, check out **Rodney's Bookstore,** 698 Mass. Ave., (617) 876–6467. It's a true-blue independent, well suited to the spirit of this feisty neighborhood, where residents picketed the opening of a Starbuck's coffee shop, denouncing it as "a corporate cafe." Rodney's is spacious and plain, with secondhand and remaindered books in virtually every category, and particularly strong in art, science, history, crafts, fiction, criticism, and biography. I've found natural history treasures here and outstanding cookbooks—ranging from references to coffee table tomes. There's also a burgeoning first editions section.

The multicultural urban village of Central Square is a perfect place for **Ten Thousand Villages,** 694 Mass. Ave., (617) 876–2414, a showcase for the work of international folk artists. Fabric art and pottery from Peru, china from Vietnam, puppets from Kenya, jewelry, clothing, furniture—over thirty developing nations are represented. The shop is one of scores of Ten Thousand Villages stores across the United States, including a sister-store in Coolidge Corner, Brookline. A nonprofit program operated by the relief and development agency of Mennonite and Brethren in Christ Churches in North America, these inviting, well-stocked stores help villagers all over the world provide food and education for their families and promote the passing-on of artistic heritage.

All this would be merely admirable if the goods were so-so. But they're vibrant, colorful, and convey the culture of the people who made them. Shesham, a glowing rosewood from India, is carved into furniture. Onyx from Pakistan becomes small animal carvings (tigers, elephants, monkeys). Some Philippine baskets are trunk-size, others designed for carrying wine. Greeting cards are small works of art; one from Bangladesh holds a tiny ceramic owl. I am fond of the ceramic figures from Peru—the complicated, familial piles of pottery people, crafted into candleholders, casseroles, and candelabra. Their intricate embraces are both sacred and funny, accurate representations of human affairs.

Farther down Mass. Ave., a municipal hub: the looming **Cambridge Post Office** (known for accepting income tax returns till the bitter end), the monumental **YMCA,** and across the street, the Romanesque-style **Cambridge City Hall,** built in 1889. A handsome, solid-looking building of gray-pink granite on a rise of land, it boasts a slate roof and an imposing 154-foot tower. Feel free to slouch on the august steps of the hall and watch the passing parade.

Everything in Central Square (if not all of Cambridge) is politicized, including the volatile matter of brewing coffee. Over the past few years, major upheavals have taken place in this formerly funky section. The arrival of a gleaming, sleek Starbuck's installation—in a treasured historic building—was picketed and the subject of newspaper editorials.

If you prefer a grittier, moodier, more Cambridge-type place, you'll find it at **1369 Coffee House,** 757 Mass. Ave., (617) 576–4600, where you can order all kinds of coffee and tea preparations, muffins, pastries, soups, and sandwiches; as likely as not, your server will sport body piercings and attitude. If you want pleasant and predictable, continue on to **Starbuck's,** 655 Mass. Ave., (617) 354–5471. Your server here will sport body piercings as well, but less attitude.

You might think **Pill Hardware,** 743 Mass. Ave., (617) 876–8310, is merely a place to buy lightbulbs. In fact, it's historic. One of the oldest businesses in Central Square, it was established by a Russian-Jewish immigrant whose name transmuted into "Pill." Some of the folksiness of the founding family lingers in the advice-to-the-apartment-dweller dispensed by store personnel. I overheard a grateful customer say, "I get better diagnoses here than I do from my doctor." A doctor standing in line overheard the remark. He reminded the other customer that the human body was more complicated than a lamp. "It's a shame," said the man behind the counter. "Lightbulbs, we got."

Take a left on Prospect Street and enter **Yoshinoya Grocery and Gift,** 36 Prospect Street, (617) 491–8221, a large Japanese market. If you cook Japanese food or eat it in restaurants—or admire the Japanese aesthetic—you'll enjoy this neighborhood fixture. On days when the world seems uncivil, I do therapeutic shopping here, ducking in for ten

Add water and Japanese dried mushrooms magically plump up.

minutes for the soothing atmosphere. Where else do people bow and smile after you've made a small purchase or run their hands over the rim of a $3.00 rice bowl you've selected to ensure it has no chips?

Anything you might need to cook Japanese food is at Yoshinoya, including fresh fish and fresh tofu, sold by the pound, and hundreds of condiments, sauces, marinades, soup bases, and flavoring salts. The produce counter is delightful, an array of very fresh cabbages, kabocha squashes, sprouts, and radishes. Design mavens could spend a half hour in the snack aisle. *Quel presentation!* Snazzy packaging with clever graphics and cartoon characters vie for the snacker's attention. Tea (both loose and in teabags) is presented in the opposite manner: restrained, elegant, the packaging emphasizing nature. Try the soothing barley tea, good for the stomach.

In the back of the store is a pleasing display of pottery: rice bowls, oblong platters for serving sushi, teapot sets with matching cups (without handles, as is the Japanese custom), and sake sets.

Carberry's, 74–76 Prospect Street, (617) 576–3530, is supposedly a bakery, but this congenial spot prepares muffins, pastries, European-style cookies, and a medley of soups, sandwiches, and specialty coffees. Customers gathered around its small tables are a human inventory of Central Square: mail carriers, academics, college kids meeting for coffee, activist writers or teachers who've pushed tables together to conduct a meeting, moms dashing out for a quick chat with a friend while the kids are in day care. A Russian baba comes in for one big pumpernickel—carrying it under her arm, without a bag—and leaves. A female bus driver grabs a sandwich. A beautician from a nearby shop runs in for six coffees, all with extra sugar. Carberry's is set a bit back on Prospect (to allow for parking). Look for a pale yellow building with purple letters.

Bread & Circus is now a small chain of natural food supermarkets, located mainly in Massachusetts. Most are showcases of organic produce, kindly killed meats, and feel-good personal care products. Those of us ancient herbalists who were around in the early, scruffy, health food store days miss the homier, more rustic, "original hippie" stores. The Central Square **Bread & Circus,** 115 Prospect Street, (617) 492-0070, was the first in the chain, taking over the space of an old independent natural food store. Today's store retains much of that granola patina.

As members of the local community include émigrés from Haiti and Latin America, you'll find many exotic squashes and fruits in the produce department, along with fibrous greens—collard, kale, mustard, chard—and veggies for Asian cuisine. The produce department people know how to cook their wares—many of the younger men are from the same countries as the exotic bananas, chayote squashes, and tomatillos—and are gracious and chatty in their cooking instructions.

At the corner of Prospect and Broadway, there's the spacious **Koreana Restaurant.** Check it out or return to Central Square on Prospect Street to explore a stretch of Mass. Ave. featuring murals, an Indian grocery takeout, and a beauty supply store with products for black men and women, plus hair ornaments and accoutrements for all.

Outdoor Art

Central Square is mural city. The Cambridge Arts Council is active and innovative, the neighborhood is teeming with artists (watch for CAOS—Cambridgeport Open Studios—a self-guided tour of artists' studios each fall), and there are lots of old buildings that could use a good side dressing. The mural form lends itself to expressions of community. Subjects (historic events, collages of historic influences, celebrations of multicultural residents) can be hashed-out in arts council meetings, and the mural making approached collectively. In Cambridge public art is often designed by a local artist in collaboration with neighborhood residents, and painted by teams of volunteers, including trained young people.

In the heart of Central Square, you can view several outstanding murals. Cambridge artist David Fichter created Potlock *in the parking lot behind Harvest Supermarket, site of a weekly farmers' market. For* Potlock, *Fichter became an urban anthropologist, for months attending neighborhood potlucks, block parties, and church gatherings to research what people ate and "how they socialized as they ate." He learned the cuisines of different nationalities and ethnicities and met scores of neighbors and extended families.*

"The large-scale kid with the cap on backwards, that's my neighbor, JR, who ran the basketball team at the Fletcher School," says Fichter of his mural. And that dignified, elderly African-American

Follow Mass. Ave. toward Boston (you'll see the shimmering John Hancock building in the distance), stopping at **Shalimar India Food & Spices,** 571 Mass. Ave., (617) 868–8311. This long, narrow store stocks a variety of Indian groceries, as well as prepared foods.

woman with a hat? "Oh, that's Aunt Gert," says Fichter. "Her daughter came by one day when I was painting and said, 'Hey, if I bring my mother by, will you put her in? She's ninety years old and has lived here all her life.' I met her mother, took her picture, and put her in. Funny thing was, everybody seemed to know Aunt Gert, or to be related to her."

After Aunt Gert, sidle down Norfolk Street at the back of the parking lot to see A Celebration of Imagination: A Tribute to Marc Chagall. This lyrical, endearing mural painted by Pasqualina Azzarello—an homage to Chagall, the power of imagination, and the people of Central Square—was created in 1997, on the occasion of the one hundredth anniversary of the artist Chagall's birth.

Cross Mass. Ave. to marvel at the mural on the side of The Middle East restaurant—a merging of Middle Eastern families and Central Square—which features a cut-out facade rising above two stories. Venture to the Cambridge Public Library, Central Square Branch, 45 Pearl Street, and you'll find shimmering mosaic murals by artist Lilli Ann Killen Rosenberg, whose work appears all over Boston, from the Freedom Trail, to Park Street Under, to the Puerto Rican community in the South End and the Portuguese community in East Cambridge.

For yet more spice, cross Central Square and follow River Street a few blocks to a tiny, packed Indian grocery (or is this an eccentric dining room filled with food?), which has many devotees. **India Foods & Spices,** 80 River Street, (617) 497–6144, not only carries a full array of Indian products—near magically arrayed in this midget market—but also prepared foods. As will be evident when you approach the store from the street, many of these delectables are prepared on the premises, including desserts flavored with rosewater and cardamon. You can also rent an Indian video to accompany your dinner; prepare for so many come-hither glances you'll fall into your vindaloo.

Venus Cosmetic, 485 Mass. Ave., (617) 492–0870, specializes in personal care products for African Americans. In the back of the store glamorous wigs are groomed and sold, and the nail enamel selection covers the visible spectrum in matte, shiny, and iridescent hues. If you don't have foxy nails, you can buy some.

Pearl Art & Craft Supplies, 579 Mass. Ave., (617) 547–6600, is a multicultural art supply store. All kinds of people—united by their artistic abilities—shop here: elderly black and white ladies gathering knitting supplies and craft components for projects with grandchildren, teenagers with black nail polish amassing beads, Indian women selecting gilded rickrack to trim saris, art students purchasing sable brushes and paints, costume designers arranging swaths of fabric and looking for just the right button.

Harvest Co-op Market, 581 Mass. Ave., (617) 661–1580, is a cooperative with many of the same products as those sold at Bread & Circus, but with lower prices. In addition, working co-op members get substantial discounts. Product display is not as elaborate as at the local capitalist competitor, but many prefer Harvest's free-form atmosphere, including the occasionally spacy assistance from store personnel ("Peas . . . ? Like what do you mean by peas?") The deli and prepared-food departments are excellent—everything fresh, tasty, and appealing to the eye—and the cosmetics and personal care section offers natural-smelling lotions, moisturizers, and night creams.

Across the street, **The Middle East** (see "Suggested Restaurants"), is a cultural and culinary mecca: a well-established, family-run restaurant, bar, and music club with a series of cozy rooms, including a basement and a former bakery, as part of its facility. Joseph and Nabil Sater opened the spot over twenty-five years ago, toughed it out through Central Square's awkward stage, and survived to prosper, helping legions of musicians in the process. At their complex you may do anything from enjoying a Levantine feast, to attending a community meeting, to rocking it out.

In addition to featuring scores of local and regional groups—live music almost nightly, often multiple acts—the club does poetry readings, dramatic fare, and occasional gallery shows. The food is reliably good.

For music lovers—world music, pop, folk, Celtic, blues—Central Square is a world of its own. In addition to the Middle East, keep an eye on the listings at **TT the Bear's Place,** 10 Brookline Street, (617) 492–2327; **Cantab Lounge,** 738 Mass. Ave., (617) 354–2685; and two handsome Irish-style pubs: **The Phoenix Landing,** 512 Mass. Ave., (617) 576–6260, and **The Field,** 20 Prospect Street, (617) 354–7345.

Another favored neighborhood place, **The Plough & Stars,** 912 Mass. Ave., (617) 441–3455, is midway between Central Square and Harvard Square. The evocative bar even became a kind of character in George Packer's novel *Central Square.*

S U G G E S T E D 🍽 R E S T A U R A N T S

Central Square has so many different kinds of restaurants—and so many different kinds of diners, whose ethnicity often contrasts with the ethnicity of the restaurant—that dining becomes a theatrical experience. In addition to the synergy of observing Indian men with turbans sipping double espressos and munching croissants, and all-American football types with their beefy fingers eating Ethiopian stews, you may also observe occupational subcultures. Software engineers eat at Indian restaurants' lunchtime buffets. MIT students and profs are at Chinese restaurants, which are quiet and good for reading. Bleary-eyed musicians are chowing down at the Middle East after waking up in late afternoon. And Carberry's is like the U.N. of bread.

In Central Square you could dine in a different Indian restaurant every day of the week. In fact, as most serve lavish, economical lunchtime buffets, you could have both lunch and dinner in restaurants du jour. Each place has something special to offer.

For reasons of size (small), decor (colorful), and quality (high), **India Pavilion ($–$$),** 17 Central Square, (617) 547–7463, has long been my favorite. For decades I was able to call the little storefront near the Cambridge police station "the quilt restaurant," as it featured beautifully embroidered Indian tapestries and quilts on every inch of wall, ceiling, and door. As there were no blank borders between artworks, the restaurant assumed the character of a textile collage, just the backdrop for its spicy, deeply hued food, especially the orange onion-pepper relish and the saffron-colored curries. A few years ago, they toned the place down. The walls are now wood-paneled with glittery paintings and textiles here and there. Still, the ancient rest room has quilts on the ceiling, as does a rear room of the restaurant, a hideaway with just a few tables.

Central Square's Indian restaurants are among the few remaining places two people can have a good meal for around $25 (sans wine).

Order two vegetarian entrees and rice, a bread, an appetizer to share, and some *raita* to cool your mouth. The *aloo paratha*—a griddle bread stuffed with potatoes and peas—is succulent and satisfying. The vegetarian entrees are highly flavored but not overly spiced. The wine list is reasonably priced.

Gandhi Restaurant ($–$$), 714 Mass. Ave., (617) 491–1104, is another tried-and-true Indian restaurant, distinguished by its huge wall mirror, daily luncheon specials, and emphasis on vegetarian entrees and over a dozen chicken specialties. In addition to the oft-served chicken *vindaloo* (hot and spicy) and chicken *korma* (cooked with cream), you'll find colorful, elegant chicken *jalfrazie,* a dish of boneless white meat combined with onions, tomatoes, bell peppers, broccoli, and ginger. Gandhi's *baingan bartha* looks a bit muddy, but it needs to be in order to convey its flavors: roasted eggplant (very smoky), peas, tomatoes, onions, and spices. These are mostly mashed together and have a wonderful flavor and texture when eaten with delicate basmati rice.

Other Indian veritables include **India Globe Restaurant,** 474 Mass. Ave., (617) 868–1866, and **Shalimar of India,** 546 Mass. Ave., (617) 547–9280. Don't be put off by Shalimar's almost garish exterior; inside it's spacious, gracious, and pleasant with pink marble-like tables and friendly service.

A few doors down from India Pavilion, please find that font of delectable protein balls, **Moody's Falafel ($),** 25 Central Square, (617) 864–0827. You cannot call Moody's a restaurant, and yet it's too big (food prep area, counter, and a few stools taking up the space of a small home kitchen) to call a hole in the wall. Imagine something slightly bigger than a streetside falafel vendor, but indoors, with the fast turnover that promotes fresh-tasting falafel, and you'll have an

Indian Cuisine

Indian food is delicious and not at all forbidding. But it is mysterious and complex. Foods that we eat all the time taste completely different. Rice is not dry and fluffy, but shiny, buttery, and fragrant. Breads are not baked in a conventional American oven, but fried on griddles or tossed onto the walls of tandoors (clay ovens) and baked. Griddle breads may be stuffed with bits of vegetables: potato, cauliflower, onion, peas. Meat, fish, poultry, and vegetables are gently simmered or stewed, flavored with clarified butter or oil that is suffused with spices, peppers, and herbs. Often there is no visual evidence of these flavorings when the dish is served because the cook has sautéed the power-packed herbs in oil, removed the pods, and used only the redolent oil.

While American cooks have good results with many European cuisines, French and Italian come to mind, those of Asia are more challenging. Many basic ingredients turn out to be subtly but significantly different from familiar American versions: Long-grained basmati rice is used instead of our shorter-grained variety. The culinary techniques are different, too. If you consider the vastness of India—its geographically discrete regions, its temperature (hot), and the religion of most of its people (Hindu, revering cattle)—the culinary characteristics fall into place.

This is piquant, salty, flavorful cooking, stimulating to the palate,

idea. With typical Central Square irony, the formal name of the establishment is Moody's Falafel Palace. The palace is open every day, 11:00 A.M. till midnight, and you can grab anything from a hot spicy falafel sandwich, to a tabouli salad, to a fortifying container of *vision, and sense of smell, and also to the metabolism. When you are feeling draggy on a sultry summer day, eat Indian. When you cannot warm up after weeks of wet winter weather, eat Indian. When you are overly hungry and at the edge of nausea, try a* lassi, *a salubrious, refreshing beverage of slightly sweetened yogurt, buttermilk, ice, and rosewater.*

In Indian restaurants, after an appetizer of spicy soup or a few deep-fried stuffed pakoras *(turnovers), served with a dot of onion relish or mint chutney, dig into the meal at hand. No matter how modest the establishment, it will always seem a banquet because all the pretty dishes are served at once: the meat or fish dish, the vegetable selection (or several such entrees if one is vegetarian), the legume stew (made with chickpeas and vegetables), the* dal *(lentil sauce),* raita *(cooling yogurt and cucumber dip), and exotic breads, stacked and steaming on a platter.*

Desserts are intensely sweet and often made with rice. Many diners opt for simply finishing their Alsatian wine, Vouvray, or Indian beer, or sipping a cup of Indian tea, a satisfying spiced black tea, cooked with cardamom seeds and milk. Though the tea is caffeinated, the hot milk offsets the stimulating effect, inducing a good night's sleep and visually rich dreams, like Indian videos, with seduction scenes and dancing.

lentil soup. You can also have a fine feed for an affordable price—lamb with Syrian salad, or chicken with rice and salad, or a well-composed vegetarian combo: falafel, tabouli, houmos, baba ghanouj, and salad.

One of the square's most welcoming restaurants is airy, informal **Asmara ($)**, 739 Mass. Ave., (617) 864–7447, with its white painted walls, folk art, and deep wicker chairs. Asmara used to serve only Ethiopian cuisine but has expanded its repertoire to include cooking from other parts of East Africa. As a result of war between Ethiopia and Eritrea, many Eritreans have settled in Cambridge and Somerville. The mix of people in the restaurant—Korean (who seem to like the spicy red pepper sauce), African, and African-American, plus students of all ethnicities and postal workers after hours— makes the atmosphere as enjoyable as the food. It's fun to eat at Asmara and then to visit Ten Thousand Villages, located just across the street.

Vegetarians and omnivores can eat happily together; the menu is divided into poultry, lamb, beef, and vegetarian entrees. I am fond of *tikil gomen-hamli*—cabbage, carrots, and potatoes in a mild sauce, served with injera, of course. A vegetarian combo in various shades of pale yellow and green makes a lovely spring dish. You'll be served a platter with dishes of cabbage, yellow split peas, collard greens, chickpeas, lentils, and a bit of potato salad, pleasant to devour as you listen to tapes of East African music. Even if you have a farm girl appetite, you won't finish it. A pity, as there are rum baba and other European pastries for dessert, one of the kinder legacies of Ethiopia's colonial past.

Picante Mexican Grill ($), 735 Mass. Ave., (617) 576–6394, is tasty and enjoyable, if not the most authentic Mexican—it's too healthy (no lard and no smoking). In this Californian-Mexican place, you'll find familiar enchiladas, burritos, quesadillas, and some nourishing special plates: grilled chicken over rice with salsa and a salad, or a veggie platter with zucchini and mushrooms, guacamole, rice,

Central Square's Middle East is a hub of food, music, and nightlife.

black beans, cheese, salad, and three tortillas. Note the fresh salsa bar; you can top your own food.

For habitués of smoky, aromatic, traditional Lebanese food, **The Middle East Restaurant ($–$$),** 472 and 480 Mass. Ave., (617) 463–EAST, is the best place in town. The cozy restaurant and bar serve from late morning to late night. It is a prized urban comfort to find pumpkin kibbe when you get the urge to devour spicy grains at 4:00 P.M. on a gloomy afternoon.

Zuzu! ($–$$), 480 Mass. Ave., (617) 492–9181, ext. 337, is a newish, sexy, stylish contemporary Mediterranean place—with an airy coral and yellow interior. It shares The Middle East's kitchen,

Finger Food

Our mothers were right: Wash your hands before eating, especially before eating Ethiopian food. The utensils you use are your fingers—period. Traditional Ethiopian food is conveyed from platter to mouth with wads of the delicate, freshly baked bread called injera, *made from t'eff flour, a nourishing grain related to millet. Injera looks like a huge pancake and is served on a handsome metal tray or in a gigantic, woven, shallow basket. Different kinds of stewy sauces (wots), made of chicken or meat, lentils or peas, are arranged around the spongy bread. Many are spiced with berbere paste, a pepper sauce. You, the clean-handed diner, twist off fluffs of injera and swipe the stew. When you become more expert, you'll be able to eat as North Africans do—deftly inserting little pockets of dough, making a quick wrist-twist, and coming up with miniature filled hot sandwiches. Your server will demonstrate, but will not feed you.*

but caters to a dressier crowd. The menu features over twenty tantalizing Middle Eastern appetizers, including oldies but goodies—grape leaves, kibbe balls, and kebabs—and more exotic fare, the likes of pan-fried spinach and yogurt dumplings, and sumac-spiced rock shrimp. The menu's Mediterranean and Middle Eastern entrees range from seared salmon and spicy yogurt to grilled eggplant with spiced lamb.

Mary Chung's Restaurant ($–$$), 464 Mass. Ave., (617) 864–1991, has a New England quality, in addition to its well-earned reputation for good Mandarin and Szechuan cuisine. Reminiscent of old Yankee establishments, Chung's does what it does honestly and well, and puts on no airs. From the outside it looks unremarkable, even a little dingy. Inside, a friendly, hospitable dining room with booths and tables, and attentive service from lovely Asian young ladies sets the tone. You'll have plenty of choices from the 204 items on the menu, not including the 42 dim sum goodies served on weekend afternoons. On fall New England evenings, you may simply want a bowl of hot and sour soup with noodles, an appetizer portion of scallion pie, and oolong tea. Regrettably, Mary Chung lacks a real wine list, but it does serve beer and a few single-serving-size bottled American wines.

Explore the side streets on this side of Mass. Ave. Authentic and hospitable ethnic restaurants pop up in smaller, easy-to-miss storefronts. **Rangzen ($),** 24 Pearl Street, (617) 354–8881, is Tibetan, an oasis of serenity, calm, and delightful cuisine, much of it vegetarian. Just a block away from the raucous music clubs and bars, Rangzen creates its atmosphere with a mural of endless mountains and sky and liberal use of wood, fresh flowers, and diaphanous curtains. The atmosphere of the restaurant and its soft-spoken host, a Tibetan woman, is consistent with the harmonious nature of the food. *Tsel temma* is a platter of chickpeas seasoned with ginger, garlic, onions, and tomatoes, served with basmati rice. *Thukpa,* a nourishing soup served in two sizes, features noodles or dumplings with vegetables and meat. At lunchtime during the week, a buffet is served from 11:30 A.M. to 3:00 P.M. At these buffets you choose among dishes such as dumplings served with a sauce of cilantro, tomatoes, and peppers; tofu with Chinese cabbage, garlic, and soy sauce; and crisp asparagus and green beans.

Don't miss the Tibetan breads. An order of *shogo phaley*, nominally whole-wheat bread stuffed with mashed potatoes and cilantro, produces two thick griddle cakes, almost like croquettes, that are both delicate and hearty.

Rangzen's dinner menu includes salads, soups, breads, entrees, and desserts. To bliss out—preferably not on a work night—share a dessert of *deshi* with your loved one. It is a simple, perfect bowl of warm, sweet, steamed white rice mixed with raisins, cashews, and butter. Or consider a tea. *Poecha* is made with Tibetan black tea, melted butter, hot milk, and a bit of salt. When I drink it and slip out of the restaurant, I barely hear the normal traffic din. Best not to drive when in this buttery, exalted state.

A few blocks down from Central Square—look for a gas station where Mass. Ave. forks to the right—an old-fashioned Italian restaurant, **La Groceria ($–$$),** 853 Main Street, (617) 876–4162, occupies a fond place in the hearts of longtime neighborhood residents. The food is not refined, but it's zesty and well prepared. The curtains are dingy, but the staff is warm, friendly, and professional. I go to La Groceria when I'm feeling depleted. It feels like a visit to a grandmother who makes a quick, assiduous assessment, asks no questions, dispenses no advice, and serves you nourishing food in quantity. Not to dignify the Mafia, but La Groceria has a cute miniroom with just one table labeled THE GODFATHER, very fun for a family to sit in, or a swooning couple, or a group of old friends telling tales.

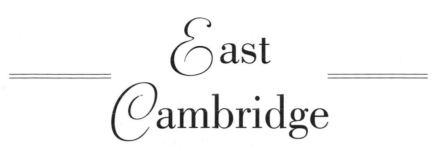

East Cambridge

A Portuguese Boulevard

*I*t's hard to pinpoint when you arrive in East Cambridge. There are no signs, no squares, no obvious monuments, other than the Portuguese bakeries, family-run groceries, and St. Francis of Assisi Church at the corner of Cambridge and Sciarappa Streets.

But for the urban wanderer, alert as an Indian tracker, the indications are clear. Tony trappings, like those of Harvard Square—mercantile glitz and showy erudition—are not in evidence. The car and bus traffic of Central Square has dissipated. Mothers and children are on foot, walking to and from neighborhood schools. There are fewer brick apartment buildings, fewer Victorian houses. This is a place of nineteenth-century wood-frame houses, known as workers cottages, and three-deckers with plastic chairs on porches. These multifamily houses line the narrow residential blocks off Cambridge Street—the main drag that leads east to the Middlesex County Court House, Lechmere Canal, the Charles River, and on the other side, Boston.

A few blocks west of this old neighborhood, Cambridge and Hampshire Streets cross at Inman Square. A splendid Romanesque-style fire station is there and the original 1369 Coffee House. Inman Square's bohemian aura radiates for several blocks, especially in the 1300 through 1200 numbers of Cambridge Street. This is a neighborhood of casual clubs and trendy ethnic-inspired restaurants: Asian, Caribbean, Southern-style, and Indian. Casa Portugal (aha!) is on Inman's edge, leading to bona fide East Cambridge.

In true-blue East Cambridge, forget trendy. Forget hip. This is a working-class neighborhood, with Iberian and Mediterranean élan. The old-timers are Portuguese and Italian. Newcomers are from the Azores, Cape Verde, Brazil: all Portuguese-speaking countries. Think churches, families, festivals—the stately seasonal processions that honor Portuguese and Italian saints. Think *Paroquia de Santo Antonio*, St. Anthony's Parish, known as the Portuguese church. For dining, it's Portuguese restaurants, bars, cafes, sub shops, and pizzerias; and simple places to eat fresh fish with cole slaw, french fries, or well-scrubbed potatoes baked in foil.

Signs of entering East Cambridge: old-fashioned furniture stores with plate-glass windows that display a whole bedroom set, with matching lamps on matching night tables. Fabric and notions stores, filled with customers studying patterns and holding remnants up to the light. Groceries where everyone speaks Portuguese. These small markets resemble 1950s-era corner stores, except there is octopus in the freezer and Portuguese sweetbread next to the English muffins.

In the heart of East Cambridge, there are five Catholic churches serving Italian, Portuguese, and Polish congregations. The Cambridge Association of Portuguese Americans is at Inman Square. The headquarters of the Dante Alighieri Society of Massachusetts is on Hampshire Street. There's a Polish-American club, and this being Boston, the club sponsors an annual St. Patrick's Day Festival.

As you make your way closer to the Charles River (Cambridge Street numbers descending), the pace on the street picks up. You reach a cluster of grand-scale redbrick buildings and a slew of coffee shops and luncheonettes. This is "downtown" East Cambridge, the seat of Middlesex County government, a world of nineteenth-century courthouses, the Registry of Deeds and Probate, and a towering modern correctional facility. Called Bulfinch Square, it is the oldest square block of buildings in the country, restored by Boston developer Graham Gund Associates. The streets around the complex look like a set where Spencer Tracy, as the cigar-smoking prosecutor, might appear. Late-model American sedans are double-parked. Crusty-looking courthouse employees rush in and out (some with fancy suits

How to Get There

By public transportation take the Green Line MBTA to
Lechmere Station. Buses are available from various locations,
including Harvard Square. A shuttle bus runs between Kendall
Square Station on the Red Line and the Cambridgeside Galleria mall.
By car from Boston take the Longfellow Bridge. From Cambridge
follow Cambridge Street from Msgr. O'Brien Highway
(Route 28) to the Lechmere area.

and running shoes, ready to be switched when the need arises to
appear in court). Well-coiffed men and women park with one hand,
holding cell phones in the other. An elderly Portuguese lady dressed
in black is perennially walking a poodle through the courthouse
plaza.

• • • *History* • • •

Though first settled by Yankees, East Cambridge became a
mecca for immigrants who arrived during the nineteenth century to
work in nearby factories. By the end of the Civil War, almost half the
area's population was Irish. Later, immigrants poured in from Italy,
Portugal, and Poland. Most of the community's churches originated
during this era.

Many of the nineteenth-century, Portuguese-speaking people
migrated from other parts of Massachusetts—especially the fishing

and manufacturing centers of Fall River and New Bedford—to work in East Cambridge's industry. Though factory workers, they were fishermen at heart. That heritage shows today in the wealth of fresh fish markets along Cambridge Street, the barrels of salt cod in groceries, and the savory seafood dishes that dominate restaurant menus.

A century before this migration, East Cambridge figured prominently in the Revolutionary War. The neighborhood was a low hill surrounded by marshland and tidal flats. In the eighteenth century, before the land was filled, the waters of the Charles River reached the present site of the Clerk of Courts building in Bulfinch Square. From a site on an East Cambridge hill, General Washington led his men during the siege of Boston in March 1776. On April 19, 1776, the British made their landing at Lechmere's Point—there's a mall located near the spot today—and began their march west to Lexington and Concord.

Crafty, convincing Dr. Andrew Craigie was the best booster East Cambridge ever had. During the 1790s he secretly bought 300 acres near Lechmere's Point and opened Craigie's Bridge in 1809, near the site of today's Charles River dam. East Cambridge and Boston were now linked. Craigie surveyed the land into lots and streets—much of the grid remains—and began the process of filling it in. A swamp became an industrial section of Cambridge. Craigie got the Boston Porcelain and Glass Company to relocate to the new community. Other industries followed: soap making, meat packing, manufacturers of woven hose. Craigie even convinced the county government based in Harvard Square to relocate to East Cambridge and donated land and money to Charles Bulfinch to design a courthouse. The Superior Court Building on Cambridge Street, built in 1814 according to Bulfinch's plans, was redone in 1848 by Ami Young and remodeled in 1898.

A good portion of the current housing stock was built as workers cottages during the nineteenth century. "Knowledge workers" who toil in the high-tech industries in nearby Kendall Square are buying up some of the fancier houses. These young entrepreneurs live in gentrified town houses and walk to work in Dr. Craigie's footsteps.

Recent immigrants have come to the area from the Azores, Cape Verde, and former Portuguese colonies in Africa, including Angola and Mozambique. The community is home to many new Americans: Haitians, Hispanics, and Portuguese-speaking people from Brazil. Now appearing on Cambridge Street and side streets: small Brazilian groceries and cafes and a cultural center on Webster Avenue.

• • • *A Walking Tour* • • •

Cambridge Street is the main thoroughfare, though East Cambridge includes sections of Hampshire Street and Broadway. To get a sense of how people in this community live, follow Cambridge Street from the courthouse to Inman Square, but also weave in and out of side streets, where churches and houses are located, everything from the typical, unadorned workers cottages, to raffish-looking converted carriage houses, to the occasional mansard. Schools are on the side streets, too, as are social service agencies and corner groceries with the basic necessities of life: milk, eggs, cigs, lighters, Portuguese soap, Portuguese bread, Portuguese sausage, lottery tickets, kitty litter (yes, for housebound kitties, but also for putting under automobile wheels stuck in slush), and devotional candles in colored glass.

Begin your explorations in the first few blocks near the courthouse, and you'll get a good dose of fish markets, firehouses, former courthouses, bakeries, churches, and sub shops.

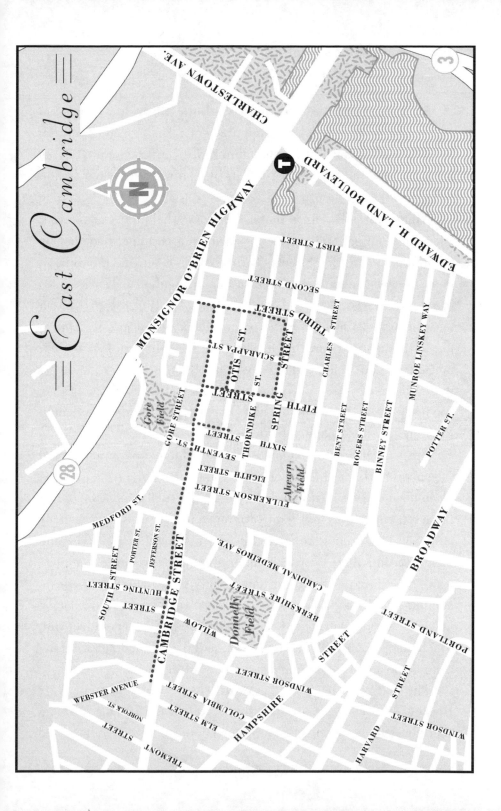

St. Francis of Assisi Roman Catholic Church occupies the corner of Cambridge and Sciarappa Streets. The graceful redbrick building has Italianate flair. The church was constructed in 1837 as a Baptist meeting house; in 1932 its Italian Catholic congregation added a bell tower for pizzazz.

Almost directly across the street—overwhelming, magisterial, and composed of a zillion bricks—**Bulfinch Square,** bounded by Cambridge and Spring Streets, Third and Fifth Streets, presents an imposing civic arena. Facing you in this monolith of redbrick buildings is the Registry of Deeds and Probate. You'll also see a golden tower with a distinctive weather vane: the scales of justice. This is the 1848 Superior Court Building; behind is a tall, grim-looking rectangular modern building, the county jail. Remember the locations of these edifices. Almost everywhere you gambol in East Cambridge, you'll see the golden tower, the high-rise jail, and Boston's Prudential Building. It's almost impossible to get lost.

Cross Cambridge Street and explore the hidden **courtyard** amid the mass of brick. All kinds of events go on here, and it's a pleasing place to sit and read, surrounded by imaginative plantings, including flowering vines and clusters of geraniums in clay urns. One Sunday afternoon I was sitting in tattered chinos reading the newspaper and had the good fortune to observe an entire outdoor wedding, complete with young bride in headgear and billowy gown, bearded groom in swallow-tailed coat, flower girls and boys, scatterers of rose petals, and beaming grandmothers. One wore an elegant blue cut-velvet suit, which she had probably made herself, as I'd seen (and admired) the material on a bolt of fabric in a store a few blocks away.

The courtyard leads to the **Cambridge Multicultural Arts Center,** 41 Second Street, (617) 577–1400, or CMAC (see-MAK), a courthouse building rehabbed as a neighborhood theater, gallery, and meeting place. Visual arts, performances, and community events are presented in an atmosphere of warmth, informality, and cross-cultural creativity. You name it, they've done it—everything from Afro-Latin jazz, to Native American drumming, to a Southeast Asian New Year's celebration. Performers are often from the community, with their families in attendance. Sometimes performances are even quasi-family affairs.

Stick mainly to Cambridge Street on your first forays, but start meandering as soon as you feel grounded. The side streets parallel to Cambridge—especially Spring, Thorndike, and Hurley—are visually fertile tributaries, even if you just follow them for a few blocks. As East Cambridge's houses are exceedingly narrow, you see a lot in a short walk—urban domesticity compressed!

In the courthouse area, at the corner of Cambridge and Third Streets, walk down Third. At lunchtime you'll find a crowd—fire-fighters, MBTA folks, truckers—chowing down at **Maria's ($)**, 43 Gore Street, (617) 876–3322, mainly on Italian subs, sandwiches, and pizza. On the way back to Cambridge Street, a decommissioned **fire station** is a show stopper: At the corner of Gore and Third Streets, the old redbrick station—Georgian Revival in style—sports natty white brick quoins and Italianate molding. It belongs to the city of Cambridge and is no doubt being watched by developers poised to pounce. A fine condo property it would make, just minutes from Lechmere Station on the Green Line into downtown Boston.

Court House Seafood Restaurant and **Court House Seafood Market,** 498 Cambridge Street, (617) 491–1213, are twin establishments. The store is a tidy old-fashioned fish market with nothing more nor less than white tiles, glass cases, whole fish on ice, and fishmongers who know their business. They cut, clean, scale, and filet the creature of your choice before your eyes. These men are virtual fish surgeons (though perhaps not as aesthetic in their appreciation as the fish artistes at Wulf's in Coolidge Corner, Brookline).

Just after you've passed Court House Seafood, take Sixth Street one block to the corner of Otis. **The Parish of the Sacred Heart of Jesus** is a block-long, Gothic-style church, built of granite and slate, a wonderful combination of textures. During Lent, straw wreaths with purple ribbon hang on the church's arch-shaped doors.

Directly across the street a charming pale-green house has a bluestone foundation like that of the church. The house was built by the architect as his project-based home. The blue-gray stone came from a quarry in Union Square, Somerville.

Next door to the pale-green house, the **Cambridge Public Library, O'Connell Branch,** 48 Sixth Street, (617) 349–4019, is well incorporated into the neighborhood. Rather than being in a municipal center with a parking lot, as is the case with newer buildings, this inviting resource is part and parcel of East Cambridge, easy to reach by the many local people who don't have cars. Inside, the library is peaceful and serene, with cozy wood paneling and walls painted a restful soft yellow. The O'Connell is the smallest branch in Cambridge, and one of the friendliest, known for providing personal service. Head librarian Judith Swarden knows her clients so well that she has learned many of their reading preferences and advises them on long-term reading programs or when a new book has come in. The library runs morning sing-alongs for seniors and a Chinese story hour on Wednesday mornings. Another Cambridge Public Library, the **Valente Branch,** 826 Cambridge Street, (617) 349–4015, closer to Inman Square, has a section of Portuguese-language books.

Another nearby interesting church, **St. Hedweg's Polish Church,** 99 Otis Street, between Sciarappa and Fifth Streets, was originally built as Second Unitarian Church in 1865. It became St.

Hedweg's for the local Polish congregation in 1907. The hurricane of 1938 destroyed it; the simple, redbrick, cast-stone-trimmed church was rebuilt in 1939.

The richly ornamented, redbrick **Putnam School,** 86 Otis Street, at the corner of Otis and Sciarappa Streets, was built in 1887 and is today an apartment house edged by linden trees. It marks the crest of land where General George Washington built Fort Putnam during the Revolutionary War. From this fortification, constructed in the winter of 1775, Washington and the patriots battled the British during the siege of Boston in March 1776.

Spring Street, parallel to Otis, is a fine residential street to explore for architecture, hideaway gardens, and community resources. Sometimes I walk it all the way to the Cambridgeside Galleria (a mall), passing the multicolored workers' cottages and the correctional facility near the courthouses, working my way to the huge, suburban-looking Sears.

Return to Cambridge Street for magenta-colored brocade and crusty bread.

Even if you have never held a needle and thread in your fingers, you owe it to your appreciation of American culture—or is it American history?—to explore **Sew Low Discount Fabrics,** 473 Cambridge Street, (617) 661–8361. Such stores, unglamorous to needlework neophytes but bright with possibility to those who sew, are passing from our landscape. I seem to find them only in working-class neighborhoods. Perhaps it's that people here watch their budgets carefully and make their own clothes. Or maybe it's that working-class neighborhoods are often ethnic neighborhoods, where tradition counts, and where sewing and tailoring skills are kept alive. In any case, viva fabric stores! This one is so crowded with bolts of cotton, rayon, silk, velvet, wool, polyester, and upholstery material in solid colors, plaids, and prints, textures diaphanous and opaque, that I can barely begin to describe the aisle of trims, which looks like a miniature, fantastical amusement park: flashing sequins, rickrack, ruffles, tassels, laces, lamé, and satin ribbons by the yard.

If you can contain yourself at Sew Low and be relatively inconspicuous, you can watch Indian ladies matching trim to silky sari fabric, and smartly dressed black women choosing African-style prints. Occasionally I see an elderly gentleman, possibly a tailor, wandering in the worsteds, fingering the fabric in the universal way of needlemen: rubbing an edge between thumb and two fingers. And I am dying to know who buys the copper-colored lamé, the hideous white fake fur, and the shag carpet fabric in avocado green, coral, and mauve.

If **Lieberman and Arcos,** 528 Cambridge Street, (617) 354–7668, sounds like a Jewish and Portuguese bakery, it is. In all the years I've been going here, I've never seen a Lieberman or an Arcos, just a string of pleasant counter employees, but I find evidence of Lieberman and Arcos. In this simple store, shelves hold bags of bagels, babke (a cinnamony coffee loaf), rye bread, and *hamentashen*, a Jewish pastry made with a sweet yeast dough and stuffed with prune jam. The Arcos family (presumably) stocks Portuguese sweetbread and rolls, slightly sweet breakfast sticks to dip into coffee, and homemade-tasting apple turnovers, made with pastry crust nicely crimped around sliced apples and plumped raisins. Prices are low, including those of hermits, those all-American spice bars. Look for them stacked on the windowsill near the door.

Speaking of stacks, look for piles of poultry in the immaculate, if slightly alarming, **Mayflower Poultry,** 621 Cambridge Street, (617) 547–9191, where the squawks of the slaughtered can occasionally be heard. In this clean, old-fashioned market, very fresh whole chicken and parts are arrayed on chipped ice, with chicken necks and backs especially well priced. Other available critters include ducks, geese, and turkeys. Mayflower's yellow chicken sign is another highly visual, geographic marker on Cambridge Street. The no-nonsense street-side sign says: LIVE POULTRY/FRESH KILLED.

A few blocks on, **Central Bakery**, 732 Cambridge Street, (617) 547–2237, is small, unadorned, and with very few products, mainly breads and rolls. The round loaves of *pao de milho* (corn bread) are Portuguese manna. Central supplies most of the restaurants and groceries in the area, as well as some local supermarkets, such as Market Basket in Union Square. Their fine-grained corn bread is delectable cut into wedges and served for breakfast or sliced and lightly toasted. It keeps for over a week, and is made of white flour, corn flour, water, yeast, and salt. That's it. Don't let them put the fresh loaf in a plastic bag, the kiss of death for crisp crust. Request brown paper.

Next door, **Royal Pastry Shop**, 738 Cambridge Street, (617) 547–2053, an Italian-American bakery, offers biscotti, sesame cookies, cannoli, napoleons, cream puffs, and an array of small-town bakery temptations: fig bars, frosted sugar cookies, and brownies. Look above the counter. Multitiered white wedding cakes with perpetual brides and grooms are displayed just under the ceiling. A thrice-divorced friend who, along with her teenaged daughter, accompanied me to the bakery, was enchanted by the festive cakes and turned momentarily sentimental.

"Maybe I'll get married again," she mused.

"Ma, just get a cake," advised her daughter.

When I first sighted the **Atomic Market**, 1010 Cambridge Street, (617) 864–9131, I thought it had something to do with MIT science models or something. It turned out to be one of the best family-run Portuguese groceries in the area. Of medium size, but well stocked, it has the typical array of breads, rolls, sausages, and salt cod, but more of everything and with a personal touch. In addition to the packaged baked goods, you'll occasionally find stacks of freshly baked Portuguese sweetbread, not the familiar round loaf, but more of a flatbread, like an overgrown Portuguese muffin, and still warm. In the rear of the store, a butcher's counter is stocked with all manner of sanguine-looking sausages, in various shades of mottled brown and red. Explore the refrigerated cases for fresh cheese, and ask the folks in the store to describe them. A particularly creamy one is made in small quantities by one of the proprietors. Atomic is closed on Mondays.

What to call **Girofle,** 1052 Cambridge Street, (617) 864–9334, a place of religious statues, pressure cookers, and gilded chandeliers dripping with crystal? At Girofle, named for a comely Portuguese flower, I recently bought a simple, elegant wine decanter with ground-glass stopper at half price and an inexpensive earthenware pitcher, hand-painted in Portugal, perfect for serving red table wine. I tried to describe the store to my mother, asking her what to call it. I told her about the silver-leafed twenty-fifth-anniversary platters, the heavily cut crystal vases, the clear wineglasses with pale-green etched-glass stems. She said to call it a fancy gift store. "But it has statues of Jesus and nativity scenes," I said. "Well then, it's a fancy-gift-store-for-Christians," said Mom. I guess that's pretty much what Girofle is, but it doesn't convey the store's eccentric charm. Side by side with Jesus, Mary, and Joseph are pots and pans, children's shoes, olive oil, mineral water, passion fruit juice, and Portuguese soup bowls. Best of all, it's occupied by Fernando Rodrigues de Sousa, proprietor. Rodrigues de Sousa, a compact, genial man who loves anything associated with farms and food, used to be in the wine business. He is an accomplished cook. Coax him a little, and he'll give you wonderful recipes (see page 188).

*Though modest in appearance, Central Bakery is the source
of the best, freshly baked Portuguese corn bread.*

Portuguese Kale Soup, Vegetarian Style

Precise measurements will never be part of Girofle proprietor Fernando Rodrigues de Sousa's verbal recipes. But if you compare them with similar fare in cookbooks, you'll do fine. Cut up potatoes, carrots, and onions, maybe some garlic, cover with water, and cook until soft. Put through a food mill or strainer, reserving broth and puree. Meanwhile, cook red beans in a pressure cooker. When they're done, spoon them into the vegetable puree broth. Add a lot of fresh kale, sliced as thinly as possible, preferably with the fancy stainless-steel slicing machine Fernando would like to sell you, but that you really don't need. A good sharp knife will do fine. (Pretend that you're slicing cabbage for cole slaw.) Add a few tablespoons of olive oil, cook the soup a little more, season with salt and pepper, and serve. You can also add some macaroni, but not rice, according to Fernando. The gracious, middle-aged gentleman, possessed of Continental manners, became chilly, even abrupt, when I once asked about rice.

"Rice?" he said. "Never. Never rice. Never rice in kale soup."

If the owner is around when you visit **Casal Bakery,** 1075 Cambridge Street, near Inman Square, (617) 547–6282, you're sure to get a friendly welcome. Blue-eyed, handsome, and chipper, Fernando Laranjeira has the distinction of being named for the orange tree. "Many last names in Portugal are from trees," he explains. Portuguese pastries *(pastal)* are what this friendly, casual shop specializes in, in addition to breads and rolls. The best selection is available on Friday. The festive, macaroonlike cupcake with a cherry is coconut *(coco)*. The miniature pie with brown edges is what it looks like—custard *(nata)*—and is lusciously loose in the middle. A tiny, toasty-brown pastry in a delicate shell is bean *(feijao)*. And, of course, there's orange *(laranga)*, a syrupy, intensely orange-tasting delicacy that I generally consume in my car, unable to wait. For days my steering wheel exudes citrus oil.

Casal carries Portuguese cornmeal bread (pao de milho) baked by Primrose Bakery in Tiverton, Rhode Island, and the taste is subtly different from that of Central Bakery's bread. It's gummier (in a good way), more succulent, with more corn flour (and less wheat flour) than Central's version. Both are habit forming, superb with tuna salad and wintry legume soups, such as lentil and split pea. If you wish to linger, a cafe with gourmet coffee drinks is part of Casal's.

If you're feeling mordant, check out **University Monument,** corner of Cambridge and Webster Streets, a few doors down from Casal's. In the midst of the city, you can select a gravestone—for yourself, a friend, an enemy—even browsing through the outdoor selection. The zoning prigs may hate me, but I love the presence of a monument business in the midst of a food shopping area. *Sic transit gloria mundi.*

Don't miss a shimmering coda to East Cambridge, a mural by artist Lilli Ann Killen Rosenberg, sponsored by the Cambridge Arts Council. The memoir panels are just over the railroad tracks near the corner of Fulkerson and Cambridge Streets outside the **Millers River Apartments,** residences for seniors. A mosaic tree filled with tropical birds and fish provides radiant color in all weather. Various panels celebrate aspects of East Cambridge's heritage: immigrant roots in farming and fishing, and varieties of family celebrations. The individual clay pieces were made by residents of Millers River and students from local schools: the Kennedy, Harrington, Agassiz, and Webster. A golden yellow Mediterranean sun glows on this part of Cambridge Street—all the time.

Salty Soul Food

Call us gluttons, but there are people who can't stop thinking about food, even when reading history.

For years I've wondered why the Portuguese use salt cod. You go into an East Cambridge grocery, buy a flat, flaky, off-white wrinkled thing, and then spend hours soaking and rinsing, rinsing and soaking. Eventually the raglike ingredient has a good taste—meaty and slightly chewy—but why not use fresh fish?

Reading The Basque History of the World, *Mark Kurlansky's saga of this individualistic Iberian people, who live in seven provinces in remote corners of Spain and France, and whose heritage is bound-up with their language, Euskera, I learned a few things about continuity and cod.*

By the tenth century, Viking seamen were quick-drying cod in Arctic air to provide food for crews on long voyages. Stores of these dry bits, a reliable but tasteless foodstuff, enabled them to extend their fishing range throughout the North Atlantic, all the way to the North American continent.

Fishing rivals of the Vikings, Basque seamen revolutionized the cod-curing process by salting the fish before they dried it. The fish lasted longer, cooked well, and tasted better. Called bacalhau *in Portuguese,* bacalao *in Spanish, and* maikaloo *in Euskera, the preserved protein enabled the Basques to vastly extend the range of their whaling expeditions.*

The seafarers created a land-based market for their product, notably in Catholic countries—Basqueland, Catalonia, France, Italy, Greece, and parts of North Africa—where meat was forbidden on holy days. And so bacalhau became not just traditional food, but Portuguese soul food. For five centuries cooks throughout the Mediterranean have been creating dishes that feature it, many of which appear on menus in East Cambridge.

S UGGESTED 🍽 R ESTAURANTS

One of the most festive restaurants I know, **Atasca ($–$$)**, 279A Broadway, which runs parallel to Cambridge Street, (617) 354–4355, always seems appropriate: for a reunion with an old friend, an anniversary dinner with an intimate, a place to cheer up a buddy who's lost a job. The setting is welcoming and warm; the food colorful, tempting, and well prepared; the service gracious and attentive. Atasca's underlying message seems to be that these are the important things in life: food, friendship, pleasure.

The place is small, and you have the feeling of being with family, an idealized family. Decor is heavy on decorative ceramics, including a collection of Iberian pottery pitchers at the bar and exuberantly hand-painted faience plates on the rear wall, along with a collection of vintage family photographs.

Consider yourself blessed if you get a seat at the bar, especially on a cold night. Perched on a comfy stool, you'll have an ideal view of the brick oven and the preparations—sizzling in terra-cotta ramekins—issuing from it. You'll be able to examine some of the bright Portuguese reds being uncorked. I have become so at home here that I ask for tastes.

A basket of Portuguese bread is served with an oval plate of shiny black olives. While nibbling, please observe the parties around you: families, first dates, local academics, a stocky European gentleman eating alone and with pleasure at the bar. These views are part of your appetizer.

Choose from an array of seafood dishes. Caldeirada de Peixe is a delicate shallow bowl of fresh fish (scallops, cod, salmon), cooked with roasted tomatoes, onions, white wine, velvety potatoes, and herbs: a golden bowl with hints of saffron. A gorgeously colorful dish, almost Christmasy—Camarao a Tasca—showcases broiled shrimp with a spicy tomato sauce, served with pungent broccoli rabe and luscious fried potatoes. Galinha a Verde is a dressy boneless breast of chicken sautéed with white wine, mushrooms, artichokes, and roasted pepper, served with nicely cooked rice.

Don't overlook the *petiscos*, Portuguese "small plates." These enticing not-so-small platters can make light entrees, especially the lusty sardine dishes. Sardinhas de Escabeche is a cold dish of grilled fresh sardines slathered with vinaigrette, served with a topping of thinly sliced onions and julienned carrots—very good with an herbaceous Portuguese white wine.

A second, newer Atasca restaurant, also run by Joseph A. and Maria C. Cerqueira, is located in a modern office building at One Cambridge Place, 50 Hampshire Street, (617) 621–6991, in the technology section of East Cambridge, just a few blocks from the original Atasca.

Everybody eats at **Court House Seafood Restaurant ($–$$),** 498 Cambridge Street, (617) 491–1213, from college students on a budget, to neighborhood folks sick of cooking, to courthouse lawyers who fax in for their lobster salad rolls. Look for a dark-green awning with vivid crustaceans and flatfish. The eatery is casual, clean, wood paneled, and ocean blue. It offers fried, broiled, and baked seafood dinners that combine sea scallops, shrimp, or bluefish—over a dozen fish choices altogether—with french fries, baked potatoes or rice, and old-fashioned cole slaw. Sautéed items are also available, as well as teriyaki chicken. You can also get grilled linguica sandwiches served on a roll with lettuce and tomato. Court House Seafood Market is next door.

Portuguese Cuisine: Food of the Sun

A hearty Mediterranean cuisine, Portuguese cooking emphasizes seafood, fresh vegetables, subtle spices, and lavish use of olive oil. This is a cuisine without pretension that puts diners at ease. Culinary techniques are simple and familiar. Presentations are vibrant and colorful. Above all, everyday ingredients are assembled with care. Even a simple omelette in a neighborhood cafe—and certainly in the kitchen of a good cook—has tang and finesse. The eggs are fresh and beaten till frothy. The omelette and mix-ins are sautéed (separately) in olive oil. Bread is a serious substance, crusty and fine-grained; cheeses are simple, often homemade, even by some storekeepers in East Cambridge groceries. The native red wines pair gorgeously with the "big tasting" soups and meats, and the fresh tasting, slightly acidic whites showcase the unctuous flavors of fish stews, mussels, and fried squid.

Aram's House of Pizza ($–$$), 345 Cambridge Street, (617) 354–5154, is unintentionally but deliciously a multicultural pizza place. They've got your basic Italian-American pie, but also Greek-style pizza ($12 for a 16 incher), Mexican, and Hawaiian. You can sit down, you can eat in, you can schmooze with the affable bakers. There's neighborhood history in their list of toppings: pepperoni for the Italians, linguica for the Portuguese, pastrami for the Poles and the Jews—or any Rumanians who wander in.

Sunset Cafe ($–$$), 851 Cambridge Street, (617) 547–2938, is a spacious, family-style spot serving Portuguese specialties: roast salted cod, octopus stew, Portuguese sausage marinated in wine, and garlicky broiled shrimp in shells. Try the succulent stewed fava bean appetizer, almost a meal if combined with the restaurant's crusty Portuguese corn bread and Portuguese soft cheese. On Saturday and Sunday nights, fado, the traditional bluesy music of Portugal, is performed.

Casa Portugal ($$), 1200 Cambridge Street, (617) 491–8880, is another traditional restaurant, almost in Inman Square, citadel of hipness, which is probably why there's a Vegetarian Plate. The rest of the menu at this white-walled, pleasant restaurant is dominated by colorful Portuguese meat and fish dishes, especially shellfish. Ameijoas a Casa Portugal, a simple dish, is a bowl of littleneck clams sautéed in olive oil, tomatoes, onions, and peppers. By contrast, Arroz de Marisco is a pull-out-the-stops cauldron of rice with shrimp, clams, mussels, squid, scallops, and a half lobster—not for the dainty eater!

Beef lovers will find intriguing preparations, such as a steak dish with a wine, mustard, and mushroom sauce, and an entree worthy of President Eisenhower, who is reputed to have eaten steak and eggs for breakfast: Bife a Portuguesa includes a fried steak with ham, a fried egg, and a wine sauce.

You wouldn't think a room with a TV mounted on the wall could be enchanting, even alluring. But what if I told you that I didn't even notice the TV the first few times I went to **O'Cantinho ($),** 1128 Cambridge Street, (617) 354–3443, a Portuguese cafe owned by Joseph and Maria Cerqueira, the hospitable folks who created Atasca. The storefront cafe near Inman Square will cause you to call in sick and spend the day reading books at a sunny table or gabbing with a friend, as you work your way through sexy little plates of Favas com Linguica (stewed fava beans with linguica, onions, garlic, and white wine), Polvo

O'Cantinho's Portuguese pastries can be enjoyed at home.

Guisado (octopus stewed with red wine), and Pasteis de Balcalau (fish cakes made of dried cod, served with a green salad). You can trundle into O'Cantinho alone—it's that kind of place—and have a hot bowl of Portuguese soup, or a tasty sandwich of fresh Portuguese white cheese and home-cured ham with a roasted garlic vinaigrette, or a vitalizing cup of cafe com laite.

I love the way this restaurant looks. The walls are painted the color of melon—soft coral, like that of ripe cantaloupe. Every time I'm surrounded by this hue, I want to rush home and paint my dining room melon. On one long wall of O'Cantinho are a series of vibrant still lifes of Portuguese interiors; on another long wall, a mélange of diminutive mirrors. Framed sepia photographs are grouped on a piece of antique wooden furniture. The back of the cafe is dominated by a pastry case with items to consume in the cafe or carry out and present at home with freshly made espresso. These delectables include flan, rice pudding, and sumptuous baked custards in pastry shells—some plain, some with coconut, some with nutty-tasting white kidney beans.

Sometimes the cafe's TV is barely audible, turned on only for atmosphere. It's perennially tuned to a Portuguese station, which appears to feature sultry women with olive skin and faux blonde hair, including the well-coiffed newscasters. Portuguese newspapers and magazines are strewn about O'Cantinho, adding to the Iberia-in-Cambridge feeling. Not at all incidentally, travel agencies specializing in trips to Portugal are near.

Taste memories are beguiling, pungent, and stubborn, and so a flavorful Moroccan-Mediterranean restaurant that was in East Cambridge but has moved to Inman Square (near O'Cantinho) demands inclusion. **Argana Restaurant ($–$$$)**, 1287 Cambridge Street, (617) 868–1247, formerly Marrakesh, offers singular ambience, informal but gracious hospitality, and a piquant yet delicate cuisine. Try one of the subtle, aromatic *tagines*—the slow-cooked Moroccan meat, fruit, and vegetable entrees simmered over charcoal in an earthenware vessel with a conical lid. Tagines can contain quail, or lamb, or a marinated salmon fillet, or seasonal vegetables and wild mushrooms. Steak frites appear on the menu in a nod to the French. Starters range from *l'harira*, a hearty chickpea and lentil soup, to chicken *bastilla*, the traditional sweet, spicy pastry filled with chicken slivers, eggs, almonds, and cinnamon. Argana's subtly exotic cuisine is particularly enjoyable in the restaurant's North African decor—a backdrop of walls painted saffron yellow and Mediterranean blue, with cushy carved wooden chairs and embroidered cushions and ornate tables with mosaic tops.

If you have an occasion to celebrate, go to **Portugalia ($$),** 723 Cambridge Street, (617) 491–5373, a gracious, festive setting lavishly decorated with Portuguese ceramics and run by a congenial staff. If you're the type who goes to sleep reading Portuguese or Iberian cookbooks, here's the place to try dishes you've only tried to imagine, especially bacalhau (salt cod). Portugalia has eight different bacalhau entrees: varieties fried, breaded, poached, baked, stewed, shredded, and grilled. Some are rustic and robust: Bacalhau a Braz is shredded salt cod scrambled with eggs, onions, and potatoes. Some are elegant: Bacalhau a ze do Pipo is baked with a gratinee of tartar sauce and served with potato puree.

A medley of Portuguese tapas that includes cod fritters, shrimp coquettes, fillet of octopus, and sardine pâté is a fun-to-share appetizer. *Caldo verde,* which a friend calls "antidepressant soup," is a nourishing bowl of creamy potato bisque, garnished with linguica and shredded collard greens. Shellfish plates are exotic and numerous here, including the marine exotica you see at local fish markets: squid, skate, assorted claws.

Regrettably, I have never had Portugalia's paella because I get deadly full when I even see it coming out of the kitchen: scads of fresh seafood, boneless chicken bits, Portuguese sausage, bacon, peas, roasted peppers, all simmered together in a saffron-suffused sauce. Someday I will ask for one tablespoonful, with a dainty serving of rice, ample Portuguese corn bread—six thick slices—and my own bottle of wine. ("Yes, waiter, you heard me right—just one glass.")

Union Square, Somerville

A Bit of Brazil, India, Asia, and the Islands

*U*nion Square, Somerville, named for its nineteenth-century incarnation as a Civil War recruitment center, is about a mile from Harvard Square. But in appearance, temperament, and energy level, it's light-years removed. This urban crossroad is a nexus of Korean, Brazilian, Portuguese, Indian, Haitian, Caribbean, and Southeast Asian markets, shops, and eateries—and also languages. According to the 2000 U.S. census, almost 30 percent of Somerville residents were born outside the U.S.; 36 percent of the community do not speak English at home.

At high noon the square has a cinematic, almost cartoonish, quality—scads of folks traversing a mesh of streets, cars loping around curves, and small, bright stores. Many of the storefronts sport alluring names. Chez Orize II, which sounds like a samba club, is a hairdresser. The Reliable Market—suggesting down-Easters in feed caps around a pot-bellied stove—is a sleek, modern Korean grocery.

In addition to proprietor-run ethnic stores, Union Square is a pastiche of old-style American outlets offering doughnuts, coffee, cigs, and mags. Towering, century-old churches are on almost every corner.

The neighborhood is located in East Somerville, just before the section of Monsignor O'Brien Highway that leads to Boston's Museum of Science. Mainly nineteenth-century and early-twentieth-century buildings have been rehabbed for current use. A fire station has been converted to a community cable TV station.

Several shops are located on the ground floors of Victorian houses, some spiffy, some shabby. Dunkin' Donuts jostles for space with family-run Korean restaurants. An ad hoc urban nursery is not only across the street from a working gas station, it stands on the site of a former gas station, with palms in place of pumps.

How to Get There

By public transportation take any of the various buses that originate in Charlestown, Brookline, Arlington, and Cambridge. The MBTA Information Line is (617) 722–3200. By car from Porter Square, Cambridge, follow Somerville Avenue east; from McGrath Highway, take the Washington Street exit, bear left under the overpass, and take a right on Somerville Avenue.

Piercing the maze, vehicles come careening: tow trucks en route to Pat's Tow, daredevil cabbies hell-bent for the airport, truck drivers outsmarting other drivers by shortcutting to Route 93 north.

And yet the square can seem like a small town. On Sundays after mass at St. Joseph's, the trucks pause for exiting parishioners. An Asian-American college kid on her bike ties up in front of the Reliable Market. A group of artists from the nearby Brickbottom Artists Studio come out of India Palace with leftover shrimp curry in paper bags. Cats preen on the still-warm hoods of cars, then saunter into corner stores.

• • • *History* • • •

Somerville, nestled between Cambridge and Boston, is a city of seven hills. Today the old neighborhoods clustered around these hills have an urban quality, or maybe it's more that of New England mill towns. In the seventeenth century the region was largely pasture.

Somerville's long colonial taproot extends back to 1629, when it was part of Charlestown, which is today part of Boston. In 1842 Somerville became an independent town. Its soil was rich with clay, leading to the development of brickworks. These factories made the bricks that helped to make Boston a redbrick city. As construction boomed during the 1840s, many Somerville farmers sold their pasturelands, which were then stripped for brickyards and rarely returned to agrarian use. By the mid-nineteenth century, slaughterhouses and the Union Glass Company had become major industries, along with the brickyards. Union Square, part of the brick-making sector, was called Sandpit Square. During the Civil War it became the site of a major recruitment office. In the fervor of enlistment, it became Union Square. After the economic devastation of the Civil War, many of the brickyards closed.

The brickyard owners had built workers cottages—homes for factory workers—many of which survive. In the present clamor for real estate in Boston, these dwellings have taken on panache. Realtors describe them as *charming* workers cottages. Those in love with the idea of domesticity acquire them, envision them, and truly re-create them as charming. (Somerville now has an active gardening club, with a wonderfully diverse membership, which stages annual tours.) Other vestiges of the brickyards survive in the Brickbottom Artists Studio.

... *A Walking Tour* ...

Union Square is small and tightly knit. You can start your walk on Somerville Avenue not far from the Market Basket supermarket, not as ordinary as it looks from the outside, or from St. Joseph's Church on Washington Street. Don't expect a nice, neat square, as in a right-angled intersection. As two of the square's three thorough-fares are curved, the square is more a spurred configuration.

If you're traveling from Cambridge, Kirkland Street becomes Washington Street when you cross Beacon Street, Somerville. (This corner is its own food mecca; see "Food Finds.") Following Washington past triple-deckers, you'll enter Union Square with St. Joseph's on your right.

Clustered in the center of the square are several markets. You can make a big sweep of the square, down to Ricky's Flower Market, exploring Washington Street ("restaurant row"), Bow Street, and Somerville Avenue. Or start with the markets in the heart of the square off the memorial plaza.

Maria's Market, 57 Union Square, (617) 666–4532, has a breezy, peasanty character, which can evoke images of Portuguese village women spreading freshly washed sheets on the lawn to dry. Maria's combines Portuguese and Brazilian products, salt cod, sardines, fresh vegetables, ornate ceramic gift items, with a rainbow (well, at least the reddish part) of sausages, and some take-out foods.

The **Reliable Market,** 45 Union Square, (617) 623–9620, a well-stocked Korean and Japanese grocery, can make non-Asian shoppers feel like Alice in Wonderland. Almost all the labels are in Korean or Japanese. When I first started shopping in "Wonderland," I had no idea what I was buying. At home I would squeeze tubes to discover toothpaste, or miso, or shampoo. Still I kept buying mystery grains and have since enjoyed sushi rice, sweet rice, wild rice, steamed barley, and soul-satisfying barley tea.

Mystery vegetables such as the buxom orange kabocha squash, I bought on faith. I subjected them to my basic *Fanny Farmer/McCall's* culinary practices and never looked back. Reliable's selection of soybean pastes (miso) has revolutionized my

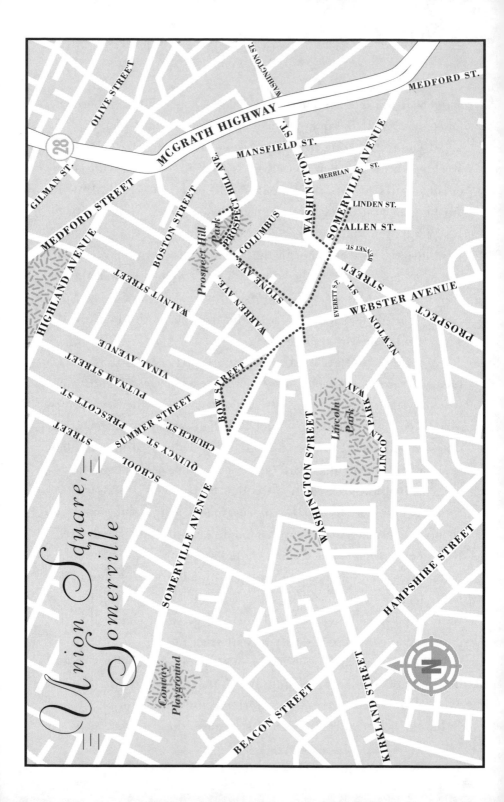

soup making. (Thin them a little. Add.) Their array of teas, including green teas, is dazzling. The Japanese snack items look cosmopolitan and hip when set on a Japanese lacquered tray near my small Sony TV. Excellent fresh fish, fascinating beers and liquors, and sundry beauty products will take a lifetime to try. Investigate the wide selection of specialty vinegars and oils.

On Washington Street, which runs behind Reliable and Maria's, you'll find several small restaurants and an ethnic urban nursery (see "The Fort and the Ferns").

From outside Reliable Market, you can see a curving street on the right: Bow Street, with its eclectic collection of restaurants, churches converted to housing, and a paean to pasta, **Capone Foods,** 14 Bow Street, (617) 629–2296. This is a genteel, immaculate shop; the proprietor has been observed washing the sidewalk in front of his store. Inside you'll find a bandbox specialty grocery with crusty breads and imported cheeses (very well priced), heavenly chocolates and biscuits, the fixings of fancy antipastos, and, above all, pasta made on the premises. Types range from basil and cilantro, to saffron, and the ineffable rosemary and garlic. In the sauce department the possibilities include alfredo, ratatouille, and porcini, which marries seductively with black pepper pasta.

Bear left on Bow to Somerville Avenue. On one side of the street, please find **La Internacional,** 318 Somerville Avenue, (617) 776–8855, the U.N. of superettes, with Spanish, Haitian, Brazilian, and Caribbean products. From plantain flour, to pigs feet, to an over-the-counter addictive substance, chunky triangles of imported Mexican chocolate (in a yellow octagonal box; used to make Mexican hot chocolate), they have it. Lively clientele, too—Haitians buying Jewish Sabbath candles, elderly ladies loading up on fresh limes, Spanish-speaking customers smelling big bunches of cilantro, kids steeplechasing down the aisles.

The Fort and the Ferns

In a way it's a shame to mention the fort steps from Maria's Market. It's best discovered by accident. But lest you miss the short but exhilarating walk to the top of a storybook fort, complete with crenelations, heed these words: Follow Stone Avenue (the corner of Maria's) to **Prospect Hill Avenue**. In another era it was a glacial drumlin. Now it's a hilly street with Victorian houses and a fort. The fort is not a mirage, but rock-solid granite, a monument. It was constructed in 1903 to commemorate Revolutionary War fortifications at this site. From its top the views of Boston and beyond are gorgeous.

On rainy and overcast days, you can't see a thing, but there's poetic compensation. A bracing sea smell floats in; sometimes, there are wisps of fog you can touch.

In the heart of Union Square, across the way from Washington Street's "restaurant row," thousands of live plants are growing: ferns, vines, trees, shrubs, veggies, houseplants, and herbs, along with holiday specialties: poinsettias and cyclamen in December, Easter lilies in April. **Ricky's Flower Market,** 9 Union Square, (617) 628–7569, would not be mistaken for a sleek suburban nursery or one of those faux barn affairs. This nursery is smack dab in the middle of fumes, traffic, and noise. Why? Because Ricky, a local boy, took over a gas station site and turned it into a plant station. He started small with outdoor stalls, built some covering, and then took over a neighboring building for pots, tropical plants, and garden supplies.

The flower market is a great sight—outdoor displays of pumpkins and mums in autumn, greens and wreaths in winter, vegetable seedlings and shrubs in spring, and flowering hanging plants and cascading vines all summer long. Local folks—especially those without cars—flock to Ricky's and call taxis to carry them and their rhododendrons home. They sit in the backs of cabs, shrubs in their laps, embracing burlapped root balls.

What novelty-loving shopper goes to department stores when she can frequent Indian grocery-video-jewelry shops? Union Square boasts several Indian variety shops, including **Bombay Market,** 359A Somerville Avenue, (617) 623–6614. Bombay Market is fun to visit after dark; from the exterior you can see that the storefront, festooned with colored lights, is actually the first floor of a Victorian house. Sometimes, tall burlap bags of basmati rice are slumped outside the store, and look like loitering pedestrians.

In a neighborhood of old houses, transition, renovation, and renewal, you can often find affordable antiques. **Londontowne,** 380 Somerville Avenue, (617) 625–2045, is like a furniture flea market under a roof. In spite of its ritzy name, this is not a snooty shop. The proprietor does not follow you about and glare when you mess with the antimacassar on the divan. In fact, the proprietor is generally invisible. On a slow rainy day, you might browse for an hour before seeing a soul. What awaits is unpredictable. Containers from the continent arrive all the time, but at irregular intervals. Inventory might be schlock, secondhand, or golden. Typically, objects include furniture, mirrors, some ceramics and clocks, bric-a-brac, lamps, loads of tables and wooden desks, carved antique doors, and salvaged stained-glass windows. Check out the basement. Its atmosphere is between that of an amusement park and your eccentric uncle's attic.

You'd have to go far to find a tippling spot with the warmth of **Tir Na Nog ($),** 366A Somerville Avenue, (617) 628–4300, an Irish pub with glowing wood paneling, exposed brick (century-old ruddy stone, not the plastic stuff), and a long, inviting bar that draws in the regulars and visitors. You can listen to acoustic music at Tir Na Nog or just knock down a pint with your mate, have a comforting supper, or share a beer with your girlfriend. Gal-pals, please note: Girls of all ages can have gabfests here without it being assumed that they're looking for love. Not only that, real men sit down at the bar and talk—to each other. Tir Na Nog is one civil place.

A supermarket is generally not mentioned in a guidebook. However, **Market Basket** (that's "MAHket" Basket in Boston parlance), just outside Union Square on Somerville Avenue, is an ethnic neighborhood in and of itself. Twice I have been asked if I was looking for a husband while I was studying products in ethnic food sections (once it was matzo, the other time it was guava jam, so maybe I'll meet a Caribbean Jew). I have been given recipes for preparing unfamiliar and scary-looking squashes and roots. I have escorted bewildered strangers who spoke no English to the dairy section, where I have tried to explain skim, 1 percent, 2 percent, and whole milk to them by puffing out my cheeks, sticking out my belly, and waddling. I have heard at least eight languages spoken, including Creole, Khmer, and Dutch. Basically, Market Basket is a big supermarket with great prices in a working-class neighborhood. And because the store is stocked to meet the needs of families of various ethnicities, all roads end here. If you're from Ecuador, you might run into someone from home stocking Quaker Oats.

FOOD FINDS

If you leave Union Square and head toward Cambridge on Washington Street, you'll reach the corner of Washington and Beacon Streets. You are on the Somerville-Cambridge line. (At Beacon, Somerville's Washington Street becomes Cambridge's Kirkland Street. Tree-intensive Kirkland leads to the world of Sanders Theatre, Harvard's Science Center, and Harvard Yard.) Rents are still relatively low in this area, allowing small restaurants, bakeries, and bars to set up shop.

True Hot Chocolate

In Union Square's Caribbean and Latino stores, you'll find bars of bitter chocolate from Mexico, Peru, and Colombia. Don't eat it. Drink it—mixed with sugar and hot milk. This is nothing like instant cocoa, but more like the ancient beverage associated with Aztec gods. The chocolate bar is scored. Break off a piece for every cup of hot chocolate you want (one cup won't be enough if you like chocolate). Melt it, whisk in a tablespoon or two of sugar, and add a cup of steamed milk. You can do the whole thing in the microwave, but don't. Do it on top of the stove in a deep metal pot (not enamel, the milk will stick). At the end of cooking, froth the beverage with an eggbeater. You can serve it with a cinnamon-stick stirrer, which intensifies the Aztec-god flavor. These aromatic rolled bark bits are available in Caribbean and Latino groceries.

Luker bitter chocolate, a common variety distributed by Goya, comes in a flat 250-gram (8.75-ounce) bar in a yellow paper wrapper.

The **Wine and Cheese Cask,** 407 Washington Street, (617) 623–8656, a corner pioneer, provides some of the most quaffable, well-priced Rhone wines, zinfandels, and Italian "finds" in the Boston area. Wine and Cheese, housed on the first floor of a residential building, just had a major facelift and is now decked out in cream and terra-cotta. The store is a pleasure to shop in, with polite and knowledgeable staff and a remarkable selection of cheeses, flat breads and loaves (a sampling of local specialty bakers), and a selection of gourmet products.

Across the way, **Panini,** 406 Washington Street, (617) 666–2770, is a bakery, coffee shop, and peaceful, artsy hangout that also supplies many local restaurants with crusty sourdough and country-style loaves, along with focaccia, ficelles, and baguettes. The ginger scones are habit forming, and the place does a thriving trade in its bags of "Panini blend" coffee (whole beans or ground) and toothsome Italian sandwiches.

Reams have been written about the Spanish restaurant **Dali ($–$$$),** 415 Washington Street, (617) 661–3254, catty-corner from Panini. Dali was doing tapas and sexy Iberian food long before it became trendy. The lively venue is what you imagine a Spanish restaurant to be—if you have a lively, florid imagination—a warm, inviting interior, tapas served at the bar, classic and regional Spanish specialties, and the feeling that you've been welcomed—maybe even summoned—into the home of an exuberant family.

EVOO ($$–$$$) (stands for Extra Virgin Olive Oil), 118 Beacon Street, (617) 661–3866, is an informal but elegant restaurant that serves sophisticated starters, soups and salads, and about ten imaginatively conceived, well-presented main courses. Other entrees are sophisticated comfort foods. A veggie entree served on an early March evening—honey-mustard glazed yams wrapped in rice paper with stir-fried vegetables—was a medley of color, texture, and taste, reminding diners of the move from winter to spring.

SUGGESTED 🍽 RESTAURANTS

Taqueria La Mexicana ($), 247 Washington Street, (617) 776–5232, a bright take-out place with walls the color of egg yolk, has a few funky tables and serves up fresh-tasting enchiladas and hearty lentil soup. Familiar Mexican foods are all here: nachos, enchiladas, tacos, tamales, burritos, and quesadillas, but so are less familiar items. Chalupas can be ordered with chicken, beef, pork, or vegetables, along with refried beans, lettuce, and pico de gallo. This snappy little place devotes a third of its menu to vegetarian fare, including a grilled mixed-vegetable plate with rice, whole beans, pico de gallo, and corn tortillas. The most expensive item on the menu, unceremoniously named Cameron Plate, features six big, plump shrimp with rice and salad, along with corn tortillas, heavenly on a hot night with a serving of La Mexicana's cantaloupe water.

Asian restaurants include **New Hometown Restaurant ($-$$)**, 9A Union Square, (617) 623–7220, and **Wuchon ($-$$)**, 290 Somerville Avenue, (617) 623–3313, both serving traditional Korean and Japanese food. Though a little hard to keep straight at first, Union Square's Asian restaurants have different atmospheres and menus.

Wuchon serves lots of Japanese dishes, in addition to Korean. Its sushi bar is open Friday through Sunday all day. Almost no one can finish Wuchon's signature "Big Bowl Rice Dishes," except the pumped-up crews from local Brazilian kickboxing studios, or the yoga students who also take classes nearby and are ravenous after ninety minutes of sustained postures. The pared-down restaurant (though with 150 offerings) offers courtesy and good value, and will prepare vegetarian versions of most dishes. Try a veggie *bibambap*. The *panchan* it's served with—including bean sprouts, broccoli flowerets, potato salad, very leafy kimchi, and seaweed—looks like a food magazine photograph when arranged on Wuchon's simple, bare, wooden tables. And those gelatinous, ridged, amber-colored cubes—mysterious to many (game pieces? Korean subway tokens? translucent after-dinner mints?)—are acorn jelly.

Korean Cuisine

For novices, eating in Korean restaurants is a culinary adventure and also an introduction to Korean culture. New inductees are surprised by how different Korean cooking is from the Asian-style restaurant food many of us grew up with, which is to say, the Chinese-American food served at suburban restaurants. Korean cuisine offers spicy barbecue, aromatic noodles, toothsome dumplings, and luscious all-in-one entrees served in deep, heated bowls or glowing stoneware pots, the latter a visual and tactile experience. Vegetarians feel in seventh heaven when served a personal tureen of bibambap, a vividly colored mélange of slivered fresh vegetables, piled over steamed rice, with a soft-cooked egg bopped on top (the diner mixes the layers and adds chili sauce).

Panchan are a plus. These small, savory dishes, served with every meal, intensify the taste, texture, and "heat" of the food and are added by the diner herself. They are intended to be condiments. But the same insatiable diners who gobble down the dal or lentil sauce, served as side dishes in Indian restaurants, may also scarf

New Hometown serves a mixture of Korean, Chinese, and Japanese dishes, though the menu is heavily Korean. The atmosphere is peaceful, truly like eating in a home. The staff is friendly but low-key, and the sparely decorated dining room has wallpaper with Korean calligraphy. A variety of stir-fried vegetable dishes are available, and noodle dishes with richly flavored, subtly spiced broth. Two people might order *chongol*, a Korean jambalaya cooked at one's table in a steel crock. The seafood version merges lobster, shrimp, cod, monkfish, seasoned vegetables, and noodles. The restaurant's *down Korean grated turnips, bean sprouts, and* kimchi, *the tangy pickled cabbage. In every cuisine that features them, these side dish "dressings" encourage the diner's playful spirit and make for a personal meal.*

If you like wilted greens, appropriate the condiment bowl that contains shiny spinach. Inform your companion, "You won't like this." Eat the whole bowl. If prepared correctly, this modest-looking dish, generally part of the panchan array or available as a side order, is a gem—very fresh, minerally-tasting, finished with sesame oil.

Carbo lovers rejoice at the possibilities of noodle and dumpling dishes. Mandoo, *or dumplings, make fine take-out fare. They can be eaten at room temperature, heated with minimal fuss, or savored in the car (en auto, a new category!) on long trips.*

Though sushi is considered Japanese, it often shows up on Korean menus because diners like it, because it is associated with Asian dining, and because the two nations have an intermingled, if often bellicose, history.

Japanese dishes are more abstemious in appearance. Salmon teriyaki is served with miso soup, rice, and salad.

Great Thai Chef ($), 255 Washington Street, (617) 625–9296, is a small, quiet spot with a mauve interior and potted plants. Palms and dracenas are bedecked with colored lights at Christmas. A few almost-real orchids are "planted" in the window. Chef serves classic Thai restaurant fare: curries, noodle dishes, rice and vegetable entrees, and some lovely desserts, including mango pie with ice cream, and taro custard. Served in a wedge, taro custard has a refined, elegant texture and a flavor reminiscent of crème brûlée. It's the kind of food so intriguing, so "other," that one comes home and stays up late consulting cookbooks and botanical references to understand it. Made from the taro root, a plant that grows all over Southeast Asia and is used for starch, the custard uses palm sugar as a sweetener, accounting for the rich, caramel flavor.

India Palace ($–$$), 23 Union Square, (617) 666–9770, just across from St. Joseph's, is a solid, no surprises, Indian restaurant, with good service, traditional offerings, and better value than similar Harvard Square and Central Square spots. The place is never crowded. It has a charming appearance. Though humble and small, it's festooned with chandeliers, perhaps a reference to its name. Beneath these scintillating lights, an affordable brunch buffet is offered. The menu offers about twenty different kinds of bread, all made on the restaurant's griddle or baked in the tandoor oven. Try the basket of breads: *nan, tandoor roti, chapati,* and *poori.* The last is deep-fried and puffed. In summer a refreshing mango *lassi*—a mango "smoothie" made with yogurt—is a nourishing pick-me-up, especially taken with spicy appetizers or a hot, salty bread.

Ethnic restaurants rule Union Square, but hip little bistros have sprung up, too. Generally, they adhere to the square's mix of people by offering eclectic international fare. In the "restaurant row" of Washington Street, tucked near the post office, **eat ($–$$),** 253 Washington Street, (617) 776–2889, is a crisp, informal spot. Its lowercase name suggests a pleasing everydayness. Intimate, warm, and with a welcoming bar, eat offers bistro-style comfort food: seared sea scallops with Tuscan white beans and pancetta, pan-roasted chicken with garlic mashed potatoes and Swiss chard, and a grilled club

Chandeliers sparkle and Indian breads abound inside India Palace.

steak. To mix it up a bit, on Monday nights eat invites visiting cooks and chefs to prepare their specialty repasts.

Taqueria Jalisco ($), 25 Union Square, (617) 623–7972, is an informal, friendly neighborhood place serving Mexican and Salvadoran cooking. Open everyday, the Taqueria offers south of the border faves—tostados, tacos, tamales—along with more unusual fare, such as burritos *mariscos* (seafood). The eatery's cheerful and economical breakfast features scrambled eggs with jalapeño peppers, sauteed onions, and sliced tomatoes.

Neighborhood Restaurant & Bakery ($), 25 Bow Street, (617) 628–2151, is, in restaurant taxonomy, somewhere between an ethnic and an American restaurant. It offers elbows-on-the-table ambience, solid feeds, and looks like something out of a Norman Rockwell painting, with a cinematic streak of David Lynch. In cold seasons junked cars (or could someone actually be driving these?) appear on the restaurant's patio dining area. Neighborhood is a checkered tablecloth kind of place, but its meat loaf is just part of the story. Big platters of Portuguese, Italian, and universal comfort food are served, along with super breakfasts. Yuppies mix with longtime residents. Nightsticks nestle near laptops. The tied-up dogs "parked" outside look like a scene from *Lady and the Tramp*, mongrels mixing with uptown pups.

East Boston

Three Urban Squares, con Salsa

*E*ast Boston is one of the biggest surprises in the city, even for those who think they know Boston. Pull off Route 1A North just before the Logan Airport exit, and you face Santarpio's, a mammoth, old-time, neighborhood pizzeria. (Consider stopping; aficionados of classic-thin-crust-no-frills pizza consider it among Boston's best.) Take a quick right onto Paris Street, and you enter what appears to be a small-scale, urban mill town, where nearly everyone speaks Spanish or Italian. A plane of light reflecting from Boston Harbor cuts across your windshield like a cinematic break between scenes. An instant later you'll see the Custom House Tower on the other side of the harbor, framed by East Boston's blocks of skinny, three-decker houses.

Continue down Paris, or Havre, or Cottage Streets to the water's edge, and you face Boston, set before you like a lavish architectural buffet: the H-shaped Federal Reserve Bank, the financial district and central downtown, Rowe's Wharf, and the prized waterfront condos in rehabbed nineteenth-century market buildings—and even the North End, with its church spires, and the edge of Charlestown.

East Boston, separated from downtown Boston by the Callahan Tunnel beneath Boston Harbor, seems like its own continent. Almost surrounded by water, and without tall buildings, it has a subtly different light than Boston, especially as you head toward its narrow waist west of Day Square.

Though known mainly as the location of Logan Airport, the intensity of East Boston has almost nothing to do with the rambling, faceless airport, except where jagged cuts and street endings denote access to the airport, which is almost universally hated by the people of Eastie. When Logan was built during the 1920s, one of the many landscape slashings eliminated an entire island, bucolic and beloved Wood Island. Its park—designed by Frederick Law Olmsted, and a

How to Get There

By public transportation take the MBTA Blue Line,
which connects with both the Orange and Green Lines, to one
of several stops: Maverick, Airport, Wood Island, Orient Heights,
Suffolk Downs, where the racetrack is located, and Belle Isle
Reservation (see "Urban Salt Marsh"). By car from Boston follow
Route 1A North as though heading to Logan Airport. Take the
local exit immediately before the airport. For the foreseeable
future, delays are likely at the Callahan and Sumner
Tunnels due to Big Dig upheaval.

mecca for immigrant workers—was demolished to create Logan
Airport. Today, Eastie is a series of "urban villages"—Maverick
Square, Central Square, Day Square, Orient Heights—each a nexus
of streets, distinguished by a landmark: a subway stop, promontory,
or shopping center.

The place is dense. Narrow three-deckers—many of them
slicked over with aluminum siding, some still showing worn clap-
boards—and the occasional dignified brownstone line the streets.
Yards are postage-stamp sized (nowhere but in Boston would they be
called yards). Parks are precious. Stores are pint-size, old-fashioned,
with stock piled up to—and occasionally hanging from—the ceiling.
Spanish is the most common language, along with Italian and Khmer.
It's hard to find a copy of *The Boston Globe*, but easy to find *La
Semana*, the Spanish-language weekly. It took several visits for me to

realize that the poodle in my favorite grocery was not So-Pedro, or Snope, but *Snoopy*, "an American dog, born here," as Francisco Portillo, his owner, proudly explained.

••• *History* •••

As is the case with other Boston neighborhoods that haven't been gentrified, you can tell a lot about East Boston's history by looking at its buildings and urban plan. The neat grid of streets and squares, and the separation between residential areas and retail hubs suggest nineteenth-century development. Modest row houses, three-deckers, and small brick apartment buildings evoke a community of working people. Grander houses on hills were built for the wealthy. Add to these surroundings the piers, docks, and bridges on the city's "edges" (East Boston is a virtual peninsula), and you might guess at a maritime past. You would be right. East Boston was once five islands. Two were filled in to become the present community, and three were filled in to become Logan Airport.

In its ninteenth-century heyday, East Boston was a center for ship-building and send-offs. Some of the great clipper ships of the day were built in Donald McKay's Border Street Shipyards, including *Glory of the Seas, Daniel Webster,* and the legendary *Flying Cloud,* which set a speed record for its voyage from New York to San Francisco (eighty-nine days). The harbor could become a stage for showy bon voyage parties; East Boston was the American port for the Cunard Line.

All through the nineteenth century, and continuing today, immigrants arrived in East Boston: Italian, Irish, Russian, Polish, Canadian. Those from overseas arrived at the Immigrant Home on Marginal Street. The legacy of these hardworking people manifests itself in the churches and settlement houses that still stand and the tunnels that connect East Boston with downtown Boston. They rest in the city's burial yards, including that of Ohabei Shalom, dating back to an era of Jewish immigration. Bakeries, shops, and restaurants with Italian connections dot the city, as do banquet facilities, such as Spinelli's.

During the last several decades, immigrants from Latin America and Southeast Asia have come to the community, opening small groceries, restaurants, bakeries, and coffee shops. These latter-day émigrés are intermixed with East Bostonians of Italian ancestry. Children of every color occupy the chairs of the East Boston branch of the Boston Public Library and sit before computers, focused and intent, navigating the World Wide Web. Above them, antique oil paintings of the clipper ships on their worldwide voyages adorn the library's walls.

Boston Buddhist Temple is tucked just outside Central Square, East Boston.

... *A Walking Tour* ...

Restaurants, groceries, and bakeries are concentrated in three squares: Maverick, Central, and Day. Along the main streets that connect these squares—Bennington, Sarasota, Meridian, Maverick, and Chelsea—you can also find stores with Latin or Italian flavor. These are residential streets as well, lined with narrow, attached houses. Lexington Street, parallel to Bennington, is purely residential and very pleasant to walk—cozy, urban, totally Eastie.

It's a short walk from Maverick Square, location of the MBTA stop, to Central Square. Day Square is several blocks away. Another urban settlement, Orient Heights, is car-distance removed, but it can also be reached via MBTA. It's probably best to start at Maverick Square, as it has everything emblematic of East Boston: harbor views, traffic, you-can't-get-there-from-here traffic patterns, bakeries (Italian and Latino), restaurants, grocery stores (Italian and Latino), a gas station, church, bar, nearby park, travel agency specializing in trips to Latin America, and Spanish-speaking people—including families with infants in strollers and youngsters in tow. It's also a transportation hub, the first MBTA stop on the MBTA Blue Line in East Boston.

Built at the turn of the last century, **Maverick Station** may not look picturesque, but it was considered an engineering marvel in its day, connecting East Boston with downtown Boston, via a tunnel under Boston Harbor.

To orient yourself, cross the street behind the station and view Boston Harbor and downtown from Lewis Mall, a public-housing complex. Within this complex is a **community garden**, a project of Boston Natural Areas Fund and residents of the apartments.

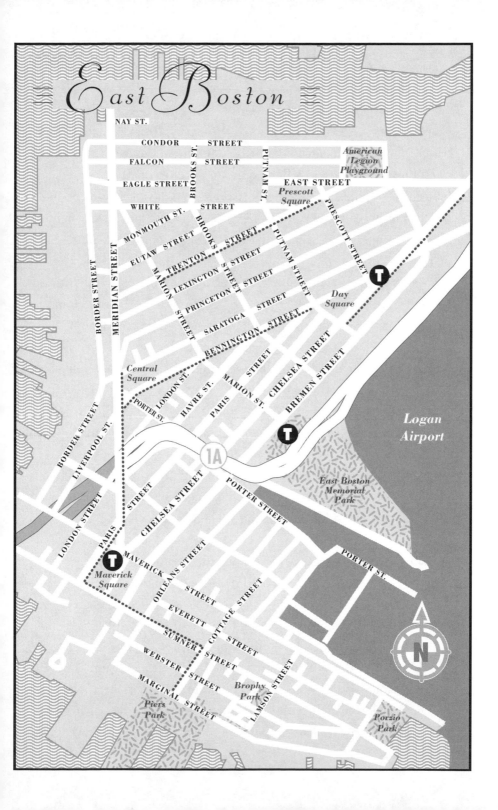

Before you conduct your food investigations, you might want to sharpen your appetite with a walk to nearby **Piers Park**. Follow Sumner Street at the edge of Maverick Square to Cottage Street. Take a right on Cottage to Piers Park, a swanky modern park with graceful buildings, seaside trellises, harbor views, and a walkway to the harbor. In warm weather the site is used for concerts, fairs, and community gatherings. At all times of year, it offers a place to perambulate and catch a breath.

Back in Maverick Square, check out small, cozy **Taqueria Cancún ($)**, 65 Maverick Square, (617) 567–4449. The restaurant is so cheery and informal, and the diners so focused on their food, it suggests a community kitchen. Even early in the day, customers are digging into platters of shrimp served with rice, beans, guacamole, and savory warm tortillas. A man is eating a tongue taco (tongue is *lengua*, lots of fun to say, if not to contemplate closely). Fruit juices— *tamarindo* (tamarind), *piña* (pineapple), *mandarina* (tangerine)—look like stained-glass windows. The soups are meals and look just like what a Colombian madre would make. No one is reading or talking as they eat their soup; they are intent, the angle and movement of their spoons as deft and purposeful as the stroke of a canoeist.

You can take out or eat in, choosing from Latino and Mexican specialties—tacos, tamales, enchiladas, flautas, burritos, and *pupusas* (corn patties)—and the different soups made each day.

Breakfast (*desayuno*) is hearty, wholesome, and inexpensive: two eggs any style, ham, beans, cheese, fried plantains, tortillas, and sour cream. Sure beats cornflakes with skim milk.

What to call **La Sultana ($)**, 40 Maverick Square, (617) 568–9999, across the street from Taqueria Cancún? Bakery, takeout, eat-in, hangout? It's all of those, a community gathering place where men drink coffee, wolf down pastries and sandwiches all day long, and order heaping platters of barbecued chicken at lunchtime. These aromatic platters are well priced and feature a quarter of a barbecued chicken, rice, beans or potato (delicious-looking, golden-brown, braised potatoes), served with the soda of your choice.

Officially a Colombian bakery, the place is a mix of elegant and down-home. A gorgeous brass espresso machine gleams; the coffee (Colombian) is excellent. Beneath the important-looking machine are scads of peasanty grilled sausages and plump empanadas with dainty crimped edges, filled with cheese or meat.

Spanish music plays from a local radio station. A customer waiting for cheeseballs, which look like deep-fried snowballs, sings along. A toddler tries to sit on the linoleum floor; her older sister picks her up. About ten people—all men—sit at a long table in the middle of La Sultana, eating and listening to the music. Buy an eggy, light cheese bread *(pan queso)* to slice and eat at home with coffee, and definitely some of the ten-inch-long crisp sugar cookies called lengua (tongue).

Follow Meridian Street a few blocks to a convergence of streets at Central Square. Those of keen visual sensibilities may be taken aback by the oversized shopping center in the heart of Central Square. You'll feel worse if you pore over period photographs of the once-lovely square, designed by nineteenth-century developers as the genteel junction of six streets (Meridian, Porter, Bennington, Saratoga, Border, and Liverpool), complete with a circular tree-shaded park. The area was jumbled by mercantile development and the construction of the Sumner Tunnel in 1933. Today's shopping center (a huge Shaw's supermarket, CVS, fast-food outlets) hardly fits the square's remaining architectural character. But the nineteenth century is long gone. And the supermarket has lots of local touches. The parking lot has great views of the Tobin Bridge—and traffic signs in Spanish. On the streets that spin out from this modern shopping center—Sarasota, Meridian, and Bennington—almost a score of varied markets and restaurants await.

Those closest to Central Square include **El Paisa Supermarket Latinos,** 34 Bennington Street, (617) 567–7082, a simple Latino general store with candles, cookware (from Colombia), utensils, baby food, spices, canned goods, and some produce.

Across the street, **Karen Market,** 41 Bennington Street, (617) 569–7382, is the tiniest grocery you'll ever squeeze into. In winter, when I'm wearing a fat, quilted parka, I am only able to slither sideways among the aisles. *"Perdóname,"* an attractive man said to me in the Salvadoran pound cake aisle. If only I'd known how to say, "Don't I know you?" in Spanish. Somehow every imaginable Goya canned good is crammed into this market, along with jars of exotic fruit, such as yellow cherries. Loofahs dangle from the ceiling. Spanish-language CDs are rack-mounted at eye level. ("Wow, there's a lot going on here," a friend, accompanying me for the first time, remarked.) Make sure you go into the very back corners of the store. Mi Ranchito Cuajada Fresca con Chile Rojo (fresh cheese with hot peppers) is a find. Look for a Styrofoam tray with six plump, egg-roll–size rolls of creamy white cheese, shrink-wrapped. Hot stuff. Perfect for a sandwich, melted on toast, or minced and added to scrambled eggs.

My two favorite sections at Karen are the Salvadoran baked goods manufactured by Genesis Specialty Bakery in Hyde Park, New York (look for a smiley face with the inscription "Jesus Loves You"), and the freezer near the cash register where you find banana leaves. I have no idea what to do with them, but I appreciate that someone does. No trouble figuring out the sweet delights in the Salvadoran cake-and-cookie section: pound cake, muffins, pineapple-stuffed pastries, and

Urban Salt Marsh

Here's a peaceful outdoor spot, near but apart from East Boston's taquerias, that is also salty and invigorating. **Belle Isle Marsh Reservation,** *off Bennington Street, near Suffolk Downs, is a little-known Metropolitan District Commission park with a boardwalk through a salt marsh. Twice a day, ten minutes from downtown Boston—and the hurly-burly of Big Dig construction—you can observe the pace of tides coming in and going out and the wildlife that feeds at various intervals in various "pantries" in the ecosystem. Blackbirds, egrets, and shorebirds take cover in the tall reeds. Muskrats build their lodges of chomped-down vegetation in the ponds. Voles scamper in the meadow. In spring the grassland habitat is whirring with butterflies and dragonflies, grasshoppers, and songbirds migrating north.*

golden rice-flour cookies *(salpora de arroz):* four in a shrink-wrapped package. These freeze well and inspire impromptu tea parties. During the Big Dig construction, I have taken to storing some in my car.

Continuing down this block of Bennington, you'll find **Peach's 'n Cream,** 69–73 Bennington Street, (617) 561–4725, on the corner. Peach's is not an ethnic bakery, it's an American-style bakery, with everything from muffins to birthday cakes to chocolate chip cookies. But as America is a melting pot, you'll also find biscotti, cannoli, fruit tortes, napoleons, eclairs, florentines, Italian rum cakes, and bagels, as well as coffee and ice cream. Locals prize Peach's 'n Cream for its fancy cakes. Many contain spirits— Amaretto, Irish Cream, Chocolate Bourbon Pecan, Grand Marnier— and can be ordered as wedding cakes.

Consider **Lolly's Bakery,** 158 Bennington Street, (617) 567–9461, between Central and Day Squares, a site for anthropological research as well as a place for pastries. The former owner was Italian and made cannoli, biscotti, and rum cakes. When a more diverse population moved into the neighborhood, he baked muffins, Danish, and fruit pies. The new owner hails from Latin America. He makes *budin* (pudding), Salvadoran quesadillas, and *champurrado*, a luscious Guatemalan drink made of coffee, hot chocolate, and cinnamon, with a dollop of whipped cream for good measure. But the versatile baker also makes some of the old Italian stuff as well as typically American goodies. Everybody who comes into the small, fragrant store tries everything. Surely goodness and mercy lie where biscotti, Boston cream pie, and *pasteles tres leches*—made with three milks: condensed, evaporated, and whole—come together.

You may wish to call it a day or, fortified by fig squares and bread pudding, continue walking along Bennington to another hub: Day Square. Two major streets come together here, Chelsea and Bennington. Sarasota, another biggie, runs parallel to Bennington a block away. It's the location of many of the city's oldest Italian restaurants, with angled parking in the center of the square and on-the-street parking on side streets.

Francisco Portillo operates a terrific little grocery in Day Square. **El-Sol Food Market,** 353 Chelsea Street, (617) 567–0287, specializes in Colombian and Salvadoran products. It will remind you of an old-fashioned corner store, with housewares and a few tools, but mostly groceries. But the groceries of El-Sol are from all over Latin America, especially Mexico, Colombia, El Salvador, and Peru: stacks of cooking chocolate from Mexico, El Salvador, and Peru for making authentic cups of hot chocolate, and shelves of dried vegetables, including Peruvian potatoes and ears of purple corn.

Try your hand at making chocobananos—chocolate-covered bananas.

Francisco, a native of El Salvador who grew up on a farm, stocks many Salvadoran ingredients. My favorite is *dulce atado:* brown sugar wrapped in a dried corn husk, neatly tied with the fiber of a banana plant. "All natural," Francisco points out. In the United States for fifteen years, he and his Colombian wife have found people in the community who are traditional cooks. One older lady supplies the store with lovely, fine-grained white cakes made of rice flour. Another home cook prepares arepas with cheese.

On my virgin visit to El-Sol, I left with many products, including a two-pound jar of byrsonima, a mysterious cherrylike fruit (as yet unidentified) in heavy syrup, and melting chocolate and wooden sticks to make chocobananos, a frozen dessert. Francisco makes these himself and sells them in the store, especially during warm weather. He, his dog Snoopy, and the grocery are so charming, I think I'll wait to buy chocobananos from El-Sol. (They're in the freezer at the front, near the register.)

Spinelli's Pastry Shoppe, 282 Bennington Street, (617) 567–1992, is the Disney World of pastry—extensive, wildly colorful,

A Typical Latin American Meal

A casual meal (the North American equivalent of a hamburger or pizza) features corn in some form and a "sandwich"—taco, tortilla, or arepa—with a "protein hit" from its topping or stuffing: rice and beans, cheese and beans, or rice and meat, generally served with guacamole, salsa, and sour cream. East Boston's taquerias generally don't have wine and beer licenses, so folks drink soft drinks or tropical fruit juices.

A more formal sit-down dinner would feature a stimulating appetizer or small bowl of soup, a meaty dish, such as round steak or chicken stew, served with a few starches—rice or potato, plantain or yuca—and salad. Dessert might include flan or fruit and aromatic Colombian coffee.

and sweet. The venerable bakery (which also offers catering and banquet facilities) sells Italian goodies, as well as pasta and red sauce take-out entrees—lasagna, ravioli, baked ziti. You can also order an American-style or hot Italian sandwich (pepperoni and eggs, or potatoes and eggs). Some days I find the place overwhelming; the lavish displays of Italian cookies, rows of high-rise cakes, and over-the-top pastries are dizzying. But it's rare that I have such a delicate day. Most days Spinelli's seems like a carnival.

S UGGESTED 🍽 R ESTAURANTS

MAVERICK SQUARE

Try **Taqueria Cancún ($)** or **La Sultana ($),** both of which are takeouts but also have table space, especially Taqueria Cancún. (See "Walking Tour.")

CENTRAL SQUARE

El Peñol ($–$$), 54 Bennington Street, (617) 569–0100, is a pleasant, family-owned, sit-down restaurant with white stucco walls and linen tablecloths. The extensive menu offers dozens of South American entrees, especially Colombian favorites. This is a meat-intensive place, with so many exotic dishes, you'll take too long to order, get ravenously hungry, eat too much, and be very happy. Cazuela de Maricos is a seafood casserole with rice and plantains. Mojarra is porgy served with tasty rice, salad, and fried plantains. Picados is a massive platter of various parts of pork and beef. Bistec a Cabbalo, a cowboy meal, suitable for eating before a roundup, consists of sirloin steak, beans, rice, sweet plantains, salad, and two eggs. Chicharron de Pollo is delectable fried chicken.

Except for the ubiquitous TV on the wall, **La Terraza ($–$$),** 19 Bennington Street, (617) 561–5200, is a lot like an inviting home dining room, with clean white walls with murals and a simple arrangement of tables. La Terraza's menu is divided among typical Latin American dishes, most featuring meat, seafood when in season, and fast foods: fried spare ribs, beef turnovers, salami with corn cake. There's a stylish bar on the second floor. The restaurant serves hard-to-find, authentic Latino desserts—*brevas con queso* (figs and cheese), *flan de coco* (coconut flan), *tomate de arbol* (tarmarillo and cheese), and even Colombian fudge. One menu item that lingers in my imagination, for its poignant Spanish name: *alas de pollo* (chicken wings).

Eating at **Saigon Hut ($),** 305 Meridian Street, (617) 567–1944, just outside Central Square, diagonally across from the library, is a peaceful, calming experience. East Boston's only Vietnamese restaurant, which also serves Chinese cuisine, is a magnet in winter for its bounteous, satisfying pho: tureen-size bowls of noodles, nourishing broth, and vegetables. I must warn you, some of Saigon Hut's menu descriptions are alarming. One manly noodle soup with flank steak is listed as containing "soft tendon." Another soup purports to contain "bible tripe." Ignore these frightening descriptions and order with impunity. Not only will you be served an opulent, subtly spiced meal, but you will spend next to nothing. Pho comes in three sizes. Extra-large is almost baby-basin size. Luscious yellow noodle combos are served; I am fond of the veggie yellow-noodle entree with tofu.

Saigon Hut is the only restaurant I have ever patronized where I am ushered to my own quiet table and served a pot of tea while I wait for takeout. "May I take your coat?," I was once asked while waiting in my slush-flecked parka. It is also that rare restaurant where you hear the vegetables being chopped (vigorously), then deep-fried (sizzle, splash, followed by aromas wafting) while you wait.

DAY SQUARE

This small, lively square is dominated by eateries, including many old-fashioned Italian restaurants—Jeveli's, Nana Cora, Mario's—as well as take-out and sit-down taquerias and a stylish Peruvian place.

Nearby, **Rincon Limeño Restaurant ($–$$),** 409 Chelsea Street, (617) 569–4942, is a cozy, festive spot with intriguing Peruvian dishes. Several marinated fish dishes (ceviche) are on the entree menu—shrimp, flatfish, mixed platters—along with seafood stews and lush platters of breaded fish with rice and french fries. Some of the more unusual dishes are appetizers: Papa a la Huancaina, a spicy dish of boiled potatoes with cheese and cream sauce, and the zippy-tasting Salchipapas, diced hot dogs mixed with french fries and a piquant sauce.

Rincon Limeño also serves breakfast. You can order your very own arcpa—a corn cake with cheese or with eggs and cheese—or a peasanty platter of refried beans, eggs, and rice. The Spanish name of this breakfast platter is beautiful, sounding like a line of a ballad, rather than a slew of protein-packed food: Calentad con Arroz, Huevos.

Everything about **Jeveli's ($–$$)**, 387 Chelsea Street, (617) 567–9539, founded in 1924, is locked in time, including the hairdos and salutations of the waitresses. Recently, one older waitress, fussing over me and my fifty-something companion, said, "Enjoy your dinners, kids!" We did.

Sophisticated Italian it's not, but Jeveli's food is homey and filling. Lasagna, ravioli, fettucini Alfredo, and pasta with sauces ranging from Alicia (garlic, oil, anchovies) to tuna sauce are part of the bill of fare, along with grilled meats and old favorites such as chicken cacciatore. Unlike many bowdlerized Italian restaurants, Jeveli's still serves tripe and traditional meat sauces, such as Vesuvio, with lots of mushrooms. The sprawling, pleasantly dark interior has stained-glass windows, giving you a sense that you and your companion are alone on a boat dining—an old-fashioned restaurant feeling I like, a far cry from today's polished minimalist decor, with tables and traffic engineered toward encounters with others.

Nana Cora ($–$$), 297 Bennington Street, (617) 569–1551, really does feel like a grandmother's place—I guess because of its small size, its old-fashioned service, and the succulent, well-presented platters. Often, the waitresses hover after serving as my own grandmother did, waiting to see how the food is received. The emphasis at

Nana Cora is on simple dishes, using fresh ingredients, cooked to order. Fish Bianco is prepared with white wine, garlic, and butter, and served with pasta or salad. Vegetable Marinara combines broccoli, zucchini, mushrooms, and olives in a light red sauce.

El Rancho Grande ($), 300 Bennington Street, (617) 561–5111, is a simple, friendly eat-in and take-out place—linoleum floors, lots of plants, and under a dozen tables with one long group table in the middle; solitary diners sometimes park themselves at this long table to eat and chat, or to eat communally but silently. Hearty soups such as *posole* (corn and pork) and *birria de chivo* (goat) are served, along with traditional Mexican items and a slew of shrimp specialties— shrimp with hot sauce, shrimp and octopus cocktail, and generous platters of crusty, crunchy, breaded shrimp.

Little Armenia, Watertown

A Middle Eastern Oasis

*F*armers note how the sun falls on fields, how a pasture slopes, and the way crops grow better in certain patches. Birders look high in the sky for hawks. Gardeners can tell if soil is acidic or alkaline by the kinds of weeds that sprout.

Similarly, urban food-finders are alert to the changing atmosphere of a city street. For blocks a street can seem nondescript, the buildings jumbled, with no apparent purpose. Then it changes. Traffic picks up. Pedestrians appear, as though from offstage. Storefronts with tempting wares begin to dot the landscape.

Driving from Cambridge to Watertown on Mt. Auburn Street, you pass a hospital, a gas station, a supermarket, a massive tan brick medical building (a former Western Electric plant), a small, well-kept historic burial ground, and suddenly enter an enclave of gastronomic activity. At the curb men parked in trucks are wolfing down spicy spinach-and-cheese *boerags*. In shops college profs in tweedy jackets study the contents of bins of dried fruit and nuts, bending low to sniff the brine of olives. Well-dressed, coiffed mothers pile plump pita bread, semisoft cheese, and sienna-colored fig jam into handheld baskets. A shopkeeper patiently explains the differences among her five types of feta cheese—sheep cheese from France, Greece, Bulgaria, Moldavia, and the United States. The huge chunks of off-white feta sit like abstract sculptures in the glass cabinets. A discerning customer slowly, methodically tries slivers of each, pausing between tastes.

"It's all good, it's all good!" says an elderly man, waiting in line. The proprietor gives him a sesame cookie—and a *mamoul*, a diminutive buttery pastry, to the child by his side.

This is "Little Armenia," a small area in Watertown near the Cambridge line. Along the residential side streets are well-cared-for wood-frame and brick houses, some modest, some august. Armenians live throughout Watertown, a community along the Charles River, the river that separates Cambridge and Boston. A three-block hub along the 500 block of Mt. Auburn Street forms a village, a confederation of groceries, bakeries, and restaurants, along with churches and cultural centers.

Each shop has its own character: from the intimacy of Sevan Bakery, with its open bins of olives—a spectrum of green, black, and brown; wrinkled and smooth; spherical and oblate—to the more subdued, mannerly Massis Bakery, with neatly packaged items, along with cookbooks and cooking implements. The stores are cosmopolitan, frequented by many non-Armenian shoppers, but the prevailing spoken language is Armenian.

Customers, many of them regulars, observe each other. In these close quarters you may, if you are lucky and bold, have the opportunity to discreetly glance at someone's shopping list. One of my treasured experiences involved sneaking a peek at the elegant penmanship of a

How to Get There

By public transportation take the Number 71 bus from the lower level of the Harvard Square Station. Many other buses are available. By car follow Mt. Auburn Street from Cambridge, or Brattle Street, which feeds into Mt. Auburn Street (Route 16).

well-dressed elderly lady. Her list, compiled in columns, was a mélange of Armenian and French words written in dark-blue ink with a fine-nibbed fountain pen. I couldn't contain my admiration.

"Forgive me—but your shopping list is so beautiful," I said. "It's like calligraphy."

The woman turned to me and said, in a deep, accented voice, "Thank you, dear. Who notices an old woman's penmanship? But as it happens I am a painter."

The proprietor of the store beamed at us. "And she speaks seven languages," she said proudly.

A small exchange while buying cheese, but among three women of three generations who were interested in each other. These meetings happen often when people are clustered around a counter of cheeses, pastries, and breads, and less often when we wait single file with our cello-packs in a supermarket.

• • • *History* • • •

The Armenians in America are not recent arrivals. Armenian bureaucrats were sent to help manage the original seventeenth-century crown colony in Virginia, according to Gary Lind-Sinanian of the Armenian Library and Museum in Watertown. But sizable numbers did not arrive until the late nineteenth century, following the Turkish massacres of the Armenians (1894–96), and in response to the need for factory workers in the Boston area. Armenians settled in Boston's South End, in Cambridgeport (once part of Watertown), and near the Hood Rubber Plant, today the site of the Watertown Mall. During the prolonged horrific period of massacres by the Turks, the genocide of 1915–22, up to 1.5 million Armenian men, women, and children were killed. According to the Armenian National Committee of American Eastern Region, half a million Armenians survived and managed to escape to Russia and the United States. Thousands poured into Watertown. The stream of immigration continued until the United States was closed to them in 1924. The Armenians settled in an area of East Watertown that became known as Little Armenia.

Watertown was established in 1640 and originally included Cambridge and Arlington. As in most Boston-area towns, housing here is old. Many dwellings have been in Armenian-American families for generations, passing from relatives and associates, providing community and stability. Though the bakeries and shops of Mt. Auburn Street are a great draw, habitual visitors wind up walking the residential streets as well. A good one to start with is Langdon Avenue, which leads to Belmont, location of Eastern Lamejun, a choice Armenian bakery and specialty shop.

Watertown is no longer a manufacturing center, employing local workers. Hood Rubber is long gone, and the old Western Electric plant at the edge of Little Armenia closed several years ago. Today's Armenian Americans are mainly white-collar workers. Still, the community remains tight. Nearly a score of organizations are based in Watertown and nearby: churches, libraries, schools, political leagues, and sports clubs, along with Armenian newspapers, radio programs, museums, performance groups, and art collections.

If you become interested in the culture and want to know more, visit the **Armenian Library and Museum,** 65 Main Street, (617) 926–2562, open Sunday, Tuesday, and Friday (call for hours). The imposing modern building, located in Watertown Square about a ten-minute drive from Kay's Market, offers ongoing exhibits on Armenian history and art, as well as changing art and textile exhibitions and lectures on everything from the Armenian coffee trade to Armenian fairy tales.

... *A Walking Tour* ...

If you are coming from Cambridge, pay attention once you pass the Mount Auburn Cemetery, near the Cambridge-Watertown boundary. Heads up at the sight of a looming tan building; the old Western Electric plant near the corner of Mt. Auburn and Arlington Streets is now a health maintenance organization.

Shops are mainly on Mt. Auburn Street, but you may want to wander onto side streets to see some of the houses in this family neighborhood: a neat mix of colonials, bungalows, capes, and three-deckers. Drive carefully: Watertown kids still play in the street.

The gleaming **Town Diner** announces the entrance to Watertown's Armenian-American food city. Take in the Town with its all-American specialties, or fortify yourself at **Sepal's** on nearby Nichols Avenue (see "Suggested Restaurants"). Rev up your appetite by visiting **Sevan Bakery**, 599 Mt. Auburn Street, (617) 924–9843, which is a lot more than a bakery. Sevan (pronounced "Se-VAHN") is a gourmet grocery, take-out emporium, caterer, and neighborhood gathering place. Its name is inspired by the Sevan, a beloved Armenian river.

As you walk in the door, you're overwhelmed by delectable aromas and vibrant colors. From the right you're seduced visually—by the bakery counter, with its diverse pastries, breads, and take-out specialties: individual cheese pies, meat pies, and pockets of spinach, walnuts, and tahini. On the left you're seduced by fragrance: a luscious waft of mint, oregano, basil, curry, cumin, and hot pepper. Some days I feel too weak, too vulnerable, to open the door to this food Xanadu (is there such a malady as the food vapors?).

Customers hover over stainless-steel trays of seeds, nuts, and dried fruit. They're supposed to be using scoops, but now and then a

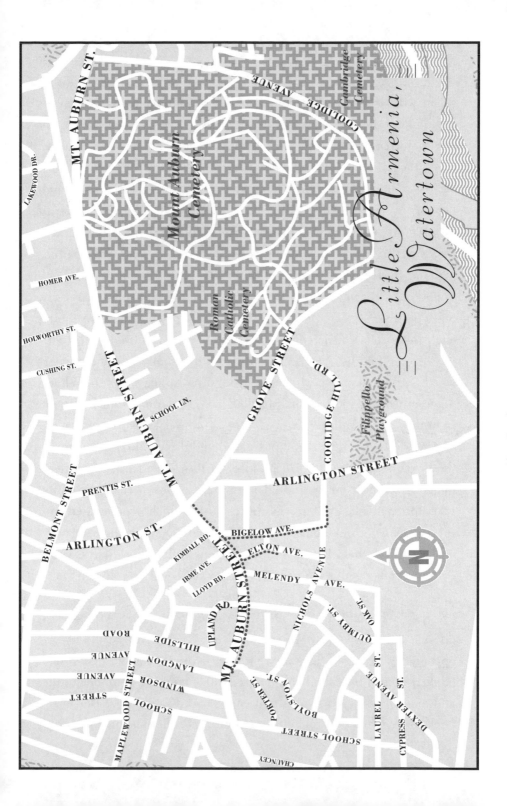

finger will be used to extract an irresistibly plump colossal cashew or to sample a macadamia nut. I catch a man's eye as he does this. He is undeterred. "This is my job," he says proudly, "I am a food detective." I ask if I can join his agency.

To appreciate Sevan you must adjust your vision, as though converting from reading billboards to reading fine print. We've all become so accustomed to overwhelming displays in supermarkets that small-scale arrangements require retraining (useful in other areas of life). Just a few of each item are on display at Sevan. Look quickly, as in the supermarket, and you'll see jam. Look carefully, and you'll see fig, quince, morello cherry, apricot, and gooseberry, each in various consistencies, in shapely jars, from multiple countries. Some jars labeled "jam" are not. Buxom and heavy as paperweights, they're exotic whole fruit, bobbing in heavy syrup. What a piece of work is international trade; here is a jar of "Young Walnuts from the Ararat Valley."

In addition to its array of preserved and dried fruit, Sevan carries the dried vegetables used in Middle Eastern cuisine. My favorite— because of their oddly animal appearance—are dried eggplants. Look for small stacks of grayish-purplish-brownish pouches tied with rubber bands. Think donkey ears. Then look for *simit,* the semisweet cookies. Take them home, and have them with coffee. If it's winter start the coffee while you're still wearing your coat so you won't have to wait too long.

Kay's Fruit Market, 594 Mt. Auburn Street, (617) 923–0523, doesn't look particularly Armenian. Fruit is fruit. At first the market appears to be an old-fashioned produce store: spacious, unadorned, banked bins of fruits and vegetables, scales hanging from the ceiling, and men in wrinkled aprons and caps stocking the bins. But in the back are caches of Armenian crackers and cheeses, in the corner

Mount Auburn Cemetery

The **Mount Auburn Cemetery**, 580 Mt. Auburn Street, (617) 547–7105, has become so integrated into the Boston-Cambridge-Watertown nature lovers' community that it has its own "friends of" organization and regular walking tours, along with lectures about landscaping and social history, and art appreciation gatherings. The carved and cast stone memorials, many by prominent sculptors, are majestic. Famous citizens of Massachusetts buried at Mount Auburn include social worker Dorothea Dix, architect Charles Bulfinch, scientists Louis Agassiz and Asa Gray, and poets Amy Lowell, Oliver Wendell Holmes, and Henry Wadsworth Longfellow.

The parklike oasis—between Cambridge and Little Armenia—was the first botanical cemetery in America, seminal in the "country cemetery" movement. The goal of reformers was to create environments where the dead could rest in harmony and beauty, and the living could stroll, pay homage and reflect, and enjoy the wonders of nature. Mount Auburn was created in 1831 on farmland overlooking the Charles River that had long been known as Sweet Auburn.

Today, botanists, naturalists, and landscape architects associated with the Arnold Arboretum use the grounds for teaching. Bird clubs and independent birders scout here early in the morning. (I saw my first screech owl in a knoll of a tree about ten feet from the entrance at 7:00 A.M.) Art students sketch the elaborate marble sculptures and headstones. History buffs are forever pointing out the graves of the rich and famous. One dewy morning I heard someone shouting, "There's Mary Baker Eddy [the founder of Christian Science]—quite a spread!"

The garden cemetery is located near the Cambridge-Watertown boundary about a half mile from Little Armenia. Look for a huge Star Market across the street. You can drive through the cemetery's main entrance and park on the paths. Maps are available. Be quiet and respectful—to honor the dead and attract the birds.

barrels of nuts, and shelves of specialty vinegars and oils. Try the string cheese: a cellophane-sealed package of what looks like braided white cheese—or a skein of yarn. When you get it home, summon your patience and unbraid the cheese rope, wash it to remove some of the salt, and pull off vertical "threads" of the cheese, which lends itself to this process. Serve as a pile of cheese strings. It looks better than it sounds.

A trove of well-priced spices is stashed in the rear right corner. Plastic containers hold triple the amount of commercially packaged varieties sold for three times the price. Kay's stocks every spice you can imagine, and more, including Syrian red pepper, *chamon* (ground cumin seeds), and hard-to-find whole mustard seeds. Amid the bins of nuts, for no apparent reason, are brightly colored gummy bears. Whatever.

If you are so fortunate as to see elderly customers shopping, keep an eye on what they're buying. A well-preserved Armenian gentleman under my surveillance bought a quantity of chubby cucumbers, lots of vinegar, mustard seed, and fresh dill and asked the proprietor whether he had any barrels he wanted to get rid of. I wish I could have watched him making his special pickles, but seeing the early maneuvers was still pretty good.

Diagonally across Mt. Auburn Street, you'll see a big modern storefront: **Massis Bakery,** 569 Mt. Auburn, (617) 924–0537, also much more than a bakery. Here you can stock up on provisions; peruse Armenian, Greek, Lebanese, and Middle Eastern cookbooks; take out a full dinner or the makings of a gourmet Armenian picnic (spreads, grape leaves, veggie salads, pastries); or, if you are a member of the truly food-obsessed class, spend a half hour studying the exotic canned goods, syrups, and spices. Where else can you find an entire aisle of pickled vegetables, ranging from baby cukes, to whole

Soorj

Nescafé it's not. Soorj is thick, syrupy, and high octane. The traditional Armenian coffee, served in demitasse cups, is thrice-boiled. It produces a lovely froth (and almost always boils over when I make it at home). Ordinary American coffee won't do as the raw material. You need the pulverized Armenian type—finer than espresso grind— combined with equal amounts of sugar. A small pot will do, but it's best to boil it in a jezveh, a tiny long-handled pitcher.

Here's a recipe based on Rachel Hogrogian's The Armenian Cookbook: *Mix six teaspoons of Armenian coffee, six teaspoons of sugar, and six demitasse cups of water in a jezveh or small pot. Stir to combine. Over moderate heat, bring the coffee to a boil three times. Watch it carefully so that each time you turn the heat up, you can remove the pot from the burner before it boils over. (This is not a recipe for the easily distracted.) After the third boiling, scoop off the foam and divide it among three demitasse cups. Pour in the coffee. The foam will rise to the top.*

turnips, to slivers of mango? If not for the bright labels, you might think you were in a nineteenth-century botany lab.

Massis's syrups are spectacular—tamarind, grenadine, rose, and *jallab* from Lebanon. Jallab—a grape, fig, and mystery-fruit concoction—is mixed with water and sipped as a cooling beverage. The shelves of spices look like an autumn landscape: brick red (pepper), mauve (sumac), gold (cumin), pale green (oregano), deep green (dill). Henna is on hand, and *lebny* (yogurt cheese) with oil and mint in jars. Massis stocks a variety of cheeses, too: *manjouri, mizetra* (for grating), Egyptian *roomi,* and a spicy version of *kasseri,* a hard Greek cheese with black pepper.

At the bakery counter you can buy lamejunes, baked fresh daily, and choose from a variety of pastries. I confess to sometimes making a meal of these. I brew a pot of espresso or Armenian coffee, eat two or three pastries, a vitamin pill, and a fresh orange, secure in the knowledge I have fulfilled my MDR of pleasure, caffeine, sugar, and citrus. Suit yourself: buttery mamouls, syrupy *paklava*, custardy *gurayba*, and the festive, bird's-nest-looking *kataifa*. For those with European tastes, napoleons, *baba au rhum*, and assorted French pastries fill out the pastry case. Nearby, to finish you off, are pistachio candies, luscious nougats, and gift boxes of Lindt and Perugina chocolates.

Massis's staff is pleasant, polite, and informative. In this store you feel more like you're in a grocery rather than a village market; it would be a faux pas to stare at someone's shopping list, which seems permissible at Sevan.

Take a turn down Elton Avenue to see one of the community's many churches. **St. Stephen's Armenian Apostolic Church,** 38 Elton Avenue, is a sprawling "modern Byzantine" building in maize-colored brick with a handsome entryway: a set of oaken doors, carved with a floral motif, beneath a marble arch.

When you enter **Arax,** 585 Mt. Auburn Street, (617) 924–3399, you may feel you are stepping into a cornucopia (the first out-of-body experience that has ever appealed to me). This is the most eye-catching, spirited grocery—a Middle Eastern general store—with produce, fresh cheeses, grains, breads, elaborate pastries, an extensive selection of appetizers and prepared foods, and even some furniture and decorative arts. How many places are there where you can find inlaid, wooden backgammon boards displayed above the spices and soaps (try the lavender and magnolia, great bargains), along with water pipes? Arax has the feeling of a bustling household. It's run by a

Armenian-style groceries and artifacts intermingle at Arax.

husband-and-wife team—she was born in Lebanon, he in Syria—and has several longtime employees. It also has little Oriental rugs in certain narrow aisles, loofahs (dried sponges) the height of small children, and a corner nook with skewers, diminutive Armenian coffee cups, and bric-a-brac.

Arax may not have as much produce as Kay's, but it has more exotic produce, more pleasingly displayed. It isn't a bakery, like Sevan or Massis, but does carry every imaginable bread and pastry, and I like the way the sweets are presented on big metal trays, allowing you to help yourself. (Yes, I am the annoying, heretofore anonymous customer who takes the corners of the sugar-steeped farina cake and only the most golden, frizzy-crusted *kataifi*.)

Armenian Cuisine

In Armenian homes you will find more exotic fare, but in Armenian-American restaurants, the choices run to relatively familiar Middle Eastern offerings, albeit with particular attention to the freshness of the vegetables, the quality of the oil, and the subtlety of the spicing. Expect aromatic appetizers that combine tahini (sesame paste) with mashed vegetables such as eggplant, or legumes such as chickpeas, served with pita bread. Entrees range from shish kebabs (lamb or beef grilled on skewers), to stuffed grape leaves, to patlijan karni yarek *(baked stuffed eggplant), generally served with pilaf (rice cooked with broth), and a Middle Eastern salad: lettuce, tomatoes, onions, and olives with an oil-and-vinegar dressing.*

If you're lucky, you may find a special dish on the menu—in autumn something featuring pumpkin. Though we think of pumpkin as typically American, and associate it with Halloween, the comely squash is grown all over the Caucasus.

Madzoon, *Armenian yogurt, is as different from supermarket yogurt as grape juice is from wine. Made with whole milk and cream, madzoon has a piquant, refreshing taste and rich, buttery consistency. Stir in a bit of honey, and you'll have a scrumptious, healthful dessert. Dilute with equal parts of ice water, and you'll have tan, a refreshing buttermilk-like drink. Madzoon is also used to make appetizers such as jajukh, a cucumber and mint side dish, and* madzoonov spanakh, *a cold spinach salad.*

Armenian desserts range from syrup-lapped pastries such as pahklava *(similar to the Greek baklava) and* bourma *(a rolled, strudel-like item with nut filling), to* gatnabour *(rich rice pudding), to* mamouls *(elegant, round, nut-filled cookies).*

S UGGESTED 🍽 R ESTAURANTS

Once Sepal was a spartan corner takeout on Mt. Auburn Street, though known far and wide for its ambrosial falafel and nourishing, well-priced soups, including the fortifying red lentil and silky, rich butternut. Now **Sepal ($–$$),** 7 Nichols Avenue, (617) 924–5753, has become a true restaurant. Nichols Avenue is off Bigelow Avenue, which runs off Mt. Auburn; outbound from Cambridge, take a left at Town Diner.

Sepal's tradition of fine falafel continues. The ground chickpea balls are crunchy on the outside, spicy and yielding on the inside, and a surprising green color because of all the parsley. In addition to a variety of falafel and Middle Eastern platters, Sepal serves tender lamb entrees, charbroiled chicken and beef, and an array of excellent vegetarian entrees. Several—grape leaves, *mujadara* (lentils with brown rice), *fatoush* (a minty green salad with toasted Syrian-bread croutons)—are to be expected. Others are exceptional and exceptionally good. Sepal's goulash is a baked vegetable stew of eggplant, carrots, tomatoes, chickpeas, and Spanish onions, served with brown rice. *Maklouba,* which means upside down, is a tofu rendering of a traditional dish: tofu chunks are layered over golden cauliflower, eggplant, and rice in a crock, baked, then turned upside down and served with Armenian tomato and red onion salad.

Uncommon Grounds ($), 575 Mt. Auburn Street, (617) 924–9625, is a cozy but hip cafe and coffee bar that opens at 6:00 A.M., just the thing to fortify birders who've watched warblers at the Mount Auburn Cemetery. Morning fare features three-egg omelette rollups, including a Greek one with feta cheese and tomatoes. Lunch choices range from burgers and tuna melts to veggie burgers and salads. Good coffee, too.

Pastry Mysteries Revealed

In most instances you can identify the foods found in Little Armenia. On menus the appetizers and entrees are described in English. In take-out places, the edibles are packed in transparent containers. But the breads, pastries, and candies in bakeries and groceries can seem mysterious. A yeast dough pocket might contain meat, spinach, or cheese—who knows? A pale chunk masquerading as cheese could actually be halvah, the sesame-seed candy cut from a block. A sesame cracker could be the size of a Ritz cracker or bigger than a vinyl record. Here's a little help:

boerag: *pastry with a filling*

bourma: *sweet pastry made of strudel-like layers enfolding chopped nuts and syrup*

choreg: *slightly sweet soft roll, perfect for serving with coffee; looks like a little bun*

jevesli: *walnut-stuffed cookies*

kadayif: *wonderful-looking pastry of shredded dough with walnut and cinnamon filling; looks like a miniature bird's nest*

khourabua: *Armenian shortbread*

Town Diner ($), 627 Mt. Auburn Street, (617) WA 6–8400, has gone hip. Taken over by new young owners, the corner landmark now has a cozy-but-cool retro look, with several menu updates. Some—an offering of a soy milk shake, in addition to the regular—are alarming to the regulars. But the friendly oldies—from western omelettes to

lavash: *savory flat bread, often sprinkled with sesame seeds; can be scored, cracker size, in a box, or can be vintage record size, wrapped in paper; may need to bake briefly to crispen*

mamoul: *buttery cookie brushed with confectionery sugar, a kind of Armenian madeleine, and more memorable*

pideh or pita: *round, flat "pocket" bread; good for stuffing as a sandwich or tearing and dipping into appetizer spreads; can be regular, with or without sesame seeds, or whole wheat*

revani: *elegant cake made of farina, crushed walnuts, and butter, lapped with syrup, and cut into diamond shapes*

rechel: *"fruit preserve" made with pumpkin, lemon, lime, and cinnamon; very good on a toasted sesame bagel with cream cheese*

simit: *semisweet breakfast cookies, generally in S shapes*

ungouyzov khumoreghen: *walnut-and-raisin-filled pastry; lovely with tea and lemon*

As the Armenian shopkeepers say (in English with Armenian hospitality), "Enjoy it!"

flapjacks and French toast—remain on the menu and are better prepared. Veggie items dot the new menu as well, and, in a nice bow to the neighborhood, Town Diner presents a Middle Eastern Sampler plate with traditional appetizer salads, feta cheese, yogurt, olives, and pita.

Armenian pastries go best with soorj—
thick, aromatic Armenian coffee.

Iggy's ($), 205 Arlington Street, (617) 924–0949, is one of the finest artisan bakers in New England. Their crusty, hearth-baked loaves, ficelles, and focaccia (plus bagels, baguettes, buns, and rolls, notably the cranberry and pecan rolls), made from mainly organic ingredients, are sold by specialty markets and served in fancy restaurants. One of just two retail outlets, Iggy's is located on a short street, almost an alleyway, off Arlington Street in Watertown. At lunchtime this little outlet makes up pizza and elegant sandwiches, including smoked salmon and the occasional prized beet and goat cheese with fresh greens. From Mt. Auburn Street, just past the tan deco building (Tufts Health Plan), take a left and be alert for a small sign on the left. Uncustomary crust will reward you.

Hyde Square, Jamaica Plain

Latin Beat

*J*amaica Plain, nicknamed JP, has at least four faces.

On sultry summer nights when girls in short-shorts and halter tops are zipping in and out of Cuban sandwich places, and radios are blasting from cruising cars, and window boxes on apartments and three-deckers overflow with red geraniums, zinnias, and petunias, it's a hot town. It's the Hyde Square area, the barrio.

On leafy Pond Street, off the curving, arboreal Jamaicaway, residents walk their friendly, groomed dogs. They mow their lawns, sweep their walks, and spruce up fading paint on the gingerbread trim of Victorian houses. It's pleasant, somewhat exclusive, almost suburban.

In the "village" part of JP, the most central, commercial part of Centre Street, folks line up at the better restaurants, including local fave, Centre Street Cafe. Some diners are in their late twenties and could be older students (possibly medical students, as JP is near Boston's Longwood medical complex), and some are undoubtedly artists (the neighborhood is thick with writers and musicians). Some are middle-aged professionals who live in the nicer local houses. A few are lesbians, one of whom is having a birthday dinner with her mom. There's a double date, too: kids in their early twenties, possibly a first date. You could be in one of those old New England towns where a contemporary college culture overlays that of a former mill town.

A fourth JP is for poets and nature lovers. Beyond the retail area and the blocks of wood-frame houses and stucco apartment buildings, a sylvan, light-dappled world awaits. Jamaica Plain is the home of the 265-acre Arnold Arboretum, an internationally known "museum of living plants," operated by Harvard University on land leased (for $1.00 a year) from the city of Boston. In this extensive preserve—tens of thousands of trees, shrubs, and ornamentals; herbaceous beds;

small ponds; and a house of historic bonsai—all JP's cultures come together (see "Olmsted's Green Shadow"). All are walking.

Our focus is on Hyde Square along lower Centre Street, a lively Latino neighborhood of bodegas, bakeries, and old houses that testify to JP's multicultural past and present.

• • • *History* • • •

During the seventeenth century, sleepy Jamaica Plain was part of Roxbury. In 1874 it became part of Boston, but well into the late nineteenth century—long after Boston had become a true city—JP continued its agrarian ways. The area, dotted with springs, ponds, and brooks, seemed favored by nature. Its soil was light and easily cultivated.

Wealthy families built weekend houses and summer villas in this charmed countryside 4 miles from Boston. Some of these residences remain, especcially those opposite Jamaica Pond and along the

How to Get There

By public transportation from Copley Square take the Number 39 bus, which runs along South Huntington Avenue and Centre Street. Or take the MBTA Orange Line subway; get off at Jackson Square or Green Street. Walk toward Centre Street. Check the numbers once you're there to ensure you're in the 300 block of Centre Street. By car follow the Riverway (carefully—it's narrow) toward the Arboretum, and take a left at the light at Perkins Street.

Arborway. The house that once belonged to Mayor James Michael Curley, number 350 The Jamaicaway, is a proper Georgian Revival with a notable departure: the wooden shutters have jaunty Irish shamrock cutouts.

As land parcels were developed for city workers, and public transportation connected JP to Boston, the community became a suburb. By 1826 you could board an hourly Boston-bound bus; in 1834 the Boston and Providence Railroad was extended through town. Grand estates that had belonged to families for generations were broken up for small-scale development, including Victorian houses that have been divided into condominiums today.

The area near Jamaica Pond is Jamaica Plain's oldest neighborhood. In 1760 its spiffy Loring-Greenough House was built for a British naval officer. During the Revolutionary War the house was used as a hospital by the patriots. The Georgian-style mansion still stands, painted buttermilk yellow, with dark-green shutters, and flanked by towering beech and horse chestnut trees. Hyde Square was another colonial outpost. Centre Street and Day Street, its spines, are among the oldest streets in town.

A mix of immigrants arrived in JP during the nineteenth century: Irish, Italian, German, and Greek families, each of whom had their own churches and parish schools. As JP was a beer-brewing center, many of the German immigrants found a familiar trade. During the last several decades, JP—especially the Hyde Square area—has become home to new immigrants from the Dominican Republic, El Salvador, Puerto Rico, and Brazil.

The appearance of lower Centre Street, its mix of residential and commercial, is much the same as it's been for a century, and the families of today's workers live in the homes built for workers during the nineteenth century. People with downtown jobs catch the T at depots with hidden 150-year-old histories. The Orange Line follows a path beneath Washington Street, one of the city's oldest thoroughfares; its stops at Stonybrook and Green Street are at old railroad depots.

On weekends families visit the Arnold Arboretum and Jamaica Pond, unwinding from their labors, as was the hope of Frederick Law Olmsted, the great landscape architect. Olmsted, whose home office was just over the Brookline boundary, could not have predicted the advent of Cuban pork sandwiches—though being a man who valued adventure and enjoyed food, he would have relished the chance to try one.

Estrella Bakery and its murals celebrate cake making.

... *A Walking Tour* ...

No big sign reading HYDE SQUARE HERE! welcomes you to the neighborhood. Located on the lower portion of Centre Street behind Angell Memorial, the veterinary hospital, Hyde Square is where Perkins and Centre Streets intersect. Perkins runs off the Jamaicaway; Centre is JP's Main Street.

The CVS at the corner of Centre and Moraine Streets is on Hyde Square's edge, as are the tracks of the Orange Line at the other end (Jackson Square). In between: pork sandwiches, pizzas, enchiladas; soul, ska, salsa; sexy-silky men's shirts, flouncy children's clothing, wedding gowns so billowy they look like floats at hometown parades.

Start your tour at the corner of Centre and Paul Gore Streets. Even if you're timid and pepper-shy, at least look in the window of **El Oriental de Cuba,** 416 Centre Street, (617) 524–6464, and see the Latino families and Anglo converts enjoying Cuban sandwiches. On hot summer nights there are traffic jams here as long sedans double-park to pick up takeout.

If you walk several blocks down Paul Gore Street, you'll reach **Spontaneous Celebrations,** 45 Danforth Street, which crosses Paul Gore Street; (617) 524–6373. Local groups rent space in the funky old house for rehearsals, meetings, dances, and workshops; classes in Afro-Cuban dance, capoeria (a Brazilian martial art and dance form), samba, merengue (which originated in the Dominican Republic), and yoga are on the menu.

As you walk back along Paul Gore to Centre, check out two thriving **community gardens** that showcase "domestic" and "imported" vegetables, testifying to the heritages of local gardeners. On your left, as you approach the corner of Paul Gore and Beecher Streets, a well-established garden has floral borders and an adjacent

Hyde Square, Jamaica Plain

Parker Hill Playground

HEATH STREET

Olmsted Park

PERKINS STREET

JAMAICAWAY

S. HUNTINGTON AVE.

DAY ST.

CREIGHTON ST.

CENTRE STREET

BICKFORD ST.

COLUMBUS AVENUE

MORAINE ST.

SHERIDAN ST.

FORBES ST.

WYMAN ST.

MOZART ST.

CHESTNUT AVE.

LAMARTINE STREET

DIMOCK ST.

PAUL GORE STREET

BOYLSTON

PETER ST.

BEECHER

STREET

ATHERTON ST.

SCHOOL ST.

28

Jamaica Pond

LOCHSTEAD AVE.

JAMAICAWAY

BEAUFORT

GOODRICH RD.

POND ST.

CENTRE STREET

SPRING PARK AVE.

ROCKVIEW ST.

CHESTNUT AVENUE

LAMARTINE STREET

ARMORY STREET

ELIOT

BURROUGHS ST.

STREET

CENTRE STREET

SEAVERNS

ALVESTON PL.

GREEN STREET

SEAVERNS AVE.

BROOKSIDE AVE.

WASHINGTON

STREET

GLEN ROAD

WALNUT AVE.

GREENOUGH AVE.

SEDGWICK ST.

SOUTH STREET

CHILD ST.

ARBORWAY

203

Arnold Arboretum

ARBORWAY

FOREST HILLS STREET

Franklin Park

JEWISH WAR VETERANS

N

neighborhood dog run that regulars have "furnished" with funky tables and chairs. As you return to Centre Street, a handsome garden at 60 Paul Gore Street is on a promontory, reminiscent of terraced farming in the Mediterranean.

Back on Centre, **Sorella's** (see "Suggested Restaurants"), was once Brown's, a German institution: the deli with the serious bratwurst, liverwurst, salami, and rye bread "like a weapon" (so crusty that if you hit someone with it, you'd knock them out). Now the spot has become another local hangout, a hip luncheonette and breakfast place that serves old-timers, newcomers, young doctors and musicians, musician-doctors, one and all. The selections are panethnic, from salsa omelettes, to stir-fries, to eggs scrambled with lox.

If you're interested in architecture and a little social history, take a right on **Sheridan Street.** Most of these houses were part of a middle-class development, a group of similar houses erected during the 1860s and 1870s. If not for the cars parked outside and the TV antennas, these houses would look much as they did when they were built. Sheridan Street is still a multicultural, middle-class neighborhood. Starting at the turn of the twentieth century, number 43 was the longtime home of Maude Cuney Hare (1874–1936), a pioneering African-American musician, teacher, and author. Hare studied piano at the New England Conservatory of Music, became a member of the local black intelligentsia, and wrote *Negro Musicians and Their Music*, a study of the African and Caribbean influences on black American music. The modest house has a charming, gingerbread-trimmed appearance. During the early part of the twentieth century, it probably overflowed with good music, good talk, and good cooking.

A few of the houses on the block are imposing, notably number 14, a Queen Anne Victorian built by a German-American architect for Adam Mock, who worked in the liquor business.

Now return to Centre Street.

A&M Jewelry Repair, 368A Centre Street, incorporates a vestige of colonial Boston. Michael Reiskind, a founder of the Jamaica Plain Historical Society and still a volunteer guide, delights in calling attention to an ancient engraved granite milestone built into the store's foundation. "B: 4," it reads, meaning that it marks a distance of 4 miles from Boston. The milestones were erected in 1734 by Paul Dudley, Esq. of the Dudley family, associated with Roxbury's Dudley Square. One mile away, natch, in the area of the **Soldier's Monument** and **Loring-Greenough House,** 12 South Street, another mile marker appears in the low wall around the monument. Finding these subtle sorts of things makes for the best kind of urban scavenger hunt.

Rocky's Barberia, 366 Centre Street, (617) 524–3420, is a real barbershop, not a fancy salon—with a pole, an open door, and a window filled with prickly cacti and flowering plants. The amiable proprietor does all types of hair and all kinds of cuts, from those of almost bald men to the edgy urban look of bladelike top and close-cropped sides.

Look's Beauty Salon, 364 Centre Street, is unremarkable in appearance, but it has ethnic and historical karma. In 1934 this little storefront was the Economy Grocery Store, founded by Sidney and Joseph Rabinowitz. This grew into a small chain of groceries, pioneers in the development of neighborhood-based variety markets, and became the Stop & Shop Company. Today's philanthropic Rabb family descended from the intrepid Rabinowitz founders. Poetically (if the presence of a supermarket can be poetic), a monster Stop & Shop is just down the street.

Whoa! Check out **Vasallo's Men's Fashions,** 362 Centre Street, (617) 522–0005. No button-down-collar oxford cloth shirts here, but flowing, silky numbers with pulsating tigers, aloha shirts with Asian

Rocky's Barberia keeps the guys and the plants lookin' good.

motifs, and sportswear with printed mottoes. Next door is an associated women's specialty shop with a cavalcade of sexy evening wear: black gowns with see-through midriffs, skin-tight yellow spandex cocktail dresses, and clingy red "active wear."

This whole neighborhood seems madly in love with children. When occasions permit, parents dress up their little ones. **Del Valles,** 360 Centre Street, (617) 522–0885, carries cribs, bassinets, and strollers, but more importantly, fancy garments and accessories. If you're crazy about sailor suits, you'll find them for infants and toddlers, along with dressy suits for little boys and tiny, flashy, excellent footwear, including gold lamé sandals, which I retroactively desire. My life would have been completely different if I'd had these instead of sensible Buster Browns.

Hyde Square kids look very cool in Del Valles's beachwear, especially the colorful caps with matching sunglasses. The bassinet that's usually in the window—tiers of lace and cascades of pale-green ribbon—must dazzle many a first-time grandparent.

Look for a corner store with a festive red-and-yellow sign. **Pimental Market,** at the corner of Wyman Street, is orderly, immaculate, and crammed with merchandise. When I dropped by one torrid summer day, Pimental had the atmosphere of a Caribbean grocery. A shipment of plantains had just arrived. Neighbors were chatting in the entryway. The owner's brown-skinned little boy was sitting (and occasionally swiveling) on the wooden counter next to the cash register, flamboyantly cracking a wad of avocado-green bubble gum. Every time his mother rang up a sale, he punctuated the sound of the cash drawer with a staccato smack of a bursting bubble. A little girl, about three, dressed in a pinafore with matching lace-trimmed socks, was trying to stock the shelves with small tins of *salsa de tomate*. The narrow store has long aisles of Goya-brand staples, including a botanical glossary of tinned beans, coconut milk, honey-with-comb, and a product new to me: hefty jars of *cajul en alimbar*, cashews in syrup from the Dominican Republic.

Modest, wood-frame **United Baptist Church,** 322 Centre Street, (617) 522–7293, is a gathering place for many neighborhood residents, including congregants who live at nearby Bromley Heath public housing. It's right next to **Mozart Park,** Centre and Mozart Streets, a small, well-used city of Boston park with a popular playground—swings, sandlot, and benches.

Olmsted's Green Shadow

The great American landscape architect, Frederick Law Olmsted, who was largely responsible for inventing his profession, did much of his best work in Jamaica Plain. As part of his commission for the Boston Parks Department, he designed a series of contiguous green spaces that stretched from the Back Bay Fens all the way to Franklin Park. The project began with the preexisting Boston Common, Public Garden, and Commonwealth Avenue Mall and continued with the sections Olmsted and his firm designed: Olmsted Park, Jamaica Pond, the Arnold Arboretum, and Franklin Park. These 7 miles of open space curving along riverways and roads became known as the Emerald Necklace.

Most of the land area of the parks Olmsted designed is in Jamaica Plain. All of it is free and open to the public. Each place is different.

Olmsted Park *on the Jamaicaway (with an access at the corner of Perkins Street)—the greensward you may glimpse as you drive along the Riverway heading to the Arboretum—is one of the lesser-known, lesser-trod parks. Time expands here, as the park's woods and ponds have a secluded, naturalistic, secretive quality.*

Jamaica Pond, *a natural kettle hole formed by a prehistoric glacier, was once a source for Boston's drinking water and a site for commercial ice harvesting. It was acquired by the city of Boston in*

Franklin's C. D., 314 Centre Street, (617) 522–9745, specializes in Latin music, which pours onto the street—tunes from the Dominican Republic, Puerto Rico, El Salvador, Guatemala, Mexico, and Colombia. In winter, when the door is shut tight, the sounds of salsa and pleña still permeate.

1892, and Olmsted incorporated it into the park system. A boathouse that still stands was built in 1910. You can rent rowboats and sailboats for a nominal fee and make your way out to a miniature island inhabited by waterfowl, including stalking cormorants.

The 265-acre **Arnold Arboretum** is the major site in the United States for the scientific study of woody plants. It's also the major site for outdoor recreation in Jamaica Plain. Once it was all farmland, part of the local Bussey family estate. They gave their land to the Arboretum (the lilac and forsythia paths are named for the Bussey family), which was planned by Olmsted and Charles Sprague Sargent, founding director of the Arb.

Olmsted designed **Franklin Park** to give us a break, and it still does. Horrified by the lives led by many factory workers and their families, and inspired by the English idea of the country park, Olmsted and his firm created a 500-acre refuge that combined natural scenery with playing fields, promenades, and bridle paths. Though shabby in places, it's still considered the jewel in the Emerald Necklace, the culmination of many Olmstedian ideas. Here you'll find mature trees and shrubs, venerable stone structures—bridges, arches, steps—and members of every ethnic group enjoying the outdoors. Golfers from all over Boston use its meadowlike public course, and the park is home to the Franklin Park Zoo, with its apes, birds, and magical house of butterflies.

If you continue to the end of Centre, you'll find a terrific fruit and vegetable stand, **Cristal Fruit,** near the corner of Centre and Bickford Streets, across from Bromley Heath. Revealing myself as a total fruit nerd, abandoning any remaining shreds of ego, I now visit this stand with a botanical guidebook. Sugarcane is instantly recognizable. It looks like trunks of bamboo. All kinds of mangos and papayas I also get, but I need help when it comes to water coconuts and impregnable-looking rhizomes.

This stand is a gathering place. Many of its customers are older island ladies who know how to prepare the fruits and vegetables. Unlike the men who run the stand, they speak English. In summer some of these women wear elegant flowered cotton dresses, straw hats with bands of fabric, decorative high-heeled sandals, and rose-pink lipstick. They look beautiful amid the tropical fruit.

Across the street a Super Stop & Shop carries a great many Latin-style groceries. More important, **Skippy White's,** 315 Centre Street, (617) 524–4500, a trove of secondhand LPs, CDs, tapes, and music videos, is in the same shopping center. (*The* Skippy White is the host of a long-running radio show, *Roots of Rhythm and Blues,* on WUMD 91.9 FM Saturday nights from 9:00 P.M. to midnight.) This Skippy's, a smaller version of the Central Square, Cambridge store, carries a larger proportion of gospel and soul, and an ever-changing mix of jazz, blues, and R&B.

This side of Centre Street isn't quite as rich as the other, but note the great views of the stores you've already visited, especially Pimental, in the first floor of a coral-pink house, and also Vasallo's— very suave. Then again, the window designers at **Sonia's Bridal Boutique,** 351 Centre Street, (617) 522–6961, need not apologize. One mannequin adorned with one bridal gown fills the entire window.

The grand doors at **Church of the Blessed Sacrament,** 365 Centre Street, (617) 522–0650, would more than accommodate the well-appointed bride. This show-stopping Italian Renaissance Revival church, originally erected for an Irish-American parish, is well worth a visit. Built in 1917 to replace a wooden church, the stately redbrick edifice has massive Ionic columns, an ornate arched door, and loads of terra-cotta trim. The building—its mass and rosy color—is an overwhelming sight. The first time I saw it, my foot unaccountably lifted off the brake of my car (aesthetic reverie?), and I nearly collided with a parked squad car. "Nice church," said the police officer. Inside Blessed Sacrament, stained-glass windows transform the light. Exterior decoration runs to murals of cherubs, pears, and grapes. Take a walk around the grounds, which encompass a rectory and a school.

Gentileza's Market, 371 Centre Street, (617) 524–4595, is another well-stocked Latino market. It has less character than Pimental (less crowded, and no toddlers stocking shelves), but it carries meats and cheeses, tortillas, and Dominican-style baked goods, including coconut cookies. Coconut is underused in gringo culture, though at least it's enshrined in Mounds bars.

Centre Boutique, 379A Centre Street, (617) 524–4839, a baby and children's clothing store, shows the tiniest tuxedos imaginable, sequined party frocks, and graceful communion dresses. I had completely forgotten about petticoats, which little girls actually wore when I was a child, until I saw these feminine little dresses in Centre Boutique's windows.

S U G G E S T E D 🍴 R E S T A U R A N T S

Centre Street runs through Hyde Square and the more central portion of Jamaica Plain (just a few blocks away), where restaurants are also located. As Hyde Square is Latino, so are most of its restaurants. In the village area, choices range from Indian, to Cambodian, to Korean. In between—at the Perkins Street–Centre Street wedge—are yuppie-hip eateries and a combo club-bowling alley.

HYDE SQUARE

Such a pleasant routine, taking a walk twice around Jamaica Pond, then heading down Perkins Street to land, just about, at **Sorella's ($)**, 388 Centre Street, (617) 524–2016. What a clever menu. If you're in a ritzy mood, you can order a lightly toasted sesame bagel with smoked salmon and all the trimmings: capers and a wedge of lemon. But if you're in a chow-down frame of stomach, platters of pancakes and waffles will soothe your hunger pangs. Some diners must have protein after walking; for them, it's Sorella's big omelettes. Lunch dishes are almost like dinner, except that Sorella's doesn't serve dinner (yet). You can choose among dozens of sandwiches, including Mickey's Special: grilled boneless chicken, portabella mushrooms, houmos, roasted red peppers, and alfalfa sprouts. Specialty entrees include stir-fries, Moroccan chicken, and home-made polenta. This is a cozy, down-to-earth, neighborhood place—cool but not slick.

Portions at **El Oriental de Cuba ($–$$)**, 416 Centre Street, (617) 524–6464, are scary: heaping platters of meat (lots of pork, but also beef, chicken, and fish), beans, rice, salad, fried plantains, and yuca, a toothsome and nourishing root vegetable. This is Cuban, Puerto Rican, and Dominican comfort food, and so to truly satisfy, the plate must be full, like at home. Entrees range from Cuban steak fried with onions and seasoned with lime, to *ropa vieja* (Spanish for old clothes). The beef in the latter dish is venerable, having simmered for hours in a garlicky red sauce with green and red peppers. Those accustomed to minimeals may feel like keeling over after one of El Oriental's stick-to-the-ribs platters, but if you can manage an additional refreshment, try a *batido*, a tropical milk shake without ice cream. Guava, mango, papaya—fine flavors to sip with a slow-simmered stew.

You can have Cuban, Puerto Rican, and Dominican homefood at **Miami Restaurant ($)**, 381 Centre Street, (617) 522–4644, or stick to American fare. Grab one of the little tables or have your sandwiches, sides, and plates packed to go. If you're not a meat-eater, Miami is probably not the place for you. In addition to the zingy Cuban sandwiches (ham, cheese, pickles, onions, lettuce, tomatoes, and mayo, pressed to become a new entity), you'll find beefsteak, pork chops, liver plates, fried fish, and chicken rinds. House specialties feature pungent, garlicy stews made with tail, tripe, or shrimp. The restaurant's array of tropical fruit shakes would make a luscious still life in oils—picture a rainbow of tall frosty glasses in apricot, rose, and garnet hues. The flavors of these shakes range from guava, to custard apple, to passion fruit and papaya, almost a dozen in all. You can also order Cuban coffee, sugarcane juice, and a drink called Dying in Your Sleep.

La Pupusa Guanaca ($), 378 Centre Street, (617) 524–4900, right across from Miami, is another small, mainly take-out place, also emphasizing home cooking, but in this case, Salvadoran fare. A *pupusa* is almost as much fun to say ("poo-POO-sa") as it is to eat. Imagine a chubby corn tortilla (with the gravitational heft of a potato latke rather than a crepe) stuffed with cheese, beans, or pork, then fried till a little crusty, and layered with pickled cabbage and chile red sauce. This bright, immaculate restaurant, the size of a kitchen, serves pork, cheese, and other renditions of pupusas, burritos, enchiladas, and tostadas, and the protein-packed *mondongo:* tripe soup with yuca, plantains, corn, and cow's feet. To drift into a happy state, order the restaurant's pineapple upside-down cake with a cup of hearty Cuban coffee. Sit in one of the four booths or, better still, at a counter that's been mounted at the corner window.

Give Us This Day Our Daily Tortilla

Do we adequately appreciate tortillas? They've been described as Mexican bread, but that's like describing cheese as dried milk.

Tortillas, thin griddle cakes, are the signature daily dish of corn-producing cultures. Historically, in these societies, time (the calendar), tools, and tasks have all been organized around the planting, growing, harvesting, drying, grinding, milling, and cooking of corn. In Latin America the corn is generally dried and ground into corn-meal. The meal—rich in B vitamins and a complementary protein when combined with beans—is mixed with lime and pounded into cakes. These are baked or grilled.

The resulting tortillas are elemental food, culinary clay that can be sculpted into snacks and entrees or eaten plain.

Tortilla preparations: Place meat, beans, or cheese in a warm tortilla, roll it into a cylinder, and you've got yourself a taco. If you fry a tortilla until it's crisp, then stuff it, you've created a tostada. A stuffed, sauced, and baked tortilla transmutes into an enchilada. Finally, a deep-fried, golden-brown, stuffed tortilla becomes a quesadilla when it emerges from the fryer, a sort of deep-fried Mexican wonton.

Don't go to **Tacos El Charro ($–$$)**, 349 Centre Street, (617) 522–2578, when you have a headache. It's not the mariachi band (weekends only); it's the big black-and-white checkerboard pattern on the walls. It's meant to jazz up the place, but it suggests a close-up of a tiled bathroom floor in a surrealistic movie. While Tacos El Charro's decor is unsettling to some, the food is deeply satisfying, and the staff couldn't be friendlier. Tacos, tamales, tostadas, burritos, quesadillas, fajitas, enchiladas—all the traditional Mexican favorites are served; the platters are big and reasonably priced. This place is homey and fun. But wear sunglasses if you're SEN-sitive.

PERKINS-CENTRE STREET WEDGE

You have to be in the right mood for **Bella Luna ($–$$),** 405 Centre Street, (617) 524–6060, an up-tempo gourmet pizza place, where there can be a little too much attitude, but where the pizzas are outrageous, and the decor is bright and whimsical. The menu lists about thirty different kinds of pizza with over forty toppings. Bella Luna runs a carefree jazz brunch, which fits in just fine. (Next door, hipster club cum bowling alley **Milky Way Lounge & Lanes,** 403 Centre Street, 617–524–3740, dominates the wedge. Days of the week are devoted to musical genres—pop, punk, soul; karaoke on Tuesdays, Latin Dance on Friday nights.)

Around the corner, **Zon's ($–$$),** 2 Perkins Street, (617) 524–9767, is a small, dark hideaway with deftly turned plates—lobster gnocchi, rib-eye steak, well-prepared catch-of-the-day, and veggies. Zon's conscious but offhand-seeming decor captures a true JP style—casual and spare, funky-retro-elegant, romance with irony and restraint. Try the surrealistic chocolate cupcake for dessert—very Magritte and also chocolatey.

If you have kids, wander up to the **Boston Public Library, Connolly branch,** 433 Centre Street, (617) 522–1960, an activity trove for young people, especially—English and Spanish movies, storytelling in Spanish and other languages, and exhibits of local artists' work. The library's Jacobean-style interior has dark wood and glass pavilions dividing the children's and adult areas, and ceilings with ornate plaster moldings.

VILLAGE AREA

Call it ethnic-inspired rather than ethnic, **Centre Street Cafe ($–$$)**, 669 Centre Street, (617) 524–9217, is a neighborhood favorite—a small, friendly, narrow restaurant with an open kitchen and international, mainly vegetarian, cuisine that comes forth fast from this tiny kitchen and a small crew. For years another favorite, Five Seasons, was located here, and much of its hippie-veggie-laid-back ethos lingers in this humble space of well-matched flavors and mismatched chairs. The fare ranges from simple, well-prepared platters of broiled fish and crisp veggies to Centre Street's hallmarks: grain- and vegetable-intensive entrees that merge culinary cultures. The unlikely sounding Southwestern Stir Fry is a gutsy mix of vegetables in chili-lime butter, served over basmati rice and smoky black beans, sprinkled with a good grade of grated parmesan. Sesame Peanut Noodles combines Chinese noodles with peanut sauce and an array of Asian vegetables. With most of these vegetable mélanges, diners can add tofu, chicken, or shrimp for an additional fee. A fowl-of-the-day dish generally uses free-range chickens, and there's a pasta of the day, often a seafood-pasta combo.

Cambodian cuisine is rare in Boston, which is a pity judging from the flavorful entrees at modestly priced **Wonder Spice Cafe ($–$$)**, 697 Centre Street, (617) 522–0200. Cambodian food tastes similar to Thai cuisine, but with more robust use of traditional flavorings, such as lemongrass, and without being fiery-hot. Mango Curry de Legumes is sublime and can be ordered with chicken or shrimp. Garlic lovers will find a gustatory home at Wonder Spice.

Blame the meat-loving British for the prevalence of northern Indian restaurants in Anglo nations. "Southern India is strongly Hindu," notes *Boston Phoenix* food maven Robert Nadeau, and thus concocts more vegetarian food than the rest of India. Well, let's hear it for the spicy veggie cuisine of **Bukhara ($–$$),** 701 Centre Street, (617) 522–2195, with its atmospheric, embroidered wall hangings and brass statue of a Hindu deity with multiple arms and breasts (several more than usual). Nifty appetizers here, including Chat Papri, made with pastry and chickpeas, served with an ethereal yogurt-tamarind sauce and lovely *dosa,* giant stuffed crepes that you slice like a jelly roll. Many Indian foods new to me show up at Bukhara, including *uttapam,* a thick pancake made with rice and lentils, topped with tomatoes, onions, peppers, and fragrant fresh coriander.

Shopper's Tip

As you make your way down Centre Street for Village-area restaurants, check out two distinctive independent bookstores—**Rhythm And Muse,** 470 Centre Street, (617) 524–6622, and **Jamaicaway Books & Gifts,** 676 Centre Street, (617) 983–3204. **Pluto,** 603 Centre Street, (617) 522–0054, is a hip boutique with cards, toys, fashion accessories, and faux fifties home decor.

For bargains, local color, and to help AIDS patients and their families, visit **Boomerangs** ("You'll Come Back, Too"), 716 Centre Street, (617) 524–5120, a stylish thrift shop, with new and recycled fashions, furnishings, housewares, and a soupcon of books and CDs. **Harvest Co-op Market,** 57 South Street—the continuation of Centre Street—(617) 524–1667, is a terrific natural foods cum gourmet store (with takeout, wine, farmstead cheeses, and real bread), a sister of the Central Square, Cambridge, co-op.

South End

ETHNIC ECHOES AND VICTORIAN PANACHE

The South End is like no other neighborhood in Boston, and like no other enclave described in this guide. It is no longer an ethnic neighborhood in the true sense. For sure, some of the best ethnic restaurants in the city line Tremont Street, Columbus Avenue, and Shawmut Avenue: Thai, Korean, Latin, French, Italian, Ethiopian. But the link between the local population and the cuisine of these eateries is largely absent. Still, the neighborhood is so appealing—its cosmopolitan blend of people, architecture, and English-style squares, and its lively art scene—that I am including it, making a baker's dozen Boston neighborhoods.

My somewhat testy preamble is not to suggest that the South End is devoid of multiethnic vitality. The alert wanderer will note many vestiges of earlier ethnic communities, as well as the presence of some current communities: African-American, Puerto Rican, Asian. But there's a difference between main streets dominated by stylish, expensive, multiethnic restaurants in the service of cosmopolitan diners, and less-gentrified streets of ethnic groceries, bakeries, and restaurants that belong to the ethnic residents of the community and are patronized by them.

If you aren't familiar with the South End, you'll be amazed. This is the largest preserved Victorian neighborhood in the United States. It fell on hard times and was largely abandoned by developers during most of the twentieth century, waiting in amber until the boom of the last few decades. A friend of mine likes to quote his canny, cigar-smoking Jewish grandfather, a man who'd had his share of ups and downs. "Sonny boy, every knock is a boost," he'd say. In real estate it can take generations for a boost to raise values. But the knocks of urban decay and economic inertia preserved the South End, saving it

How to Get There

By public transportation take the Orange Line MBTA to
Back Bay Station; walk down Dartmouth or Clarendon to
Columbus Avenue. The new Silver Line buses run along Washington
Street from Downtown Crossing to Dudley Square, Roxbury. By car
follow Storrow Drive to the Copley Square exit, then take
Clarendon Street through Back Bay to Columbus Avenue or
Route 93 south to the East Berkeley Street exit.

from Boston's "urban renewal" and the fate of the old West End,
razed during the 1960s to create Government Center.

Approach the South End from the Back Bay, the land of glitzy
Copley Place—Tiffany's, Neiman Marcus, Louis Vuitton—and the
scene seems to change energy bands. It quiets down and becomes more
residential, with bowfront brownstones, period streetlights, Edwardian
squares. Any skyscraper you can still see is somewhere else.

• • • History • • •

Imagine the South End as a ribbon of land, the Neck, connecting
downtown Boston with Roxbury. During the Colonial Era, the Neck—
the entrance to Boston, complete with toll-taker—was near today's
intersection of Washington and East Berkeley (formerly Dover)
Streets, where the peninsula of Boston was just 100 feet wide and
obscured at high tide. Washington Street, once Orange Street, was the

Neck's first major street. Murky water lapped at its sides. Then enterprising locals began filling in the area. By the 1830s there was sufficient landfill to allow the laying of three more streets, all parallel to Washington: Tremont Street, Shawmut Avenue, and Harrison Avenue.

Like all vintage neighborhoods that've been left alone, the South End tells its story through architecture. As the Neck was broadened and plumped, developers began to build elegant English-style housing, brownstones surrounding groomed rectilinear gardens. These are stately, eloquent designs, models of communal yet private urban life. Throughout the South End, the pattern was repeated—redbrick row houses, often with bowfronts, fancy balustrades, and twirling cast-iron fences.

In addition to its residences, the community became a place for the hospitals constructed to serve the growing population of Boston: Boston City Hospital, Massachusetts Homeopathic Hospital, and the Boston University School of Medicine were all in place by 1875.

Though this admirable urban district was completed well before the Back Bay, the South End never reached the prominence of its fashionable neighbor, also constructed on landfill. Following the financial panic of 1873, there was little additional development. The neighborhood became a region of rooming houses and immigrant ghettos. Local African Americans who lived on the western slope of Beacon Hill moved here, along with immigrants from Ireland, Germany, the Middle East (Syria, Lebanon, Armenia), Italy, and Greece.

By the 1960s the area was one of the shabbiest in Boston. But the deteriorated brownstones still stood, and the English-style street plan remained intact. Starting in the late 1960s and 1970s, urban homesteaders—many of them college-educated young people who wanted to make a stake in the city—started to buy the old row houses. Slowly, the South End came around. Attracted by its faded glamour,

Some of Boston's grandest doors are on Columbus Avenue.

Protest Makes Perfect

*Two symbols of today's South End are almost directly across from the MBTA Orange Line Back Bay Station. A modern apartment building doesn't usually merit attention, but in Boston, where every building seems to have a story—and often one associated with history—**Tent City**, 130 Dartmouth Street, tells a tale. This is a residence built by protest and cohesion, as well as bricks and mortar, and is symbolic of the persistent community activism that typifies the South End. The name of the complex commemorates a 1968 demonstration by community residents, many of them low-income, to protest the lack of affordable housing in the increasingly gentrified South End. Under pressure, a site was donated for affordable housing, creating a precedent for future linkage projects, and permitting funds to be siphoned from lucrative development deals to serve community needs. Tent City, designed by the Boston firm Goody, Clancy & Associates, took twenty years of community struggle and agitation to materialize. But in 1988 the 269-unit mixed-income complex went up—next door to Neiman Marcus. Twenty-five percent of the*

low rents, and the possibilities for creating a new kind of neighborhood, artists and members of the gay community moved in. They used sweat equity as capital and creativity for decor. Civic pride developed. The neighborhood made demands on city services. And community organizers couldn't have asked for a better villain than the threat of an interstate, which would have sliced through Boston if not for their vociferous and ultimately effective opposition.

Today, the most obvious parts of the South End are the upscale restaurants and fashionable bistros, and gutted, rehabbed condos *units are reserved for low-income people. As Tent City stretches from the Back Bay to the South End, its mass of brick steps down from twelve stories to four stories, blending into Columbus Avenue.*

Tent City is a residence built by protest; **Southwest Corridor Park** *(starts adjacent to Tent City) is a 4½-mile-long linear park fueled by the same juice. During the late 1960s a 4-mile-long swath—from the Back Bay, through the South End and Roxbury, to Jamaica Plain—was cleared for a new interstate. Following a decade of protest, the project was canceled. Half a billion dollars in federal money was redirected into public transportation (the Orange Line) and a park, the Southwest Corridor Park. In 1988 both opened. The park, a green ribbon passing through and uniting neighborhoods, is designed to serve communities along its way. Some "nodes" have tot lots, some hoops, some landscapes worthy of South End gardening fanatics. Boston Globe architecture critic Robert Campbell has described the Southwest Corridor as "one of the outstanding public works in Boston history."*

that start at half a million dollars. But walk slowly. Look closely. Examine the churches, many of which have passed from Protestant to Catholic to Jewish and Eastern Orthodox congregations, before settling into Baptist and A.M.E. affiliations. Follow side streets. If you can, walk beyond the gentrified boulevards onto Shawmut Avenue. Over the harvest of the community gardens—plots of winter melons, jalapeño peppers, Kentucky Wonder beans—see the John Hancock tower, a ravishing sight against moving clouds, despite all the trouble it's caused.

... *A Walking Tour* ...

The spines of the South End are four long, parallel avenues and streets: Columbus Avenue, Tremont Street, Shawmut Avenue, and Washington Street. To get your moorings, consider: Shawmut Avenue starts just outside Chinatown near the new Quincy School. Washington Street passes through Chinatown, as does Harrison Avenue.

Enterprises along Columbus, Tremont, and Shawmut attest to the South End's ethnic history and more prosperous, if homogenous, present. Follow these streets to get the lay of the land, making periodic forays at cross streets, especially when you see small parks. These are the English-style squares.

COLUMBUS AVENUE

A half block from the Amtrak and MBTA Back Bay Station, Columbus Avenue is at a slight diagonal to Clarendon and Dartmouth Streets, the Back Bay thoroughfares that lead to the South End. Initially, you'll be in the land of hip restaurants and pricy condos, but if you continue west along Columbus toward Mass. Ave., ethnic flavors scent the air.

Take a right onto Columbus and proceed, perhaps taking a break at Charlie's (see "Suggested Restaurants"), a beloved sandwich shop and luncheonette run by a Greek-American family. A few doors down, Anchovie's, a little Italian place, is another neighborhood standby (see "Suggested Restaurants"). As you continue along Columbus, glance to the right on Holyoke Street. You'll see the Prudential Building in the background, folks ambling through Southwest Corridor Park in the middle distance, and redbrick Victorian row houses with copper roofs.

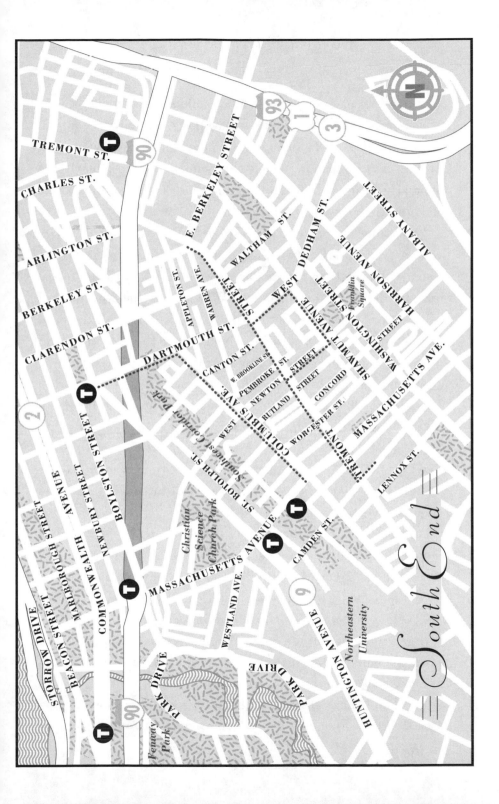

In the artsy part of the South End, nothing is left alone. Rarely will you see so many fire hydrants, signposts, and city tree lots so adorned with flowers. In summer a business enterprise, **Artist Sign Carving,** 435 Columbus Avenue, has sunflowers and other bright perennials growing in front, and morning glories creeping around the stained-glass windows and oak door.

Across the street near the corner of West Newton, Harriet Tubman Square holds two works of art by African-American women sculptors. Fern Cunningham's *Step on Board* is an elegiac work that depicts Tubman, the great black activist who led her people out of bondage, figuratively as author, speaker, and teacher; and literally guiding them along the Underground Railroad. From the North, Tubman traveled into slave-holding territory repeatedly. In bas-relief are a group of men and women following her; she strides forth, breaking from the relief, holding a Holy Bible in her right hand, beckoning her people forward with her left. Meta Warrick Fuller's work, *Emancipation,* dramatizes the struggle out of slavery. Information about Harriet Tubman and the two artists is available at **Harriet Tubman House,** 566 Columbus Avenue, a social service agency.

Diagonally across the street, **Union United Methodist Church,** 485 Columbus Avenue, (617) 536–0872, is set majestically on a corner and stretches onto midblock: a Gothic-style church built in 1870 as Union Congregational Church. The building's nubbly blocks of gray and golden stone are puddingstone.

Here, as throughout the South End, keep your vision peeled for remarkable buildings and gardens. At 488 Columbus Avenue, a red-brick row house with brownstone trim and a spiffy oak door has a wildly colorful, English-style patch with a sign that exhorts, Grow, Dammit! At the corner of Columbus and Greenwich Park, a four-story

Lotus Designs' floral displays overflow onto the pavement.

redbrick and stone Gothic Revival row house features a reclining stone lion and ornate iron gate.

The whole neighborhood is mad for plants. Every florist in the burg tries to create a different magical kingdom. At **Lotus Designs,** 547 Columbus Avenue, (617) 262–7031, one of the store's designers is Thai, and it shows in the synthesis of beauty, sensuality, and spirit that characterizes everything from the sidewalk display, to the fanciful entryway (passion flowers overtaking trellises), to the window designs. On a sea of flowers, Buddha resides adjacent to palms, vines, and small potted trees. Inside is a palace of plants, including orchids. Those in need of inspiration should visit weekly.

Like all urban wanderers, I have love affairs with certain corners, especially those intersections of class, ethnicity, and time. Near the intersection of Columbus and Mass. Ave. are a settlement house, serving African Americans on the former site of a jazz club; a church that was a synagogue; a hole-in-the-wall jazz club a few blocks from Symphony Hall; and a soul food place that has long been one of the most integrated spots in Boston. Something really does happen when people break bread, especially hot corn bread, together.

Bob the Chef's restaurant (see "Suggested Restaurants") has a natty exterior that plays against the **Columbus Avenue A.M.E. Zion Church,** 600 Columbus Avenue, (617) 266–2758, formerly Adath Israel. The cornerstone in the house of worship reads July 8, 1884. The old synagogue, established by German Jews, is not only one of the oldest Jewish houses of worship in Boston, but marks an interesting juncture.

The mid-nineteenth-century arrival of German Jews in the South End created Boston's Jewish community. In 1842 Ohabei Shalom (Lovers of Peace), the first congregation, was formed, and a simple wooden synagogue was dedicated on Warren Street (now Warrenton). In 1854 a group seceded to become Adath Israel (House of Israel). The congregation later moved from the Columbus Avenue synagogue to Commonwealth Avenue outside Kenmore Square (the mosquelike building is today Morse Auditorium at Boston University), and later to the modern building on the Riverway: Temple Israel, a Reform synagogue fronted by a Louise Nevelson sculpture. In 1858 part of the Ohabei Shalom congregation broke off to become Mishkan Tefila—with a synagogue in Roxbury and, today, Newton. As noted in the *Guide to Jewish Boston,* published in 1986, Boston is the only city that can claim three "original" synagogues. All began in the South End.

The African-American congregation that purchased Adath Israel were members of the North Russell Street African-American Methodist Episcopal Church, located on the western slope of Beacon Hill. Their spiritual descendants are at Columbus Avenue A.M.E. Zion Church today.

It is both possible and advisable to view a Jewish temple and a temple of barbecue in one delicious heart-and-nostrils-open glance: Take in the Mogan David (Star of David) on Columbus Avenue A.M.E. Zion Church and the big block letters promoting CHITTERLINGS on Bob the Chef's. What a corner.

Newcomers wonder how a chitterlings place got to the South End. It didn't get there, it was there, as part of the jazz club scene that once existed in the neighborhood. Bob the Chef's has been gussied up just this side of too tasteful, but the greens are still fine, the corn bread crumbly, and jazz music is part of the bill.

Harriet Tubman House, 566 Columbus Avenue, (617) 536–8610, is a big, cheerful, modern building, constructed in 1976. Inside, it's like a combination clubhouse, art gallery, and preschool. Light pours into an atrium space. Seniors, mainly African Americans, hang out and play cards. Children get computer instruction. Preschoolers learn to read, and adults work on reading and math skills toward taking a high school equivalency exam.

The South End was the first Boston neighborhood to have a settlement house: Andover House, opened in 1891. Harriet Tubman House opened on Holyoke Street soon after. Today, United South End Settlements is composed of Harriet Tubman House; the Children's Art Centre, 36 Rutland Street; Youth Resource Center, 48 Rutland Street; and Camp Hale, a summer program founded in 1900 in Center Sandwich, New Hampshire.

On the exterior of the settlement house, a mural of jazz musicians commemorates the old High Hat, a jazz club formerly located on the same spot as Harriet Tubman House. At this side of the building, you're near the Mass. Ave. intersection. Diagonally across the street is Wally's.

Wally's, 427 Mass. Ave., (617) 424–1408, a true-blue jazz club, is hard to find by its address. But look just to the right on Mass. Ave.; under a fat "Bud" sign is a smaller one denoting Wally's Cafe. A sub-culture of the city gathers here: music lovers of all colors and stripes, including students from Berklee College of Music on the uptown part of Mass. Ave., released from composition class into the real world. "Gigs and grit, man," as one player put it to me.

Near the Mass. Ave. portion of Columbus Avenue, wander onto Tremont, another long boulevard, and the first to be gentrified, though you'll be starting on the nongentrified end.

TREMONT STREET

Take a right and continue up to the old Chickering & Sons build-ing (near the corner of Tremont and Camden), which now houses artists in its lofty spaces. The South End was a major, nationally known piano-building center. This block-long factory, built in 1853, manufactured 4,000 instruments per year. Three other piano facto-ries were located on Harrison Avenue and Washington Street.

Next door to **Club Estelle,** 888 Tremont Street, (617) 445–7572, a supper club offering African, Latin, and Caribbean music, **People's Baptist Church,** 134 Camden, (617) 427–0424, sits on a small plot of land, planted with flower gardens. The people and spirit of this place go back almost 200 years, when the congregation met at the African Meeting House near Smith Court on Beacon Hill. People's Baptist is the oldest continuous African-American church in New England.

Continue along Tremont heading toward Boston, the direction from which you began on Columbus Avenue.

Though the Back Bay has the reputation for "most churches," the South End seems lots more churchy to me. Many of these buildings are huge and old, constructed of rusticated stone, and would be much less astonishing if sited in the English countryside, as opposed to along city blocks and residential side streets.

New Hope Baptist, 740 Tremont Street, (617) 536–9332, is one of the most remarkable in appearance: august, yet friendly. (It's that nifty Roxbury puddingstone; New Hope, formerly Tremont Street Methodist Episcopal Church, was the first Boston church to use it.) With Gothic-style, pointed-arch stained-glass windows and similarly shaped arched doors, the 1862 building is a showplace—in summer with its bobbing sunflowers, planted in flower beds just off the street, and in winter when the drab skies are a foil for the stained-glass windows, dominated by cobalt-blue and turquoise figures.

Across the street, take a load off your feet at the spacious **Boston Public Library, South End Branch,** 685 Tremont Street, (617) 536–8241. Opened in 1971, this well-designed library has an adjoining reading park: shady, pleasant, and welcoming. The earlier South End branch on Shawmut Avenue (opened in 1905), which moved to Blackstone Square (1923), served thousands of immigrants, providing a vital stage for education and community.

A grand and well-established community garden is on Worcester Street between Columbus and Tremont.

Villa Victoria, bounded by Tremont, Shawmut, West Brookline, and West Dedham, is not one place, but a host of places, all associated with the indigenous Puerto Rican community, and another tale of urban activism. During the 1960s the city of Boston targeted sixteen acres, occupied by a mainly Puerto Rican community, for its urban renewal plan. A few dozen outraged families rallied, gathered support, and became politically savvy. IBA (*Inquilinos Boricuas en Acción*— Puerto Rican Tenants in Action) was born. Following yet another long haul, the sixteen acres were returned to the community and an affordable-housing project created. Today, Villa Victoria—home to 3,000 residents, including some leaders of the 1960s revolt—is a subsidized housing complex with stores, services, and a plaza.

In the middle of Villa Victoria (on Aguadilla Street, formerly West Newton Street), you'll see *Betances,* a massive mosaic celebrating Dr. Ramon E. Betances (1827–98), "the Abraham Lincoln of Puerto Rico." The inspiring mural, another Lilli Ann Killen Rosenberg piece, was assembled with over 300 colorful clay pieces handmade by the adults and children of Villa Victoria. Made almost twenty-five years ago, *Betances* was Rosenberg's first Boston work. (The artist, whose works have enlivened the greater metropolitan area, is now in her seventies.)

Catty-corner to *Betances,* look for *Cultural Legacy and Our Latin Pride,* a grand-scale painted plywood work by Nora Valdez and local teenagers. Valdez, born in Argentina and brought up under a military dictatorship, was in her twenties when she worked as a community-based sculptor and carver in Boston during the early nineties. *Cultural Legacy* was controversial. Reflecting the views of the Boston high school students who conceived it, the mural illustrates problems teenagers deal with, including a scene depicting heroin addicts shooting up. Despite some opposition, the vivid, high-energy mural stayed in place.

Jorge Hernandez Cultural Center, 65 West Newton Street, (617) 867–9191, a gathering place for Latin music, neighborhood meetings, weddings, samba lessons, and parties, is also snug in the bosom of Villa Victoria. Once, the yellow-brick building was All

Saints' Lutheran Church, built in 1899. In 1959 its congregation moved to a low-slung, low-key modern building on Marlborough Street in the Back Bay. The same year, a newly formed All Saints' Lutheran Church was organized in the South End. In 1969—a radical year in Boston, all around—they dedicated the Shrine of the Black Christ. In 1986 the neighborhood church became a cultural center, serving the Latino community, especially residents of Villa Victoria.

Flash back 150 years: Designed by engineer Ellis S. Chesbrough, elegant **Union Park Square,** between Shawmut and Tremont Streets, was built in 1851, a model of Victorian elegance. Rows of redbrick town houses surround a verdant square. Today, it looks much as it did 150 years ago, down to the ornate cast-iron fences, which resemble black lace. As you wander around Boston and start to mentally "connect-the-dots," please note that 5 Union Park was the home of Samuel Stillman Pierce, founder of S. S. Pierce & Company, the gourmet purveyor in Coolidge Corner.

Within its cavernous round sanctum, The Cyclorama has been providing entertainment for over a century. The 1884 building was designed to house a 400-foot-long, two-story-high circular painting of the Battle of Gettysburg. In later lives it became an automobile factory and the Boston Flower Exchange. Since 1970 it's housed the **Boston Center for the Arts** (BCA), 539 Tremont Street, (617) 426–7700, which hosts theater companies, artists' studios, galleries, and rehearsal spaces, and has been instrumental in the economic and cultural revival of the South End. The BCA takes its heritage and community seriously. It is home to such companies as Sugan Theatre Company, (617) 426–2787, which presents Irish repertory and new work. The BCA is the cultural anchor of today's South End. And through the growing and harvest seasons, a farmers' market gathers on its paved outdoor plaza.

Across Tremont, the **Berkeley Street Community Garden** beckons. The garden's sign is in English and Chinese characters, which pretty much tells the story of its gardeners. Winter melons grow with sugar pumpkins. Walk along the long central garden path, and you'll emerge on a propitious corner of Shawmut Avenue.

SHAWMUT AVENUE

The moving finger writes, and having writ, moves on. This atmospheric street, long associated with Boston's nineteenth-century Middle Eastern community, once housed Lebanese and Syrian restaurants, grocery stores, and shops. Only a few of these remain, and the street is slowly but surely going high-hat.

If you walk through the community garden from Tremont Street to Shawmut Avenue, you'll exit near a little-known church (take a left), **Holy Trinity German Catholic Church,** 140 Shawmut Avenue, constructed in 1844. Even today, it offers a Sunday mass in German and English.

Formaggio, 268 Shawmut Avenue, (617) 350–6996, a fancy cheese store—sister to the West Cambridge Formaggio—is just a few years old, but its food history goes back. Tony, as in Tony's Produce, ran the small store for almost thirty years. The place was basic boxes of fruits and vegetables on sagging tables; the prices hard to know, in Tony's head mainly, and on a sliding and mounting scale, some said. Formaggio doesn't have that kind of personality, but, boy, does it have cheese—expensive, high quality, most of it imported from farmstead operations. One of the more exotic and comely is a Spanish cheese with figs soaked in muscatel. An aromatic display of olives ranges from tiny oil-cured Ligurian beauties, onyx-black and sparkling, to heroic-looking *Bella di Cerignola,* big, crisp, and green. Formaggio also offers prepared food: lentils with roasted carrots and goat cheese, black-eyed

pea salad, celery root remoulade, and the like. In the front are confec-
tions—nougats, bon-bons, candied violets—as well as pastries,
breads, and the D'Abruzzo line of imported pastas.

Next door to Formaggio, **Syrian Grocery,** 270 Shawmut
Avenue, (617) 426–1458, is a pleasing contrast, cozy and old world
as opposed to instant chic. The Mansour family has owned this tidy
store for over three decades. Syrian Grocery's gemlike interior
derives from its wooden appointments, shelves painted deep
turquoise, and touches of brass, such as those of the coffee beakers.
The store's aroma derives from freshly ground coffee, bins of olives,
salty cheeses (including lebane—yogurt cheese), sesame candy, halvah, pistachio nuts, and fresh pita. The grocery also carries jams,
fancy oils and vinegars, tins of Middle Eastern ingredients, and
assorted imported irresistibles, ranging from Scottish shortbread to
Swiss gooseberry jam.

WASHINGTON STREET

Way south in the South End, Washington Street is at the onset of
revival—with galleries, restaurants, and hip shops emerging from the
dust of dilapidation. Urban visionaries knew it would happen; the
street has karma. Washington is one of the oldest thoroughfares in
Boston, the original connecting road from downtown all the way to
Roxbury, then out to Dedham. (If you started at the Old State House
at the corner of State and Washington Streets, you could continue to
the South End, and Roxbury, and onward.) Boston's old elevated railway ran here, thundering over movie palaces, outdoor markets, and a
Yiddish theater, connecting Dudley Station in Roxbury to Sullivan
Square in Charlestown, the route of today's Orange Line.

Even the street's numbers tell a story. Those in the South End are
in the thousands, which seemed impossible to me when I first came

to Boston and would look up addresses in the South End. The spots I sought must be in Roslindale, I thought. But no—the numbers had started downtown.

In the South End, Washington Street holds an architectural, historical, and spiritual treasure: **Cathedral of the Holy Cross,** Washington Street at Union Park Square. Completed in 1875, the Gothic Revival structure—a true cathedral in structure and scope— seats 3,500 people and accommodates twice that number of standing parishioners. It, too, is a member of the Roxbury puddingstone family, smoothed and ordered with granite and limestone trim.

A new Mediterranean restaurant, **Gallia ($$–$$$),** 1525 Washington Street, (617) 247–4455, across from the cathedral, opened last year, and some old storefronts are sprucing up. The **Red Fez ($$),** 1222 Washington Street, (617) 338–6060, a venerable Middle Eastern restaurant—closed for over a decade, and much missed—has been rejuvenated and reopened. **Flour,** 1595 Washington Street, (617) 267–4300, a bakery with attitude, offers homemade Oreos, Lemon Lust tarts, and lovingly produced dog biscuits, along with soups and salads (for humans). If you follow Washington away from Chinatown and the South End, you'll soon wind up at Tropical Market in Dudley Square.

Beyond Washington Street, Harrison Avenue is dominated by **Boston City Hospital,** now incorporated within Boston University Medical Center. The classical center pavilion, designed by Gridley J. Fox Bryant, is an architectural relative of French-style Boston City Hall, which Bryant also designed along with Arthur Gilman. The pavilion was built between 1861 and 1864 and is a grand sight. Over time, it has hovered over the wounded: In the collection of the Boston Public Library, a stark black-and-white 1898 photograph shows a sea of tents behind the pavilion, an outdoor hospital for the soldiers of the Spanish-American War.

Boston City Hospital was founded in 1851 at the bequest of Elisha Goodnow, a public-spirited South Boston merchant, to serve "the economically disadvantaged." It still does.

S U G G E S T E D 🍽 R E S T A U R A N T S

Everybody has their own idea of what authentic means. To me, in the South End the most authentic ethnic restaurants are those associated with the people who live there now.

Botucatu Restaurant ($-$$), 57 West Dedham Street, between Tremont Street and Shawmut Avenue, (617) 247–9249, is an informal, attractive little place that serves Brazilian, Peruvian, and Latin-American specialties. And why not? It's in the heart of Villa Victoria. Appetizers include an array of empanadas, from those with spicy meat to spinach-cheese combos, and succulent *mandioca,* bite-size bits of deep-fried cassava root—crisp on the outside, velvety within—served with creamy carrot sauce. Choose from chicken, fish, beef, and pork entrees, and on Saturday and Sunday, *feijoada,* Brazil's national dish: a black-bean stew with pork, sausage, and dried beef, served with rice and collard greens.

Addis Red Sea Ethiopian Restaurant ($-$$), 544 Tremont Street, (617) 426–8727, is another "real place," one of the few North African restaurants in Boston. Addis attracts Ethiopian and Eritrean expats and other devotees of spicy Ethiopian stews and injera, the fluffy crepelike bread you dip into the meat and veggie stews. No utensils are used, just the bread—lots of fun. The decor features woven tables that neatly support the fragile injera.

On the Park ($–$$$), 1 Union Park, 312 Shawmut Avenue, (617) 426–0862, is another kind of ethnic restaurant, expressing the ethos of those who live in the South End now: a racial and ethnic mix of educated people with lively outlooks, including gay people, artists, young professionals, and the so-called urban pioneers who settled in the city thirty years ago. On the Park cooks a mix of international comfort foods, nicely but unpretentiously served in this sunny corner restaurant near Union Park Square. Choose from Asian, Latino, and northern Italian fare (not to mention Elaine's Chocolate Cake, a creation of the owner's mom), and enjoy the array of artwork done by neighborhood painters, photographers, and designers.

You can call **Charlie's Sandwich Shoppe ($),** 429 Columbus Avenue, (617) 536–7669, a red-checkered-tablecloth kind of place with no fear of mouthing a cliché. Charlie's is a typically South End hybrid: a neighborhood luncheonette with an ethnic heritage that's morphed into a hip spot that maintains its ethnic je ne sais quois. Long run by a Greek-American family, Charlie's has a few Greek items on the menu, but mainly it's the usual favorites—cranberry pancakes and omelettes for breakfast; cheeseburgers with trimmings, franks and beans, and turkey hash for lunch.

Even in the South End, African Americans were not always welcome in restaurants, a particular problem for traveling musicians. Discrimination was not practiced at Charlie's. Duke Ellington and other jazzmen drank their joe and ate their eggs here all through the 1940s. Breakfast and lunch only. No credit cards. Closed Sunday.

It's not true that you can't be a couch potato in public. **Anchovie's ($–$$)**, 433 Columbus Avenue, (617) 266–5088, a neighborhood bar with pizza, calzone, and fresh pasta, makes us all feel like taking our shoes off—and some of us do. The appetizer portion of mussels with garlic-herb butter is enough for dinner. The ziti and meatballs and eggplant parm make me feel like I'm in college again, a memory zone I thought I'd lost, but honest red sauce brings it back. And when was the last time you were able to order a side of meatballs?

You're dating yourself if you refer to **Jae's Cafe and Grill ($–$$)**, 520 Columbus Avenue, (617) 421–9405, as the original Jae's. It means you've been around long enough to have watched this fashionable Korean restaurant spawn three more: in Cambridge, Brookline, and Boston (though the Jae's in Brookline is more a grill). The original Jae's is still the best—Korean specialties, grilled fish, loads of noodle and veggie dishes, Thai-style curries, stir-fried rice, and sushi. What's not to like? Upstairs, the restaurant is cool, with a saltwater fish tank of sleek, gorgeous creatures that make you feel drab, not to mention awkward in water. Downstairs, the upholstered booths and soft lighting convey a quieter, more grown-up ambience, a restaurant where you can actually converse.

Bob the Chef's ($–$$), 604 Columbus Avenue, (617) 536–6204, used to be shabby but homey. Now it's bistro-ized but retains a cozy feel. Catfish fingers, crab cakes, and sweet-potato pie are on the menu, along with barbecued pork ribs and mustard fried catfish. Bob's also serves meat loaf, chicken livers, and jambalaya, and on the weekends, chitterlings. Vegetarians can compose a soulful meal of greens, mac and cheese, red beans and rice, and the overly sweet gotta-have-'em yams.

Festive, elegant, romantic **Icarus ($$$–$$$$)**, 3 Appleton Street, (617) 426–1790, is one of the oldest, most-respected members of the culinary new wave that helped to revitalize the South End. Located on a pretty side street near the Back Bay, Icarus's menu runs to polenta with wild mushrooms, grilled shrimp with mango-jalapeño sorbet, and venison with juniper and cranberries.

House of Siam ($–$$), 542 Columbus Avenue, (617) 267–1755, is a gracious, inviting restaurant with a rouge-colored interior and gold-silk-draped lanterns. The extensive menu features Thai soups, salads, curries, noodles, and fried rice, with lots of seafood and duck specialties, and vegetarian entrees. Try for the cozy corner table near the door. Perch, then, at the lively corner of Columbus and Claremont, where you'll observe the passing pedestrian cavalcade and the restaurant owner's glowing Buddhist shrine. Its offerings— food, wine, flowers—are changed daily, and little candles are kept perennially alight.

Other pricy and prestigious restaurants include **Hamersley's Bistro ($$$–$$$$)**, 553 Tremont Street, (617) 423–2700, a treasured French bistro—classy rather than trendy—now lodged at the Boston Center for the Arts complex; **Aquitaine ($$–$$$)**, 569 Tremont Street, (617) 424–8577, a French bistro serving platters such as hanger steak and fries, permeated by truffle demiglace (you're a long way from Kansas); **Masa ($$–$$$)**, 439 Tremont Street, (617) 338–8884, with a bistro feel and Southwestern influence; and **Rouge ($$–$$$)**, 480 Columbus Avenue, (617) 867–0600, a new Creole- and Cajun-style bistro with jazzy entrees such as steamed cod and clams in Dixie Beer broth with hominy, New Orleans BBQ shrimp, and Boudin sausage served with frisée (a crunchy, frilled salad green) doused with a Creole mustard vinaigrette.

$\mathcal{B}$ibliography

Bladholm, Linda. *The Asian Grocery Store Demystified*. New York: Renaissance Books, 1999.

Boston Landmarks Commission. *Exploring Neighborhoods Series: Publications on Historic Neighborhoods*. Boston: Boston Landmarks Commission, The Environment Department, City of Boston, 1996.

Cook, Mary Alice. *Traditional Recipes from Provincetown*. Provincetown, Mass.: Shank Painter Publishing Company, 1983.

Feldman, Steven, ed. *Guide to Jewish Boston*. Cambridge, Mass.: Genesis 2, 1986.

Hardwicke, Greer, and Roger Reed. *Images of America: Brookline*. Charlestown, S.C.: Arcadia Publishing, 1998.

Harris, Jessica B. *Iron Pots and Wooden Spoons*. New York: Ballantine Books, 1989.

Harris, John. *Historic Walks in Old Boston*. Guilford, Conn.: Globe Pequot Press, 2000.

Harris, Patricia, and David Lyon. *Boston*. New York: Fodor, Compass American Guides, 1997.

Hogrogian, Rachel. *The Armenian Cookbook*. New York: Atheneum, 1971.

Jaffrey, Madhur. *Indian Cooking*. New York: Barron's, 1982.

———. *An Invitation to Indian Cooking*. New York: Vintage Books, 1975.

Kurlansky, Mark. *The Basque History of the World*. New York: Walker & Company, 1999.

Marks, Gil. *The World of Jewish Cooking.* New York: Simon & Schuster, 1996.

Novas, Himilce, and Rosemary Silva. *Latin American Cooking Across the U.S.A.* New York: Alfred A. Knopf, 1997.

Passmore, Jacki. *The Encyclopedia of Asian Food and Cooking.* New York: Hearst Books, 1991.

Rettig, Robert Bell. *Guide to Cambridge Architecture: Ten Walking Tours.* Cambridge, Mass.: The MIT Press, 1969.

Rosenblum, Mort. *Olives: The Life and Lore of a Noble Fruit.* New York: North Point Press/Farrar, Strauss & Giroux, 1996.

Rosten, Leo. *The Joys of Yiddish.* New York: Pocket Books, 2000.

Routhier, Nicole. *Foods of Vietnam.* New York: Stewart, Tabori & Chang, 1989.

Rybczynski, Witold. *A Clearing in the Distance.* New York: Scribner, 1999.

Sammarco, Anthony Mitchell. *Images of America: Boston's South End, Boston's West End, Cambridge, Dorchester,* Volumes I and II, *East Boston, Jamaica Plain, Roxbury, South Boston.* Dover, NH: Arcadia Publishing, 1996–2000.

Southworth, Susan, and Michael Southworth. *AIA Guide to Boston.* Guilford, Conn.: Globe Pequot, 1992.

Uvezian, Sonia. *The Cuisine of Armenia.* New York: Harper Colophon Books, 1974.

Wilson, Susan. *Boston Sites and Insights.* Boston, Mass.: Beacon Press, 1994.

Wurman, Richard Saul. *Access Boston.* New York: Access Press, 1997.

Zaitzevsky, Cynthia. *Frederick Law Olmsted and the Boston Park System.* Cambridge, Mass.: Harvard University Press, 1992.

$\mathcal{G}$ l o s s a r y

Arborio rice: The type of rice used to make risotto; it's white, shiny, short-grained, almost chubby in appearance, and when slow-cooked absorbs volumes of tasty broth without losing its texture or shape.

Arepa: A type of tortilla (can be plump or thin, made with white or yellow cornmeal), served with melted cheese or an egg-and-cheese combo, and sometimes filled with meat.

Baba ghanouj: A Middle Eastern appetizer based on mashed eggplant, tahini (sesame paste), garlic, and onions; the best versions use smoky-tasting eggplant that has been cooked over an open hearth.

Babke: A sweet Jewish yeast bread with lots of cinnamon, raisins, and sometimes grated chocolate swirled into the dough.

Bacalhau: Filets of dried, salted codfish that withstand long storage without refrigeration, used in Mediterranean cooking; in Spanish salt cod is *bacalao*, in Italian *bacalla*, and in the Basque language (Euskera) *maikaloo*.

Bibambap: A Korean meal in a bowl; essentially a large bowl of white rice and layers of artfully cut crisp-cooked vegetables and tofu or meat. Served with a soft-cooked egg on the top, it's tossed together at the table and spiced with pepper sauce.

Binaeduk: Korean pancakes.

Boerag: Bready, calzonelike Armenian pastry with filling, which could be anything from cheese, to spinach, to meat.

Carne assada: Grilled steak; ubiquitous on Latin American menus.

Cassava: A nutritious tuber used in South American cooking; very versatile, can be pounded into flour, or cut into slices for deep-frying, and even forms the basis for tapioca.

Ceviche: Raw seafood, generally scallops, which has been marinated in citrus juice (lime or lemon), then tossed with cut-up vegetables and spices.

Champurrado: A mocha-tasting Guatemalan beverage made of coffee, hot chocolate, and cinnamon, topped with whipped cream.

Chitterlings: A prized African-American soul food dish: pig intestines that have been stewed, then fried.

Dosa: A giant-size crepelike Indian pancake.

Durian: An Asian fruit prized more for its aphrodisiac powers than its sweet, garlicky taste; looks like a pineapple with thorns, or a primitive weapon.

Egg kichel: A very light Jewish pastry, sometimes in the shape of a bow tie, sprinkled with sugar.

Falafel: Deep-fried croquettes made of mashed chickpeas, bread crumbs, and spices, generally served in a Middle Eastern–style pita bread sandwich; a tasty "meatball" that contains no meat.

Ficelle: A very skinny French bread (baguette-shaped, but leaner).

Focaccia: An Italian flat bread, almost as shallow as a pizza crust; can have simple toppings, such as onion and rosemary.

Grits: A southern-style side dish; dried corn cooked into a creamy cereal and served with a pat of butter or a little well of gravy.

Hamentash (plural: hamentashen): Triangular pastry stuffed with apricots, prunes, or poppyseeds, sweetened with honey; the pastry is the tricolored shape of an evil ruler's hat associated with the Jewish holiday of Purim.

Houmos: A Middle Eastern appetizer so popular it can now be bought in supermarkets; made of mashed chickpeas and sesame paste, it's used as a sandwich spread and as a dip for pita bread or raw vegetables.

Kimchi: Korean pickled cabbage, served as a relish; soon you will crave it.

Lamejune: A kind of Armenian pizza with a soft, crepelike base and simple topping of ground lamb, tomatoes, onions, and spices.

Lassi: An Indian milkshake made with yogurt or buttermilk, ice, and rose-water; can be ordered salty or sweet, and sometimes in fruit flavors, such as mango.

Lavash: Armenian flat bread, generally round in shape; can be as crisp as a cracker or softened with water to use as a roll-up or to dip into appetizers.

Lebane: Middle Eastern cheese made of yogurt.

Linguica: A spicy sausage, used in the Portuguese-inspired cooking of Brazil, Cape Verde, and the Azores; generally included in kale soup.

Longan: A small Asian fruit, often sold in a can with syrup.

Loquat: An apricot-size fruit with a quincelike aroma; can be found in Asian markets and sometimes Armenian groceries. (If you are a very patient window box gardener, you can grow the shiny black seeds into delicate trees.)

Mandoo: Korean dumplings; if pale they've been steamed, if golden, fried.

Pajon: A Korean seafood and scallion pancake; very tasty.

Pakora: Indian appetizer; a triangular, crimped, stuffed pasty that is deep-fried and served with sauces, chutneys, and relishes; generally vegetarian.

Panettone: A round, dome-topped, buttery Italian Christmas bread with lots of golden raisins, currants, candied peels, and almonds. When it gets stale, it can be used to make divine toast.

Pao-de-milho: Portuguese corn bread, which is nothing like panbaked American corn bread, but is instead a round, crusty, fine-grained bread made of wheat flour and cornmeal.

Pasteles: Puerto Rican tamales; instead of the more usual cornmeal dough, the coating around the meat filling is a mix of mashed root vegetables and plantain; the filling is shaped, then wrapped in plantain or banana leaves, and boiled.

Pho: Vietnamese noodle soup, classically made with beef broth, topped with meat slivers, and served with bean sprouts and fresh coriander; sometimes seafood- or chicken-based soups are also referred to as pho.

Pupusa: A corn patty stuffed with cheese or pork.

Rambutan: A small Asian fruit, native to Malaysia, with a thin red skin and hairy, pliable spines; the fruit within is grapelike in texture and slightly tart.

Rapini: Italian for broccoli rabe, a vegetable in the broccoli family with long, edible stems (about the width of a string bean) and broccoli-like flowers.

Ropa viejo: A slow-simmered Latin beef stew where the venerable, tender meat is cooked in garlicky red sauce with green and hot peppers; literally means "old clothes."

Tahini: Sesame paste, used as an ingredient in Middle Eastern appetizers, such as houmos, baba ghanouj, and falafel.

Tamale: A spicy meat mixture wrapped in corn flour dough, then placed in a corn husk and steamed; remove husk before eating!

Thukpa: A very nourishing Tibetan soup, made with vegetables and meat, served with noodles or small dumplings.

Torrone: An Italian candy made of chocolate, nougat, and nuts shaped into a log.

Wots: Ethiopian stews made of chicken or meat or vegetables, eaten with torn-off pieces of warm spongy bread (injera).

$\mathcal{I}ndex$

About the Author

Lynda Morgenroth is a Boston-area feature writer and essayist. Her articles on food and popular culture, art and architecture, and nature and the environment have appeared in publications including *The Boston Globe, The New York Times, Yankee, The Atlantic, Orion,* and *New Age.* Morgenroth lives in a "quirky, 113-year-old house" just north of Boston.